Skateboarding

This book explores the cultural, social, spatial and political dynamics of skateboarding, drawing on contributions from leading international experts across a range of disciplines, such as sociology and philosophy of sport, architecture, anthropology, ecology, cultural studies, sociology, geography and other fields. Part 1 critiques the ethos of skateboarding, its cultures and scenes, global trajectory and the meanings it holds. Part 2 critically examines skateboarding in terms of space and sites and Part 3 explores shifts that have occurred in skateboarding's history around mainstreaming, commercialization, professionalization, neoliberalization and creative cities.

Kara-Jane Lombard is Senior Lecturer in the School of Media, Culture and Creative Arts at Curtin University, Western Australia.

Routledge Research in Sport, Culture and Society

1 Sport, Masculinities and the Body
Ian Wellard

2 India and the Olympics
Boria Majumdar and Nalin Mehta

3 Social Capital and Sport Governance in Europe
Edited by Margaret Groeneveld, Barrie Houlihan and Fabien Ohl

4 Theology, Ethics and Transcendence in Sports
Edited by Jim Parry, Mark Nesti and Nick Watson

5 Women and Exercise
The Body, Health and Consumerism
Edited by Eileen Kennedy and Pirkko Markula

6 Race, Ethnicity and Football
Persisting Debates and Emergent Issues
Edited by Daniel Burdsey

7 The Organisation and Governance of Top Football Across Europe
An Institutional Perspective
Edited by Hallgeir Gammelsæter and Benoît Senaux

8 Sport and Social Mobility
Crossing Boundaries
Ramón Spaaij

9 Critical Readings in Bodybuilding
Edited by Adam Locks and Niall Richardson

10 The Cultural Politics of Post-9/11 American Sport
Power, Pedagogy and the Popular
Michael Silk

11 Ultimate Fighting and Embodiment
Violence, Gender and Mixed Martial Arts
Dale C. Spencer

12 The Olympic Games and Cultural Policy
Beatriz Garcia

13 The Urban Geography of Boxing
Race, Class, and Gender in the Ring
Benita Heiskanen

14 The Social Organization of Sports Medicine
Critical Socio-Cultural Perspectives
Edited by Dominic Malcolm and Parissa Safai

15 **Host Cities and the Olympics**
An Interactionist Approach
Harry Hiller

16 **Sports Governance, Development and Corporate Responsibility**
Edited by Barbara Segaert, Marc Theeboom, Christiane Timmerman and Bart Vanreusel

17 **Sport and Its Female Fans**
Edited by Kim Toffoletti and Peter Mewett

18 **Sport Policy in Britain**
Barrie Houlihan and Iain Lindsey

19 **Sports and Christianity**
Historical and Contemporary Perspectives
Edited by Nick J. Watson and Andrew Parker

20 **Sports Coaching Research**
Context, Consequences, and Consciousness
Anthony Bush, Michael Silk, David Andrews and Hugh Lauder

21 **Sport Across Asia**
Politics, Cultures, and Identities
Edited by Katrin Bromber, Birgit Krawietz, and Joseph Maguire

22 **Athletes, Sexual Assault, and "Trials by Media"**
Narrative Immunity
Deb Waterhouse-Watson

23 **Youth Sport, Physical Activity and Play**
Policy, Interventions and Participation
Andrew Parker and Don Vinson

24 **The Global Horseracing Industry**
Social, Economic, Environmental and Ethical Perspectives
Phil McManus, Glenn Albrecht, and Raewyn Graham

25 **Sport, Public Broadcasting, and Cultural Citizenship**
Signal Lost?
Edited by Jay Scherer and David Rowe

26 **Sport and Body Politics in Japan**
Wolfram Manzenreiter

27 **The Fantasy Sport Industry**
Games within Games
Andrew C. Billings and Brody J. Ruihley

28 **Sport in Prison**
Exploring the Role of Physical Activity in Penal Practices
Rosie Meek

29 **Sport and Nationalism in China**
Lu Zhouxiang and Fan Hong

30 **Rethinking Drug Use in Sport**
Why the war will never be won
Bob Stewart and Aaron Smith

31 **Sport, Animals, and Society**
Edited by James Gillett and Michelle Gilbert

32 **Sport Development in the United States**
Edited by Peter Smolianov, Dwight Zakus and Joseph Gallo

33 **Youth Olympic Games**
Edited by Dag Vidar Hanstad, Barrie Houlihan and Milena Parent

34 **Safeguarding, Child Protection and Abuse in Sport**
International Perspectives in Research, Policy and Practice
Edited by Melanie Lang and Mike Hartill

35 **Touch in Sports Coaching and Physical Education**
Fear, Risk, and Moral Panic
Edited by Heather Piper

36 **Sport, Racism and Social Media**
Neil Farrington, Lee Hall, Daniel Kilvington, John Price and Amir Saeed

37 **Football and Migration**
Perspectives, Places, Players
Edited by Richard Elliott and John Harris

38 **Health and Elite Sport**
Is High Performance Sport a Healthy Pursuit?
Edited by Joe Baker, Parissa Safai and Jessica Fraser-Thomas

39 **Asian American Athletes in Sport and Society**
Edited by C. Richard King

40 **Pierre Bourdieu and Physical Culture**
Edited by lisahunter, Wayne Smith and elke emerald

41 **Reframing Disability?**
Media, (Dis)Empowerment, and Voice in the 2012 Paralympics
Edited by Daniel Jackson, Caroline E. M. Hodges, Mike Molesworth and Richard Scullion

42 **Sport and the Social Significance of Pleasure**
Richard Pringle, Robert E. Rinehart and Jayne Caudwell

43 **A Sociology of Football in a Global Context**
Jamie Cleland

44 **Gambling with the Myth of the American Dream**
Aaron M. Duncan

45 **Inclusion and Exclusion in Competitive Sport**
Socio-Legal and Regulatory Perspectives
Seema Patel

46 **Asia and the Future of Football**
The Role of the Asian Football Confederation
Ben Weinberg

47 **Football and Accelerated Culture**
This Modern Sporting Life
Steve Redhead

48 **Researching Embodied Sport**
Exploring movement cultures
Edited by Ian Wellard

49 **Female Fans of the NFL**
Taking Their Place in the Stands
Anne Cunnningham Osborne and Danielle Sarver Coombs

50 **Sport in Islam and in Muslim Communities**
Edited by Alberto Testa and Mahfoud Amara

51 **Endurance Running**
A Socio-Cultural Examination
Edited by William Bridel, Pirkko Markula and Jim Denison

52 **Mega Events and Globalization**
Capital, Cultures and Spectacle in a Changing World Order
Edited by Richard Gruneau and John Horne

53 **Beyond Sport for Development and Peace**
Transnational Perspectives on Theory, Policy and Practice
Edited by Lyndsay Hayhurst, Tess Kay and Megan Chawansky

54 **Ethics and Governance in Sport**
The future of sport imagined
Edited by Yves Vanden Auweele, Elaine Cook and Jim Parry

55 **Skateboarding**
Subcultures, Sites and Shifts
Edited by Kara-Jane Lombard

Skateboarding
Subcultures, sites and shifts

Edited by Kara-Jane Lombard

LONDON AND NEW YORK

First published 2016
by Routledge
2 Park Square, Milton Park, Abingdon, Oxon OX14 4RN

and by Routledge
711 Third Avenue, New York, NY 10017

Routledge is an imprint of the Taylor & Francis Group, an informa business

© 2016 selection and editorial material, Kara-Jane Lombard; individual chapters, the contributors

The right of Kara-Jane Lombard to be identified as author of the editorial material, and of the individual authors as authors of their contributions, has been asserted by them in accordance with sections 77 and 78 of the Copyright, Designs and Patents Act 1988.

All rights reserved. No part of this book may be reprinted or reproduced or utilised in any form or by any electronic, mechanical, or other means, now known or hereafter invented, including photocopying and recording, or in any information storage or retrieval system, without permission in writing from the publishers.

Trademark notice: Product or corporate names may be trademarks or registered trademarks, and are used only for identification and explanation without intent to infringe.

British Library Cataloguing in Publication Data
A catalogue record for this book is available from the British Library

Library of Congress Cataloging-in-Publication Data
  Skateboarding : subcultures, sites and shifts / edited by Kara-Jane Lombard, senior lecturer in the School of Media, Culture and Creative Arts at Curtin University, Australia.
     pages cm
  1. Skateboarding—Social aspects.   I. Lombard, Kara-Jane.
  GV859.8.S56 2016
  796.22—dc23
  2015019626

ISBN: 978-1-138-82982-4 (hbk)
ISBN: 978-1-315-73757-7 (ebk)

Typeset in Times
by Apex CoVantage, LLC

To my parents, Anton and Reona, and my big brother, Merrill

Contents

Notes on contributors xiii
Acknowledgements xvi

1 The cultural politics of skateboarding and the rise of skate urbanism 1
KARA-JANE LOMBARD

PART 1
Cultures and scenes 15

2 No one standing above you: Rodney Mullen and the ethics of innovation 17
BILL SCHAFFER

3 Skateboard philanthropy: inclusion and prefigurative politics 30
PAUL O'CONNOR

4 Skateboarding activism: exploring diverse voices and community support 44
INDIGO WILLING AND SCOTT SHEARER

5 He catches things in flight: scopic regimes, visuality, and skateboarding in Tyneside, England 57
MICHAEL JEFFRIES, SEBASTIAN MESSER, AND JON SWORDS

6 Posing LA, performing Tokyo: photography and race in skateboarding's global imaginary 73
DWAYNE DIXON

xii *Contents*

PART 2
Sites and space
89

7 **Southbank skateboarding, London, and urban culture: the Undercroft, Hungerford Bridge, and House of Vans**
91
IAIN BORDEN

8 **The 'legitimate' skateboarder: politics of private–public skateboarding spaces**
108
MATTHEW ATENCIO AND BECKY BEAL

9 **Spreading the Skirtboarder stoke: reflexively blogging fluid femininities and constructing new female skateboarding identities**
121
STEPH MACKAY

PART 3
Skate shifts
137

10 **Skateboarding as a technology of the collective: Kona Skatepark, Jacksonville, Florida, USA**
139
MICHAEL J. LORR

11 **Steep transitions: spatial-temporal incorporation, Beasley Skate Park, and subcultural politics in the gentrifying city**
152
SIMON ORPANA

12 **Trucks, tricks, and technologies of government: analyzing the productive encounter between governance and resistance in skateboarding**
169
KARA-JANE LOMBARD

13 **Transformative improvisation: the creation of the commercial skateboard shoe, 1960–1979**
182
THOMAS TURNER

Index
195

Contributors

Matthew Atencio, PhD, is an assistant professor of kinesiology at California State University East Bay in Hayward, CA. His teaching and research pertain to the fields of sport sociology, as well as physical education and outdoor education pedagogy. Dr. Atencio has published extensively in these fields, drawing upon theories reflecting feminist, post-colonial, post-structural and complexity systems perspectives. Dr. Atencio has worked in several international contexts including Australia, Singapore, the United Kingdom and the United States.

Becky Beal, EdD, is a professor of kinesiology at California State University, East Bay in Hayward, California, where she teaches courses in the sociology and philosophy of sport and serves as the associate director for the Center for Sport and Social Justice. Dr. Beal has been actively involved in the North American Society for the Sociology of Sport and served on the editorial board for the *Sociology of Sport Journal*. Beal has been researching the cultural and political dynamics of skateboarding for more than twenty years and has published several articles and book chapters and a reference book on the topic.

Iain Borden is professor of architecture and urban culture and vice-dean of education at the Bartlett, University College London. Iain's authored and co-edited books include *Forty Ways to Think About Architecture* (Wiley 2014), *Drive: Journeys through Film, Cities and Landscapes* (Reaktion 2012), *Bartlett Designs: Speculating with Architecture* (Wiley 2009), *Manual: the Architecture and Office of Allford Hall Monaghan Morris* (Birkhauser 2003), *Skateboarding Space and the City: Architecture and the Body* (Berg 2001/ Bloomsbury 2017), *The Unknown City: Contesting Architecture and Social Space* (MIT 2001) and *InterSections: Architectural Histories and Critical Theories* (Routledge 2000).

Dwayne Dixon is a visiting lecturer in the Asian and Middle Eastern Studies Department at Duke University. His research focuses on young people in Tokyo and their relations to globalized urban space, their use of visual technologies and their understandings of self amid changing conceptions of adulthood and limited economic possibility. His work is intertextual, combining ethnographic

xiv *Contributors*

video along with traditional scholarly writing, presented digitally using Scalar, an open-source publishing platform. His writing has been published in *The Journal of Postmodern Culture* and *Pastelegram*, and his photographic and video works have been exhibited internationally. He has been skateboarding since 1987.

Michael Jeffries is an ecologist with a particular interest in the spatial and temporal dynamics of wetland wildlife and the interplay of chance versus deterministic events, which is not so very different from the world of skateboarders and how they recreate and reinvent the city.

Kara-Jane Lombard is Senior Lecturer in the School of Media, Communication and Creative Arts at Curtin University, Western Australia. Her research interests include youth culture, gender, governmentality and creative industries. Most recently, her work has been published in the *Journal of Men's Studies*, *Visual Communication Quarterly* and the *Journal for Cultural Research*.

Michael J. Lorr is the director of the Community Leadership Program and Associate Professor of Sociology at Aquinas College in Grand Rapids, MI. His work on urban, environmental and cultural sociology has recently appeared in the *Journal of Contemporary Ethnography*, *Nature & Culture*, *Humanity and Society* and the *Journal of Youth and Adolescence*.

Steph Mackay is a Social Sciences and Humanities Research Council (SSHRC) Postdoctoral Fellow at Carleton University in Ottawa, Canada. She has published in a range of scholarly journals and books on the topics of gender in skateboarding media, social theory, obesity and digital media. Her current project explores the opportunities and limits of identity building in and through digital media and the extent to which online communities can play a role in increasing lifestyle sport participation among women.

Sebastian Messer is a chartered architect. He is interested in alternative forms of practicing architecture and 'Live Projects' in architectural education. His work is informed by narratives, to understand the lives that take place between walls, and he is researching the representation and tactics of appropriation and activism and how these might inform the profession of architecture.

Paul O'Connor is originally from the UK and received his PhD in sociology from the University of Queensland on the subject of the everyday hybridity of young Muslims in Hong Kong in 2009. He has various publications, including a book *Islam in Hong Kong* with Hong Kong University Press in 2012. As an interdisciplinary scholar, Paul's work includes a focus on social theory, religious and ethnic minorities and the body and urban space. He teaches a variety of courses at the Chinese University of Hong Kong's department of anthropology on ethnicity, Islam, religion and culture, anthropology of the body and globalization. He has lived in Hong Kong for the past twelve years. Paul is also a veteran skateboarder and follower of skateboard academia and insists on taking his board on all his travels.

Simon Orpana, PhD, has published articles on skateboarding, subcultures and film in such journals as *Psychogeographies*, *Topia* and *The Review of Education, Pedagogy, and Cultural Studies*. He currently holds a SSHRC post-doctoral fellowship at the University of Alberta working on a project about biopolitics, finance capital and the corporeal turn in contemporary film and culture. His illustrated zine *The Art of Gentrification* is included in *Popular Culture: A User's Guide*, third edition.

Bill Schaffer has published widely in film and animation studies. He has held permanent positions at universities in Australia and the UK but is not currently attached to any institution. He has been a skateboarder for forty years, was part of the small group that pioneered pool skating in Australia in the 1970s and still can't do any decent tricks.

Scott Shearer has a Bachelor of Environmental Planning from Griffith University and Master of Social Science (Social Planning) from the University of Queensland. He is also president of the Brisbane Skateboarding Association and Director of Bearings Social Planning and Research.

Jon Swords is a geographer with interests in the cultural economy, cartography and visual methodologies. Most recently, he's been researching film and TV production, arts patronage and urban sports.

Thomas Turner currently teaches cultural and historical studies at London College of Fashion, University of the Arts London, and previously taught American history at Birkbeck, University of London, where he also completed a PhD on the history of sports shoes. Thomas is interested in the histories of popular culture, consumption, products, youth subcultures, music, and style. He has published work on the confluence of music and sportswear and on the history of jazz.

Indigo Willing earned a PhD from the University of Queensland. She is formerly a Rockefeller Research Fellow in the Humanities at the University of Massachusetts, Boston, and is currently an ARC Research Fellow (Sociology) at the Griffith Centre for Cultural Research at Griffith University and a Research Affiliate for Bearings Social Planning and Research.

Acknowledgements

Thank you, first of all, to those who have contributed to this book – Bill Schaffer, Paul O'Connor, Indigo Willing, Scott Shearer, Michael Jeffries, Sebastian Messer, Jon Swords, Dwayne Dixon, Iain Borden, Matthew Atencio, Becky Beal, Steph MacKay, Michael J. Lorr, Simon Orpana and Thomas Turner. It has been wonderful working with you all and a thrill to find such an engaged, critical community of skate scholars. Your work inspires me.

My sincere thanks to my editor at Routledge, Faye Leerink, for her guidance and support in helping us all realize this project.

I am very grateful to the individuals and organizations who granted permissions for the reproduction of images and quotes, including O'Reilly Media; Lemelson Centre, National Museum of American History, Smithsonian Institution; Ben Armsen; Lewis Ellenden; Søren Nordal Enevoldsen; Johnny Haynes; Derek Lapierre; Euan Lynn; Simon Orpana; Adam Thirtle; Adam Todhunter; Wig Worland, Every effort has been made to obtain identify, obtain permission from, and make appropriate citation to the original copyright holders. If there have been any accidental errors or omissions, we apologise to those concerned.

To two of the best friends a girl could ask for – Alzena MacDonald and Kristen Phillips. Thank you for all the encouragement, support and advice. Alzie, I will never forget your reaction when I told you we had gotten a contract for the book – thank you for being so excited for me! And to Special K, thank you so much for offering to help me in these final weeks – despite the fact that you are working as an academic and a lawyer and studying at the same time!

Mark Gibson, my Honours and PhD supervisor, it is a pleasure to thank and honour you. I would never have explored skateboarding without your guidance.

David Pyvis, I really appreciate all the time you took to mentor me.

Rachel Robertson, Head of Department for Communication and Cultural Studies at Curtin University, thank you so much for your support and kindness since I joined your department. I really appreciate you fighting for me to have time to work on this book this year.

To Lucas Marie, whose scholarship inspired me to think about the framing of this book.

There are no words for the gratitude and love I have for my family. Mom, Dad, Mez – thank you for the endless time you have taken over the years to listen to me, encourage me, help me in various ways with my academic endeavours and other things in life. This book is dedicated to you.

1 The cultural politics of skateboarding and the rise of skate urbanism

Kara-Jane Lombard

The contributors to this book have long known that skateboarding is significant because of its culture, politics, creativity, innovation, unique perspective of architecture and space, engagement with commercial culture, and, perhaps most importantly, the sheer joy and form of self-expression it affords those who skate. When I first began researching skateboarding just after the new millennium, it seemed that the popular media reports I discovered often construed skateboarding as increasingly 'respectable' and mainstream. For instance, in 2002, an article by American journalist Chris Springsteen (2002) commented, 'Punks? Criminals? Athletes. A shift in thinking about skateboarders has taken the better part of four decades'. In February 2003, the Australian Broadcasting Corporation's Radio National broadcast featured an interview with several professional skateboarders on *The Sports Factor* titled 'Skateboarding . . . seeking respectability'. The summary for the program noted, 'it's had its ups and downs over the years . . . now skateboarding is seeking just a little respectability' (Hadfield 2003). In April 2005, Canadian *The Record: New Westminster's Hometown Newspaper* ran an article on skateboarding titled 'Riding a wave of respectability' (Kurucz 2005). Similarly, a *60 Minutes* piece which aired in Australia on 30 November that year acknowledged skateboarding as a respectable sport, as well as a billion-dollar industry. During this time, there was also much discussion of skateboarding as an 'extreme' sport, although many involved in skateboarding resisted that label, including Sean Holland (2003) in his editorial for the April 2003 edition of *Australian Skateboarding Magazine*.

The representations of skateboarding I come across in the news media fifteen years later reveal discussions of skateboarding as an integral part of urban life and culture and the value it has in terms of socially inclusive and progressive ends. In reviewing these media reports, I've particularly noticed the emergence of three themes. The first is a recognition of the multitude of ways skateboarding impacts urbanism and our everyday life, from popular culture to the economy. As an example, an article from UK newspaper *The Telegraph* in March 2014, while still insisting that skateboarders view their practice as resistant and see commercial incorporation as exploitation, argued that, 'Today's skaters might just have to accept that their sport is rolling into its fifth era of mainstream popularity' (Leitch 2014). The article pointed to skateboard decks with prints by fashion

2   Kara-Jane Lombard

designers such as Christian Louboutin, Stella McCartney, and Jil Sander being sold at Selfridges as evidence of skate's mainstreaming.

Wired Magazine, the monthly US publication which reports on technological trends and their impact on culture, published two articles on skateboarding in the first few months of 2015. Both discussed skater Rodney Mullen's engagement with the tech and business worlds. One article explored Mullen's venture into commercial software with an app he is involved in while also noting that,

> The Smithsonian's Lemelson Center wants to make him a fellow, with an eye toward having him star in a video series about his research; venture capitalists are urging him to get involved in funding startups; the 'resident futurist' at Seattle's Intellectual Ventures Lab wants him to devise a program that explores the relationship between hacking and skateboarding.
>
> (Koerner 2015)

The second piece pointed out that 'Rodney Mullen believes skate culture has something positive to offer the tech world, and the tech world is paying attention' but warned that in order to do so, Mullen needs to be decoupled from the sexism in modern skateboarding (Sierra 2015).

A second trend in contemporary media representations is the sense of skateboarding's social benefit to society. In a 2015 article in *The Guardian*, Iain Borden noted that there is increasingly a 'realisation of the positive role skateboarding can play in education, entrepreneurship and community cohesion'. Borden gives several examples of this which illustrate how skateboarding is being utilized for ends such as providing young people with design and technology skills, building social capital, and countering societal issues from addiction to unemployment, violence, gender issues, and access to education. As he concludes, 'Skateboarding here is part of an answer to complex social conditions in the city' (2015).

One of the most frequently reported-on instances of this trend is Skateistan (for example: Ellis-Peterson 2015; Lister 2015). The non-profit skate school created by Australian skater Oliver Percovich in 2009 provides educational and empowerment opportunities for Afghanistan's youth. It is particularly noted for empowering girls. One article explains that Skateistan gives 'girls between the ages of five and 16 the opportunity to skateboard – in a country where they are not allowed on bicycles' (Ellis-Peterson 2015). Similar initiatives in other countries are also being explored in the media (Cornelius 2015).

A third theme I've noticed in more recent media portrayals of skateboarding explores 'skate urbanism' or the 'skate city'. As one news article published towards the end of 2014 noted, 'We may be nearing the day where skateboard urbanism is a thing . . . And with the diversity found among skateboarders, building a new bowl in the neighborhood may not stir fears of gentrification as other projects might' (Owens 2014). Borden's (2015) article in *The Guardian* outlines two ways in which skate urbanism, or the skate city, is occurring. The first is through skateboarding's DIY movement, which adds to existing urban spaces to create new skate opportunities. Second, he points out that the skate city is also

The cultural politics of skateboarding and the rise of skate urbanism 3

being cultivated through a skate infrastructure building boom and spaces created by skate-architects who include skatable designs in their work (2015). Clearly skateboarding is, as sports, music, lifestyle, and skateboarding photographer Atiba Jefferson puts it, an 'influential culture' (Lasane 2015).

Skate studies

As these media representations demonstrate, skateboarding is a significant part of urban and cultural fabric in contemporary global society, and thus there is a serious academic case for addressing it. *Skateboarding: Subcultures, Scenes, Sites and Shifts* provides the first wide-ranging introduction to the theoretical understandings and critical explorations of the meanings, practices, and cultures surrounding skateboarding. It is theoretically and methodologically diverse in approach. The contributors, many of whom are seasoned skaters, include international scholars and leading figures in skateboarding scholarship with expertise in sociology and philosophy of sport, architecture, anthropology, ecology, cultural studies, sociology, geography, and other fields. Chapters explore skateboarding in places such as the United States, UK, Australia, and Asia and sites such as skateparks, streets, and websites.

Many of the chapters in this volume are concerned with skateboarding's social and cultural dynamics and thus explore its identity politics. For instance, MacKay's chapter examines gender, Dixon discusses aspects of race, O'Connor's chapter touches on race, gender, and sexual orientation, while Lorr analyzes multi-generational identity. Some chapters investigate its engagement within urban sites (Borden, Atencio and Beal, Dixon, Lorr, and Orpana). Other contributions explore representations of skateboarding (Jeffries, Messer and Swords, Willing and Shearer, MacKay, Dixon). A further thematic concern among some chapters is a consideration of the numerous stakeholders involved in skateboarding, such as city planners and managers, multi-national corporations, parents, and adult volunteers (Atencio and Beal, Willing and Shearer, Lorr, Turner). The normalization and commodification of skateboarding is a significant theme (Lorr, Turner), as is the discourse of neoliberalism (Atencio and Beal, Orpana, and Lombard). The organization of this volume represents one attempt at giving the heterogeneous questions surrounding skateboarding a thematic structure. A review of skate media over the last fifty years as well as skateboarding scholarship reveals that some of the main themes of concern revolve around the cultures and scenes of skateboarding, spatial issues and skate sites, and the changes that have occurred such as around mainstreaming, commercialization, and normalization. Thus this volume is divided into three parts.

Part 1: Cultures and scenes

Part 1 contains five chapters that specifically address the cultures and scenes of skateboarding. Those unfamiliar with skateboarding and its scholarship might be surprised to find it discussed in terms of innovation, philanthropy, activism,

4   *Kara-Jane Lombard*

and creativity. Innovation and creativity are at the heart of so much of skateboarding – from its appropriation of diverse terrain over the last six decades to the invention of new tricks and equipment to the various media that have sprung up around it. Thus Bill Schaffer's chapter is the ideal starting place for a book on skateboarding. The book also commences with the so-called 'godfather of street skating', professional skater Rodney Mullen. Widely considered the most important innovator in the history of skateboarding, having invented several fundamental moves, Mullen practices both freestyle and street skating. According to Mullen, skateboarding should be regarded more as an art or mode of expression than as a sport, and it is an inherently innovative practice that works to create transformative relationships between environment and body, community and individual, brain and body.

Schaffer begins with the suggestion that skateboarding is a discipline with its own implied *ethic* in the sense given by Spinoza. He argues that such a 'skaterly' ethics is articulated in a recent series of lectures by Rodney Mullen. Schaffer finds that Mullen's approach to skateboarding stresses the need to break apart established mental and physical habits so that their 'parts' may enter into new and unexpected relations, which has important implications for understandings of innovation more generally.

The next two chapters are concerned with aspects of skateboarding's civic engagement. Paul O'Connor's chapter argues that the various ways in which skateboarders help and encourage each other has influenced a variety of charitable projects that use the values of skateboarding in order to make a positive impact on communities and young people. The chapter argues that skateboard philanthropy is a macro version of micro processes in skateboard culture. At the same time, he argues that skateboard philanthropy can be understood as a type of prefigurative politics in which skateboarders seek to communicate and demonstrate the key values of skateboarding and maintain control and authenticity in skateboard culture.

Indigo Willing and Scott Shearer's contribution to skateboarding literature aims to broaden understandings of skateboarding as a subculture beyond its core of young males to build recognition of the diverse populations at the periphery. Their chapter demonstrates how diverse voices challenge the subculture's traditional associations with deviance, anti-social masculinity, criminality, and other negative assumptions. They argue this not only paves the way for more inclusive representations of skateboarding but also highlights the role skateboarding plays to different people and the need for skateboarding facilities to reflect that.

The following two chapters examine the visual culture associated with skateboarding – albeit in quite different ways. Michael Jeffries, Sebastian Messer, and Jon Swords acknowledge that skateboarding is often explicitly credited with being creative (e.g. Beal 1995; Borden 2001; Howell 2005). However, as they point out, the specific nature of this creativity and its importance for individual skaters goes largely unexplored. Thus their chapter argues that skateboarding has a powerful visual culture, primarily reproduced through photography and video, and they aim to examine the motives of skaters who create. They explore this neglected topic through the concept of the scopic regime, which includes not only what is created

The cultural politics of skateboarding and the rise of skate urbanism 5

but also the practices, motivations, and discourses involved. They categorize the photography and video of six skateboarders from Tyneside in England. Although their subjects and intentions are diverse, capturing the technical perfection of tricks, social reportage, or politically engaged activism, in each case, skateboarding has been the foundation for their personal creativity.

Dwayne Dixon begins and ends his chapter recalling two photo shoots in Japan – one with a Japanese pop star, the other with a pro skater. These photo shoots ethnographically triangulate skateboarding's rich intersection of architecture, youthful (raced) bodies, and images. For the star, white skaters are necessary to authenticate his posing in styles imitating scenes from the Hollywood film *Lords of Dogtown*. For the skater, grimy Tokyo architecture confers a legitimizing aura to his skateboarding performance across the surfaces of the global city. Thus Dixon finds that skateboarding communicates desirable authenticity within global capitalism because it connects youthful energy and urban cool. He argues that in tension with fantasy and history, skateboarding's mediated visibility produces the commodified contours of a global imaginary.

Part 2: Sites and space

The field of skateboarding literature has often focused on the importance of space and the sites where skateboarding occurs. As Borden has explored in *Skateboarding, Space and the City* (2001), the different eras of skateboarding can be defined in terms of the different sites which predominated. Varying terrain means varying modes of engagement and forms of repression – changing the meaning of skateboarding. The three chapters in Part 2 of this collection are concerned with some of the sites of skateboarding – pools, streets, skateparks, and websites.

Iain Borden's chapter analyzes three different spaces at or near London's Southbank Centre to explore the connection between skateboarding and wider societal conditions in this city: the Undercroft at the Southbank Centre itself, the proposed Hungerford Bridge skate space, and the nearby House of Vans venue. His chapter shows how skateboarding is now becoming an ever-more-established part of urban life and culture. These three spaces demonstrate that skateboarding is vital to thousands of skaters, is appreciated by even greater numbers of the public, and is even essential to wider artistic and commercial operations. In these three spaces, skateboarding is at once indispensable, desirable, and necessary.

For Matthew Atencio and Becky Beal, it is the spaces directed by public–private partnerships that are of interest. Their chapter explores how the discourse of neoliberalism has created skateparks directed by private–public partnerships. They investigate three instances of this: the Rob Dyrdek Foundation's Safe Spot Skate Spot skate plazas, Town Park and affiliated Hood Games festival, and the Bay Area Skatepark. Atencio and Beal suggest that each of these skate sites intends to benefit the general public, although they still privilege and exclude certain groups.

Steph MacKay moves away from urban space to analyze digital space. Her chapter explores the discursive constructions of gender circulated on a skateboarding blog, Skirtboarders.com, by a group of women skateboarders in Montréal,

6 *Kara-Jane Lombard*

Canada. She also examines the Skirtboarders' reflexivity in the production of their blog and how users perceive Skirtboarders.com. Her findings reveal that the Skirtboarders reflexively create and circulate fluid definitions of skateboarding femininity on their blog. Thus the Skirtboarders and blog users see Skirtboarders. com as one of many political tools for challenging male-dominated skateboarding media organizations.

Part 3: Skate shifts

Becky Beal's EdD dissertation *The Subculture of Skateboarding: Beyond Social Resistance* (1992) stands on the cusp of two eras – concerned with the resistive potential of skateboarding but still able to connect with the increasing mainstreaming of skateboarding. This tension has since been a consistent topic in much skate scholarship and media, and the mainstreaming of skate in all its forms has become more prominent in discussions of skateboarding. The four chapters in Part 3 examine shifts that have occurred in skateboarding's history around mainstreaming by specifically referring to commercialization, professionalization, neo-liberalization, and creative cities.

This section of the book begins with Michael J. Lorr's chapter, which utilizes the recent normalization of skateboarding as a way to compare how different generations of skateboarders at Kona Skate Park in the United States conceptualize and embody their individual and collective identities. Two skateboarding practices, street skating and park skating, illustrate the similarity and difference between generations and highlight how skateboarding becomes a multigenerational resource skaters draw on and into the constitution of social life. His chapter pinpoints how skateboarding works as an iterative multigenerational 'technology of the collective' by focusing on skateboarding practices, thereby contributing to the ongoing dialogue about how practice and identity matter to individuals and communities.

Simon Orpana's chapter follows on from Lorr's, and he is similarly focused on a skatepark – this time Beasley Skatepark in Canada. Orpana examines Beasley in order to investigate how skateboarding has become a more celebrated, integral part of urban culture. Key to understanding this change is the gentrification strategies of cities that are trying to assert a neoliberal vision of the 'creative city' as remedy to a faltering industrial economy. In navigating the shift to a neoliberal, 'post-industrial' culture, Orpana coins the term *spatial-temporal incorporation*, arguing that this form of incorporation plays an important role in socializing subjects and reshaping urban spaces. Concurrently, he finds that skateboard culture retains traces of the collaboration, solidarity, and community of industrial society – values that might help transform our current situation.

Like Orpana's, my chapter examines skateboarding in relation to neoliberalism – this time in terms of advanced liberalism and the governance of skateboarding. Governmental programs, strategies, and technologies arise out of a complex field of contestation and are inscribed by many voices – including the subjects of governance. My chapter argues that it is important to theorize the productive encounter between governance and resistance. Consequently, it examines a

The cultural politics of skateboarding and the rise of skate urbanism   7

particular aspect of resistance in the governance of skateboarding by considering the incorporation of indigenous governance (governance based in the everyday lives of subjects and not imposed from the outside). Indigenous forms of governance are increasingly appropriated to achieve ends sought by political programmers. In the process, however, it is also apparent that resistance can alter the programmed vision of rule, and the subjects of rule are able to bring the governors into alignment with their wills and their governances.

The book concludes with Thomas Turner's examination of the development of specially designed skateboard shoes in the United States in the 1960s and 1970s. His chapter argues that by improvising with shoes intended for other purposes, skateboarders subtly reconfigured perceptions of existing sports and leisure footwear but that the creation of the skateboard shoe as a specific entity relied on producers replicating and reinforcing these creative re-imaginings. It demonstrates how small groups of consumers can affect the way in which products are understood and highlights the way in which consumers and producers collaborate in the generation of new practices and their associated goods and ideas. Turner's attention to the creative improvisation in the development of skateboarding means that, in many ways, the book ends as it begins – discussing the creative and innovational tendencies of skateboarding.

The meanings of skateboarding

> Skateboarding, contradictorily, is at once 'criminalized' as a night-time activity (as US President George Bush remarked of skateboarders 'just thank God they don't have guns') and represented as 'child's play' at other times.
>
> (Borden 2001, p. 253)

In the early 1990s, a 'skate and destroy/skate and create' sticker war arose between two of the most prominent skateboarding magazines in the world. While *Transworld Skateboarding* tried to promote a respectable image for skateboarding as a reputable sport with its 'skate and create' slogan, *Thrasher* magazine had a more destructive 'skate and destroy' punk ethos. The stickers tended to polarize the skate community and also pointed to two of the opposing tendencies still inherent in skateboarding today – a respectable, 'extreme' sport and a means of creative expression which enacts a form of resistance. The meanings that skateboarding encompasses are more numerous than this, however, and these meanings have also evolved over time.

Thus the remainder of this chapter is concerned with the cultural politics of skateboarding. By cultural politics, I adopt social geographer Peter Jackson's (1991, p. 200) definition: 'the domain in which meanings are constructed and negotiated, where relations of dominance and subordination are defined and contested'. To prepare the ground for a discussion of the way meanings have evolved in skateboarding, it is useful to turn to the first book-length academic study of skateboarding, Iain Borden's book *Skateboarding, Space and the City: Architecture and the Body* (2001). Constructing an historical account of skateboarding, Borden exposes four distinct eras of skateboarding – sidewalk surfing, the pool era

8 Kara-Jane Lombard

inspired by the Z-Boys, skateparks, and street skating. While Borden conducts a theoretical history of skateboarding in order to identify a new kind of architectural history, his book is also useful in demonstrating the ways in which the meanings of skateboarding are evolving. As he accounts for the four eras of skateboarding, Borden explains that varying terrain means varying modes of engagement and forms of repression – changing the meaning of skateboarding. For instance, he notes that the latest phase of urban skating is more political than the street skating of the 1970s due to the varying spatiality and temporality (p. 242).

Borden also notes that the different stages of skateboarding have produced skaters from different backgrounds. For example, 'where the vertical riders of the 1970s and 1980s were often from the "suburban recreation grounds", the later streetstyle skaters tended to come from 'the worst parts of towns and know the true meaning of street life' (p. 185). Over the years, the ethnic origin of skaters has also changed. As Borden notes, 'while skaters in the 1970s tended to be white, blond-haired and called Chip or Brad, in the 1980s skaters were generally of more varied ethnic origins, and called Caballero or Kasai, or in the 1990s Barajas, Hassan, Lieu or Santos' (p. 141). Furthermore, the demographics of contemporary skateboarding now cross multiple generations, as noted by several chapters in this volume.

The early form of the skateboard can be dated back to the early 1900s and featured roller skate wheels attached to a 2 × 4 board or box. In the 1950s, skateboarding became increasingly popular throughout the world, and although boards were still homemade, modifications to the trucks made it easier to manoeuvre. In the late 1950s, the first commercial skateboards by Roller Derby and Humco began to appear on US department store shelves, and three years later, the first retail skateboard shop opened in California. Skateboarding also began gaining popularity in other parts of the world.

In the 1960s, skateboarding gained a following among surf crowds, and in 1965, it appeared on the cover of *Life* magazine. The first skateboarding competition was held at a Pier Avenue Junior High School in California in 1963. A year later, the first outdoor skatepark was built in Florida. In 1963, Larry Stevenson's company Makaha designed the first professional modern skateboards. A lifeguard and the publisher of surfing magazine, *Surf Guide*, Stevenson's prototype was a cross between a homemade skateboard and a surfboard. As Michael Brooke (1999, p. 23) notes,

> It was Stevenson who had the insight that skateboarding could be a part of surf culture. *Surf Guide* laid the foundation for the roots of surfing to mesh with skateboarding . . . Surfers were the first to embrace skateboarding and realize its potential.

The same year, *Surf Guide* began to promote skateboarding (or sidewalk surfing, as it was then called), and included full-page advertisements for Makaha Skateboards. A team of skaters called the Makaha Skateboard Exhibition Team toured America to promote skateboarding and the product, and the company also sponsored the first official skateboarding competition in Hermosa, California.

The cultural politics of skateboarding and the rise of skate urbanism   9

Skateboarding was considered an activity for children when it first emerged. The first wave of popularity during the 1960s saw its meaning evolve into a fad. Despite its increasing popularity throughout the sixties, skateboarding remained a dangerous activity, with poor design contributing to numerous accidents. 'As a result of these problems, cities and towns began banning skateboards. By August of 1965, 20 [American] cities had banned skateboarding from sidewalks and streets' (Brook, 1999, p. 24). Suddenly in 1965, after skate contests, a movie, magazine and immense popularity which saw more than 50 million boards sold in just a few years, the skateboarding boom crashed. It was autumn 1965, and Larry Stevenson was getting 75,000 cancellations for Makaha boards in a day (p. 24). Stevenson never gave up on skateboarding, however, and continued to promote it. The invention of the kicktail in the late 1960s, largely credited to Stevenson, made the skateboard easier to manoeuvre.

In the following decade, the emergence of the Zephyr Skate Team (or Z-Boys) saw the development of skateboarding as an outlaw, alternative, and underground activity. The 1970s also saw the next phase of professionalization and commercialization of skateboarding, partly initiated by the Z-Boys. Zephyr was a surfboard manufacturing company started by Jeff Ho, Craig Stecyk, and Skip Engblom. In a neglected area of Santa Monica known as Dogtown (due to its rundown urban beachfront with a legacy of outlaw surfing, gangs, and graffiti), the Zephyr Production Surf Shop made unique customized boards and gathered local teens to form the shop team. Over time, this surf team became a skate team and the Z-Boys were formed (Peralta 2001).

The Z-Boys debuted at the Bahne-Cadillac Skateboard Championships (also known as the Del Mar Nationals) in 1975. Their unique and aggressive styles caught the skating world off guard and reinvigorated it. Soon afterwards, the Z-Boys split, some to pursue more lucrative opportunities. Skateboarding was becoming more professional, with numerous skateboarding teams started and countless competitions held. As Borden (2001, p. 110) notes, 'in the 1970s most professional skaters were keen to see skateboarding developed as a professional sport'.

In the 1970s, the commercial sector responded to the popularity of skateboarding as new technology was developed and thousands of skateparks were built around the world.

> Throughout the 1970s, there were contests of many descriptions and disciplines . . . skateboard-specific companies stepped up their promotion and advertising campaigns, making substantial investments outside of just production costs. By the late 1970s, massive skateboard parks were opening faster than the cement could dry.
>
> (*Thrasher* 2001, p. 18)

Skateboarders began exploring the vertical limits of skateparks, pools, and drainpipes. Skateparks became one of the most profitable businesses of the 1970s (Borden 2001, p. 4).

10 *Kara-Jane Lombard*

In the 1980s, skateboarding became even more professional. As a business, it was quite profitable and estimated to generate between US$300 and $500 million per annum by the late 1980s (Borden, 2001, p. 156). While skateboarding was becoming more mainstream and professional, many skateboarders continued to skate on their own terms, resisting the campaign for skateboarding to be included in the Olympic Games (Borden, 2001, p. 5). The mid-1980s saw the emergence of street skating (the first professional street contest was held in April 1983 in San Francisco's Golden Gate Park) and the jump ramp era. Contests in the 1980s saw involvement from corporations like Ocean Pacific and Swatch. Not only were large corporations involved in skateboarding by sponsoring riders and contests, but television networks were successfully organizing their own 'extreme sport' events. Events like NBC's Gravity Games and events run or sponsored by the likes of Mountain Dew, Microsoft, T-Mobile, Target, Slim Jim, Ford, and Red Bull became abundant.

Despite the interest by large corporations, in the 1980s, many skateparks began to close. Brooke (1999, p. 117) writes, 'by 1981, skateboarding had entered another slump. Only the truly dedicated stayed with the sport. In Florida, as elsewhere, the skateparks had all closed, except for Kona in Jacksonville'. This led to a rise in street skating, with younger skaters preferring to street skate concrete benches, stairs, rails, and other features. Along with the demise of vert (ramp) skating, manufacturers began working on various innovations, such as smaller wheels. Cities around the globe cracked down on street skating, issuing fines, confiscating boards, and charging skaters with trespassing.

Skateboarding's status as a resistant and underground activity became more entrenched with the rise of street skating in the 1990s, while at the same time skateboarding was also becoming more professional and respectable. The war of the television networks' extreme games during the 1990s sought to cement skateboarding's outlaw status as an 'extreme' sport but did more to develop skateboarding as a legitimate sport. It was largely due to ESPN2's X Games that skateboarding became considered an 'extreme sport.' As Jim Fitzpatrick (2000) notes,

> skating gives the X-Games a legitimate 'extreme sport'. . . it showcases the personality of the sport, establishes respectability from non-skaters, and creates celebrities. ESPN legitimizes the sport to people who would never be exposed to it other than kicking skaters off their property.

Skateboarding thus emerged as a legitimate sport, attracting the interest of the corporate world, boasting worldwide competitions and numerous associations. Professional skateboarders emerged, and several of them started their own companies to manufacture skateboards, accessories, and even apparel.

The more recent shifts in skateboarding's meanings revolve around its integration into urban and cultural life and its utilization as a tool for socially progressive and inclusive ends. To quote Borden (2015),

> skateboarding is increasingly central to debates about the value of public spaces, while simultaneously adding artistic, cultural, educational and

The cultural politics of skateboarding and the rise of skate urbanism   11

commercial value to our urban lives. It is even helping to address some of our most difficult social challenges, and providing hugely disadvantaged children and youths with new hopes, skills and futures.

Despite this trend, contemporary skateboarding continues to comprise ambiguous and often opposing meanings. For journalist Luke Leitch (2014), skateboarders cherish an outlaw aura, for academic Becky Beal (2013) it is participant run and thrives on a DIY ethic while being a part of the mainstream, while for skater Tait Colberg (2012) it is personal expression and art. Academic discussion reveals various and often contradictory understandings of skateboarding: it is a multi–million-dollar industry, recreational activity, sport, children's pursuit, fad, underground movement, criminal activity, form of transport, aesthetic practice, and much more. And the question of whether skateboarding is a subculture is a key debate in academic literature, the media, and within skateboarding itself.

The chapters in this volume must negotiate this crucial question – what is skateboarding? Rather than impose a uniform understanding of it across all chapters, each chapter defines skateboarding in its own sense or investigates some of the different ways in which it is framed and inscribed with meaning. This includes the ways in which these meanings are translated to various contexts and evolve over time. For example, Paul O'Connor's chapter details and qualifies some of these contradictions that exist in skate culture. Michael J. Lorr's inquiry into how skateboarding has become a multi-generational resource explores many of the shifts that have occurred in its meanings. Bill Schaffer defines skateboarding as a discipline with its own implied ethic as he explores its innovation. Indigo Willing and Scott Shearer and Simon Orpana describe skateboarding as a subculture, while Steph MacKay investigates it from the perspective of sport.

The chapters by Thomas Turner and Michael Jeffries, Sebastian Messer, and Jon Swords explore the creative aspects of skateboarding. For Turner, it is the creative improvisation of skateboarding that is then commercialized that is of interest, while the latter trio analyze the practice and motivation of skaters who also create photography, video, and zines. Jeffries, Messer, and Swords note that there are often vague and general assertions that skateboarding is inherently creative, coupled with representations which often inadvertently undermine the claims that it is alternative and transgressive. Thus they are also, in many ways, concerned with the understandings of skateboarding as resistive versus mainstream. Matthew Atencio and Becky Beal's chapter on skate initiatives propelled by private–public partnerships examines the ways in which skateboarding is framed as a socially inclusive and recuperative activity.

Conclusion

Shortly before this book was submitted for publication, two of its contributors, Iain Borden and Michael Jeffries, wrote media pieces commenting on the increasing realization of the positive role of skateboarding in society and the development of the skateboard city. As Jeffries (2015) put it, skaters are 'a mysterious and

12 *Kara-Jane Lombard*

often invisible presence busily making the city a better place to live'. This volume hopes to render the urban practice of skateboarding and those who engage with it in various ways a little more visible. But it is not, in any way, a 'summary text' or the 'final word' on skateboarding. It is simply part of the conversation. By its nature, a book is static and fixed, but as this chapter demonstrates, skateboarding is a fluid, dynamic field, a global phenomenon whose participants have strong connections to local scenes, a rebellious activity and commercialized form. So how do we make sense of skateboarding, its place in urban sites and cultures, and those who participate and engage with it?

References

Beal, B 1992, *The subculture of skateboarding: beyond social resistance*. PhD thesis. University of Northern Colorado.

Beal, B 1995, 'Disqualifying the official: an exploration of social resistance of skateboarding', *Sociology of Sport Journal*, vol. 12, no. 3, pp. 252–267.

Beal, B 2013, *Skateboarding: the ultimate guide*, Greenwood, Santa Barbara, Denver and Oxford.

Borden, I 2001, *Skateboarding, space and the city: architecture and the body*, Berg, Oxford.

Borden, I 2015, 'The new skate city: how skateboarders are joining the urban mainstream', *The Guardian*, 20 April. Available from: www.theguardian.com/cities/2015/apr/20/skate-city-skateboarders-developers-bans-defensive-architecture. [25 April 2015].

Brooke, M 1999, *The concrete wave: the history of skateboarding*, Warwick Publishing, Toronto.

Colberg, T 2012, *The skateboarding art*, Tait Colberg, USA.

Cornelius, J 2015, 'Hope ramped up at skateboard school', Times Live, 30 March. Available from: www.timeslive.co.za/thetimes/2015/03/30/hope-ramped-up-at-skateboard-school. [25 April 2015].

Ellis-Peterson, H 2015, 'For Kabul schoolgirls, learning to ride a skateboard is pathway to liberation', *The Guardian*, 20 April. Available from: www.theguardian.com/world/2015/apr/19/kabul-girls-liberation-skateboard-skateistan. [25 April 2015].

Fitzpatrick, J 2000, 'As seen on TV', *Transworld Skateboarding*, 24 February. Available from: www.skateboarding.com/skate/magazine/article/0,12768,200809,00.html. [3 September 2004].

Hadfield, W 2003, *Skateboarding . . . seeking respectability*, Sports Factor. Available from: www.abc.net.au/rn/talks/8.30/sportsf/stories/s795027.htm. [2 March 2004].

Holland, S 2003, 'Intro: skateboarding is not extreme', *Australian Skateboarding Magazine*, 12 April, p. 12.

Howell, O 2005, 'The "creative class" and the gentrifying city: skateboarding in Philadelphia's Love Park', *Journal of Architectural Education*, vol. 59, no. 2, pp. 32–42.

Jackson, P 1991, 'The cultural politics of masculinity: towards a social geography', *Transactions of the Institute of British Geographers*, vol. 16, pp. 199–213.

Jeffries, M 2015, 'In praise of skaters – elves saving cities' forlorn and forgotten corners, *The Conversation*, 28 April. Available from: http://theconversation.com/in-praise-of-skaters-elves-saving-cities-forlorn-and-forgotten-corners-40859. [28 April 2015].

Koerner, BI 2015, 'Silicon Valley has lost its way. Can skateboarding legend Rodney Mullen help it?', *Wired*, 27 January 2015. Available from: www.wired.com/2015/01/rodney-mullen/. [26 April 2015].

The cultural politics of skateboarding and the rise of skate urbanism 13

Kurucz, J 2005, 'Riding a wave of respectability', *The Record*, 20 April. Available from: www.royalcityrecord.com/issues05/044105/sports/043205sp1.html. [2 May 2005].

Lasane, A 2015, 'Atiba Jefferson talks the cultural influence of skateboarding and the art of skate photography', *Complex*, 31 March. Available from: www.complex. com/style/2015/03/atiba-jefferson-talks-influence-of-skateboarding-and-the-art-of-skate-photography. [25 April 2015].

Leitch, L 2014, 'Skateboarding has gone mainstream (again)', *The Telegraph*, 29 March. Available from: www.telegraph.co.uk/men/fashion-and-style/10729536/ Skateboarding-has-gone-mainstream-again.html. [26 April 2015].

Lister, K 2015, 'Skateboarding makes Afghan girls feel free', *Vice*, 29 January. Available from: www.vice.com/read/skateboarding-makes-afghan-girls-feel-free-881. [25 April 2015].

Owens, C 2014, '"Skateboard urbanism" could change park planning', *Next City*, 1 October. Available from: https://nextcity.org/daily/entry/skateboard-urbanism-draft. [25 April 2015].

Peralta, S (director) 2001, *Dogtown and Z-Boys* (DVD). Columbia Tri-Star Horn, United States.

Sierra, K 2015, 'Silicon Valley could learn a lot from skater culture. Just not how to be a meritocracy', *Wired*, 23 February. Available from: www.wired.com/2015/02/ silicon-valley-thinks-can-learn-skater-culture-terrible-idea. [26 April 2015].

Springsteen, C 2002, 'Skateboarding gains respectability', *Battle Creek Enquirer*, 26 November. Available from: www.battlecreekenquirer.com/news/stories/20021126/local news/448519.html. [27 January 2004].

Thrasher 2001, *Thrasher: insane terrain*, Universe, New York.

Part 1
Cultures and scenes

2 No one standing above you

Rodney Mullen and the ethics of innovation

Bill Schaffer

I suggest that skateboarding is a discipline with its own implied *ethic* in the sense given by Baruch Spinoza, for whom 'good' is defined as a positive capacity for *increasing power through relationships*. As Gilles Deleuze (1988, p. 22) explains, for Spinoza:

> That individual will be called *good* (or free, or rational or strong) who strives, insofar as he is capable, to organize his encounters, to join with whatever agrees with his nature, to combine his relation with relations that are compatible with his, and thereby to increase his power. For goodness is a matter of dynamism, power, and the composition of powers.

An ethic in this sense does not consist of a set of norms imposed from above. Instead, it becomes a matter of exploring the power of the body to enter into unexpected relationships with other bodies, environments, and social groups. I will argue that such a 'skaterly' ethics is articulated in a recent series of lectures presented by Rodney Mullen, widely viewed as the most influential innovator in the history of skateboarding. Mullen repeatedly begins these presentations by recalling the aspect of skateboarding that he felt first distinguished it from more traditional sports: 'there was no one standing above you'. This affirmation refers to the fact that skateboarding requires neither submission to coaches nor conformity to pre-defined goals but may also be taken to suggest a general rejection of 'transcendent' authority. Like Spinoza's ethical system, as we will see, Mullen's approach to skateboarding is thoroughly *relational* and *immanent* insofar as 'goodness' *emerges* in the interaction between things.

My ambition, then, is to precipitate an encounter between philosophy and skateboarding; more specifically, between Spinoza/Deleuze and what I am calling *Mullenology*. The point of this project is not to reduce Mullen's reflections to a mere confirming 'example' of Spinozist or Deleuzean concepts. To the contrary, I will conclude by exploring the possibility that Mullenology may open up a new critical perspective on some aspects of the rhetoric of Deleuze, particularly in relation to the concept of *centering*, and suggest that the implications of such a critique may extend well beyond the domain of skateboarding.

18   *Bill Schaffer*

Innovation as expression

At least since 1976, when the Z-Boys began to overshadow older freestyle champions, skateboard culture has been marked by a polarity between style and technique (Peralta 2001). Style was everything to the Z-Boys. Their skating emulated the 'new' short-board surfing style and valued flowing *lines* – patterns of movement implicitly 'drawn' by the moving skater – and 'soulful' or 'radical' body shapes. By contrast, Mullen argues that some of the most inventive and influential skaters tend to look awkward on their boards, as if this very lack of ease in the relationship between body and deck is conducive to innovation.

Mullen became famous in the early 1980s as a world champion of freestyle, the extremely technical form of skating which the Z-Boys already seemed to have left behind. Indeed, Mullen happily mocks his own style as 'robotic'. Nonetheless, for Mullen (cited in Lemelson Centre 2012), as for the Z-Boys, 'skateboarding is as much, or more, of an art or mode of expression than it is a sport'. For Mullen, however, expression is less about sexy lines than the process of *inventing tricks*. The sole stylistic imperative for Mullen is the pragmatic one of 'minimizing movement', keeping all his moving parts suspended and ready to respond at every instant in order to maximize opportunities for innovation. Mullen's signature style is the apparent absence of style. It is *skating degree zero*, almost 'modernist' in the way that function dictates form. Mullen's process, however, concerns much more than just the way he holds his body while on a board – it amounts to a theory of the way thought and action relate across different levels of organization.

Finding the centre

Very early in his skating career, Mullen experienced a kind of epiphany, one he would later describe as 'finding his center' (Mullen cited in Louison 2011, loc. 384). This insight allowed him to spin up to twenty '360s' – spinning while balanced on the back wheels – taking him to the level of top freestyle competitors. The implications of this lesson didn't stop at this one trick. For Mullen, this would turn out to be a lesson about the very process of innovation. It was a lesson about the need to break open and reconfigure apparent unities within oneself.

The lesson Mullen learnt on the day he finally 'found his center' was that just 'trying' or 'willing' yourself to make a move doesn't get you anywhere. It's the wrong kind of repetition. The willpower approach is wrong at both ends: it mistakenly assumes that the body is commanded by a unitary will; it also mistakenly assumes that the trick is a unitary entity. Everything in the process Mullen has since developed implies the rejection of these two suppositions. From this point on, he would never just repeatedly 'try' or attempt to 'will' a trick. Instead, 'every motion would be taken apart and cycled over and over in my mind, whether I was on my board or lying in bed, from foot plant and weight distribution to where I held my shoulders and eyes' (Louison 2011, loc. 391). In this sense, it can be said that Mullen established a 'new center' by renouncing any assumed privilege

No one standing above you　19

as a puppet master pulling the strings of his own body through acts of will. In effect, he centered by giving up the center.

The analogy between the body and puppetry is Mullen's own: 'We are sophisticated puppets' (Mullen cited in TEDx Talks 2013). The important point of the analogy, however, is not that the puppet is controlled from outside itself but that its jointed parts can be disassembled and put back together in new ways. Indeed, there can be no external control, since we are all our *own* puppets. It is the way that parts are connected, more than the properties of the parts themselves, that determines what we can do with our bodies. The only hope for making something new happen in this context is to attend to the *organization* of your body. This process is not one of physically breaking up the body (although anyone familiar with Mullen's biography will know that at a certain point, he was forced to do exactly that as a result of an inoperable injury to his hips). The parts in question here are not limbs or organs. The terms Mullen uses to describe those elements are 'sub-movements' or 'executive functions' (a term he borrows from cognitive science).

Many executives

> Tricks are made of sub-movements, executive motor functions, more granular to a degree which I can't quite tell you.
>
> (Mullen cited in Mr1hmm1 2013)

> By the time you have this trick down you can call it executive, it's unthinking, it's more or less white noise going on in your head with a sort of a flick. At that stage you have to be able to crack it open and break it apart.
>
> (Mullen cited in O'Reilly 2014)

For Mullen, as I read it, executive function is the way the body is organized to automate already established capacities: the mechanism of bodily habits. The body has many executives, many of which function outside awareness; many executives, but no CEO. In terms of the puppet analogy, the capacities of our bodies seem to be determined at any point by pre-defined possibilities of movement, each controlled from a center of command and pulled by a single string, but in reality the hands pulling the strings are themselves pulled by other strings. These controlling strings can be disconnected and reconnected, allowing for the formation of new movements, new habits, and new degrees of freedom for the flesh-and-blood puppets that we are. Skateboarding is exactly this serious and joyful form of self-puppetry.

Mullen relates his personal penchant for breaking things down into 'pieces' to his university training in physics; nonetheless, his approach is neither reductive nor mechanistic. His method is about connections and breaks sensed 'internally'; 'integration of a feel combined with an analytic ability to chase down everything else that might work while holding down the rest' (Mullen cited in O'Reilly 2014). Mullen articulates this relationship between analysis and 'feeling' in terms

20   *Bill Schaffer*

of what we might call 'the tablecloth principle': 'that's how it works for me: stack, stack, stack, stack, stack, rack it, and put like a tablecloth on it, and focus on that last little bit' (Mullen cited in *Rodney Mullen: from the ground up* 2013).

This principle responds to the problem Mullen encountered when he first tried to spin more '360s': tricks are too complex to be directed by conscious control in real time. There is too much going on too fast to be consciously coordinated by an individual consciousness. Once a trick is 'wired', it is taken care of 'automatically' by executive function, but the invention of new tricks happens *between* the disengaged parts of already-established functions. Performance of established tricks is automated; the emergence of new functions happens spontaneously once parts are detached from their established roles through the process of analysis and feeling. Mullen therefore does as much thinking as possible when not on the board and as little thinking as possible on the board. When the time comes to go for it, he achieves the narrowest possible cognitive focus by thinking about just one simple aspect of bodily movement, such as the angle of a shoulder or the direction of his gaze at a particular point. He repeatedly stresses the need for 'being able to tune in and tune out' (Mullen cited in O'Reilly 2014). After the analysis and re-sequencing of your bodily habits ('stack, stack, stack') you need to 'rack it, put a tablecloth over it', let go of cognitive control, and just trust or believe in the body itself, 'then everything else is taken for granted and runs on autopilot' (Mullen cited in *Rodney Mullen: from the ground up* 2013). It is your body that will make or not make the move, according to its own capacities, not the 'you' who wants to hold and control all the strings. Thus sometimes you don't know you've made it for several seconds (Mullen cited in O'Reilly 2014). Skateboarding constantly demands a kind of faith in the body.

Bodies are infinite

Mullen consistently refers to 'movements' and 'sub-movements' as if they were relatively autonomous individuals. Executive functions are capable of 'looking after themselves' and 'running on autopilot'. Tricks are composed of movements that are in turn composed of sub-movements in a process that Mullen (cited in TEDx Talks 2013) says is 'granular' to an 'indefinite degree'; we could say they are like a Russian doll that contains infinitely more Russian dolls, all the way down. Our bodies are *puppets made out of puppets*. In Deleuzean/Spinozist terms, our bodies are 'composite to infinity'. Explicating Spinoza's understanding of the body, Deleuze (cited in *On Spinoza* 2007) writes:

> a body is necessarily composite to infinity . . . for example, my eye and the relative constancy of my eye are defined by a certain relation of movement and rest through all the modifications of the diverse parts of my eye; but my eye itself, which already has an infinity of parts.

The practical implication of this is that 'sub-movements are floating around and connect themselves' (Mullen cited in Mr1hmm1 2013). The very act of sensing and articulating sub-movements frees up habitual patterns of movement (already-mastered tricks). Instead of 'you' commanding the body, *the body teaches you*: 'as they become more rarefied and branched out . . . [they] educate you as they branch out' (Mullen cited in Lemelson Centre 2012). Everything depends on the way that wholes relate to parts and parts relate to each other. Mullen uses words like 'holistic' and 'synergy' and 'totality' to describe the way parts form a functional unity that is greater than the sum of those parts. When asked if he approaches his skating in a non-linear way, Mullen (cited in Andrews 2010) replied, 'It's a good word to describe it, but holistic is better, and synergistic even better. The totality of the whole is greater than the sum of its parts'.

Even as Mullen evokes the familiar rhetoric of holism, he also advises 'don't look at the whole' (Mullen cited in *Rodney Mullen: pop an ollie and innovate* 2013). He tells us that creative possibilities are always seen 'in your peripheral vision . . . it doesn't happen when you're looking directly at it' (Mullen cited in Lemelson Centre 2012). Mullen thus posits a whole or totality, but then tells us to forget about it, put it out of mind, avoid confronting it at all costs. He explicitly dismisses appeals to 'the organic': 'you can dissect what is organic to the point it dissolves into nothingness' (2012).

Asked to define a 'rule of innovation', Mullen (cited in Lemelson Centre, 2012) replies that 'it comes from recognizing voids . . . make things simpler . . . more minimalist . . . filling voids'. He exhorts us to 'recognize voids and go after them'. It seems these voids do not consist in the mere absence of something but are more like potentials that emerge *between* things. They are the intervals 'across which' parts reconnect when executive functions are disassembled. It is exactly by dissolving what at first seems 'organic' that one finds the gaps that allow for new connections. It is here that the concept of the *assemblage* might assist in conceptualizing Mullen's approach to innovation. In explicating a form of 'assemblage theory' directly inspired by Deleuze, Manuel De Landa (cited in European Graduate School 2012) defines the more traditional conception of 'whole' as one determined by an 'interiority' of parts which prohibits their disengaging from the totality and contrasts this to the 'exteriority of parts' in an assemblage, which allows parts to unlock from the whole and recombine. From this perspective, the whole may be greater than the sum of its parts, but the part is sometimes also greater than the whole, insofar as change happens between parts that have disengaged from the whole.

Environmental dust: how context shapes content

Mullen's lectures constantly return to the question of *how context shapes content*. Context here refers to 'terrain' or environment; content means 'tricks'. Specific environments, then, shape tricks, that is, *what the body can do*. Mullen treats environmental features as 'active' parts entering into new connections with the board and parts of the skater's body. This is clear in Mullen's recollections regarding his invention of the 'dark slide'. This highly unlikely trick involves flipping the board upside down, wheels upward, sliding in that 'wrong' position on a curb or

22 Bill Schaffer

ledge, then flipping back onto the wheels and riding away. The crucial moment in developing the full move for Mullen came when he realized that a certain footing could allow the obstacle itself to do the flip for him:

> I had seen someone slide on the back of the board like that, and I was like 'how can I get it over?' Because that had not yet been done and then it dawned on me . . . I had an infrastructure, I had this deep layer . . . it's just your foot. It's just the way you throw your board over, just let the ledge do that and it's easy. The next thing you know, there's twenty more tricks based out of the variations.
>
> (Mullen cited in *Rodney Mullen: pop an ollie and innovate* 2013)

The context/content dynamic, then, exhibits the same logic of coupling and uncoupling we have already seen operate between the parts of the skater's own body, extended now to the relationship between body, board, and designed environments. It is ultimately not the skater who 'shapes' the tricks but the skater/environment coupling. Moreover, the context also emerges anew through interaction with content. Terrain that has been designed to limit movement is transformed to allow for new possibilities of movement. Skateboarding effectively reconfigures the world in which it takes place, not by physically demolishing and reconstructing but by revealing previously unperceived *affordances*. James Gibson (1986, p. 127), the founder of ecological psychology, defined affordances in terms that seem entirely consonant with Mullen's reflections on skateboarding:

> The affordances of the environment are what it offers the animal, what it provides or furnishes, either for good or ill. The verb to afford is found in the dictionary, but the noun affordance is not. I have made it up. I mean by it something that refers to both the environment and the animal in a way that no existing term does. It implies the complementarity of the animal and the environment.

This complementarity of the animal and the environment is exactly what Mullen (cited in Lemelson Centre 2012) assumes in his approach to innovation:

> Go to some context or go to some area that you are slightly unfamiliar with and you start doing what is familiar to you . . . Something will connect with one of these branched relatives of some other sub-movement that naturally goes with it.

Skateboarding is thus a practice of revealing unintended affordances of designed environments: a picnic table is no longer something to eat at, a downhill road is no longer just a way of getting from A to B, a handrail is no longer just a way of steadying a walking body, a pool is no longer a just a thing to fill with water and swim in.

As De Landa has shown, Gibson's affordances can be viewed as the same thing as Spinoza/Deleuze's *affects*. Both are possibilities of connection that affect the

No one standing above you 23

body, and both are therefore always relational and 'double'. A knife affords cutting only in relation to something else: there needs to be something that cuts and something that is cut (De Landa cited in European Graduate School 2012). In this sense, affects and affordances are emergent events rather than intrinsic properties. They happen *in between*. This is exactly why *we do not know what a body can do*. The capacities of a body are determined not only by its intrinsic properties, which we can identify and enumerate, but also by concrete and singular interactions that cannot be determined in advance. In another turn of this open feedback loop, the skater, too, becomes another element of the creative process, at once transformed and transforming. As Mullen (cited in TEDx Talks 2013) says, 'All this environmental dust that gets baked in and becomes executive motor function, that marks us, that we don't even know is there'. According to Mullen, then, the environment is literally *folded* into the body as 'environmental dust'.

The metrics of respect: individuation and collectivity

The most impressive thing about the list of tricks invented by Mullen is not their sheer number but the fact that many of them are, in his own words, *foundational*. Above all, the 'flatland ollie' is the foundation of modern street skating, even though Mullen invented it while still committed to the mode of freestyle. The 'ollie' is a way of making board and body jump into the air together, without any need for the rider to grab the board. It would be left to other skaters to take the 'ollie' to the street and open up the city anew as a 'smooth space' in which obstacles are transformed into affordances. Suddenly you could 'ollie' up gutters, onto curbs and grind them, onto handrails and slide them, cross gaps, and keep riding in a single flowing line. A trick Mullen considered one of his more trivial freestyle moves transformed skateboarding around the world, subsequently transforming Mullen's career as the freestyle scene was killed by his own freestyle move. In a sense, the 'ollie' eventually transformed the world itself, as evidenced in the form of the massive, ongoing global investment in 'skate stopper' technologies – metal bars and studs added to ledges, rails, and footpaths – by architects and urban planners.

All this prodigious innovation began with Rodney Mullen, alone with a board and a slab of concrete, trying to command his body to spin more '360s'. As we have seen, the approach Mullen has subsequently developed is to treat his own body as a set of 'movements' and 'sub-movements' that can be divided and re-organized to create new habits. That is exactly his 'praxis', yet this praxis is also intrinsically collective. At this level, too, the whole is greater than the sum of its parts, yet the parts are never fused or fully integrated with the whole. So there is another level of coupling and uncoupling, another level of assemblage, at which an individual relates to the global skate community.

> Real respect is given by how much we take what other guys do, these basic tricks, 360 flips, we take that, we make it our own and then we contribute back to the community in a way that edifies the community itself. The greater

24   *Bill Schaffer*

the contribution, the more we express and form our individuality, which is so important to a lot of us who feel like rejects to begin with. The summation of that gives us something we could never achieve as an individual.
>   (Mullen cited in *Rodney Mullen: pop an ollie and innovate* 2013)

Mullen, as we have seen, is an extraordinarily articulate individual, in defiance of all the typical clichés about 'slacker dudes'. Nonetheless, he was formed by the experience of not being able to communicate, as a result of both geographical isolation and the eccentricity of his personality. Even today, Mullen's own practice remains intensely solitary – he mostly skates at night and by himself, like a kind of skate hermit – yet he is driven by the need to contribute to a community. He refers to himself as a permanent outsider, even in relation to his own skate culture, yet this non-belonging is also a form of belonging. This paradox is possible because the 'basic ethos' of skateboarding is to form 'collections of people that really don't belong in collections . . . yet we seek a sense of belonging' (Mullen cited in Lemelson Centre 2012). Thus 'the metrics of respect' is determined 'how we individuate ourselves by what we do' and respect is earned 'by the degree to which you make yourself different' (2012).

It is in this sense that Mullen (cited in *Rodney Mullen: pop an ollie and innovate* 2013) draws a parallel between skate culture and the culture of hackers. Skaters and hackers, for Mullen, are the model of a creative community, and the lessons they teach go far beyond their respective fields. Like skaters, hackers reveal unexpected connections and affordances in designed environments. Like skaters, they gain respect from their community by sharing their innovations and allowing them to be mutated by others. Skaters, I would say, are *space hacker*s. They hack cities and suburbs.

Individuation as both Mullen and Deleuze envision it is therefore intrinsically collective. 'Individuality' is not something given in advance and awaiting an opportunity for expression. Instead, individuation emerges through interaction with environment and community. Expression is also a process of interactive transformation. If context *shapes* content, as Mullen stresses, then content *expresses* context. In this sense, far from being vandalism, *skating expresses designed space*, something that was very apparent to Edmund Bacon, one of the heroes of modern urban planning (Skaters for Public Skateparks 2006).

Thank you, thank you, thank you: urban planning, vandalism, and skateboarding

In 1965, Bacon commissioned the design of Philadelphia's JFK Plaza, now known as LOVE Park. The only concessions to any anticipated human presence incorporated into this Brutalist space were a few fountains and a set of granite benches designed more for their integration with the overall scheme than for comfort. All that changed with the advent of modern street skating in the 1990s. The very qualities that made LOVE Park an unlikely place to just sit and relax made it perfect for street skating. Predictably, the mayor of Philadelphia mounted a war against street skating after first trying to cash in with a corporate skate event, ordering constant police patrols to chase down skaters and confiscate their boards. When that failed, the mayor resorted to his own form of sanctioned vandalism, redesigning benches and planters in ways that he hoped would render them impossible to skate.

It was at this point that Edmund Bacon became involved. Far from dismissing street skaters as vandals needing to be controlled, Bacon saw that they had discovered the secret to making dead spaces come alive; they were the truly creative force and the mayor was the vandal. In this light, skaters are the leaders of a movement against alienation. They make it their daily business to explore the hidden possibilities of cities and suburbs, reinventing the designed world they live in as a zone of freedom and expression. They really 'live' in the city instead of just moving from A to B. 'You – skateboarders', Bacon declared, 'are the leading edge of a revolution of the human being's relation to his or her environment' (Skaters for Public Skateparks 2006). At the age of ninety-four, barely able to walk, Bacon staged one of the most moving gestures of support for the culture of skateboarding ever witnessed. With the aid of two men supporting his aged shoulders, Bacon summoned the media to LOVE Park and had himself filmed illegally riding a skateboard in the very same space that he had commissioned thirty years earlier. The unrestrained joy which overcame the frail body of this once-powerful man taking his first ever ride on a skateboard is palpable.

Get into something: Deleuze, centering, and the question of control

I have emphasized what I take to be deep affinities between Mullenology and Spinoza/Deleuze. There is a point, however, at which tensions between these discourses cannot be suppressed. These tensions concern the question of *centering* and emerge precisely when Deleuze comes closest to directly addressing the ethos of skateboarding. As a 'philosopher of the new', Deleuze showed an active interest in the phenomenon of innovation within sports. Towards the end of his life, he became fascinated with surfing, recognizing that it represented a radical alternative to traditional forms of sport. According to Deleuze (1992, p. 7): 'everywhere *surfing* has replaced the older *sports*'. These reflections on the logic of surfing are offered in a very brief yet highly influential essay in which Deleuze laid out a theory of *control societies*, seen as supplanting the disciplinary societies described by Michel Foucault (1977, 1978). To summarize an already densely argued thesis: to move from discipline to control is to move from spatial isolation to constant communication, from assembly line to network, from docility to mobility, from individual to dividual, from discrete enclosures to continuous tracking, from identity to debt, from moulding according to fixed norms to incessant modulation. It is in this context that Deleuze evokes the image of surfing.

Deleuze's account of control societies is already ambiguous. The very same concepts that in his earlier work seemed to be allied with resistance and creativity, such as deterritorialization and dividuality, seem now to have become the very principle of power. While the 'control' model retains an indisputable descriptive

26 *Bill Schaffer*

power in the context of our online world, it also 'feels' as though Deleuze has exhausted all his conceptual resources merely *describing* the operations of domination in its new expression, leaving no visible gaps or room for the possibility of escape. The role of surfing in this account of the emerging logic of domination is thus deeply ambiguous. It is not at all clear whether it represents resistance to the new system or its most subtle form of mobile control. If surfing is replacing the disciplinary model of conventional sport 'everywhere' and mobility is now a function of domination, which has become 'free floating', might not the joy of surfing be the ultimate ruse of power itself?

It is here that Deleuze's references to surfing become interesting in tension with Mullenology. Deleuze (1995, p. 121) writes,

> The kind of movements you find in sports and habits are changing. We got by for a long time with an energetic conception of motion, where there's a point of contact, or we are the source of movement. Running, putting the shot, and so on: effort, resistance, with a starting point, a lever. But nowadays we see movement defined less and less in relation to a point of leverage. All the new sports – surfing, windsurfing, hang-gliding – take the form of entering into an existing wave. There's no longer an origin as starting point, but a sort of putting-into-orbit. The key thing is how to get taken up in the motion of a big wave, a column of rising air, to 'get into something' instead of being the origin of an effort.

It is surprising that Deleuze does not mention skateboarding in this context. After all, it is skateboarding that 'deterritorializes' surfing in a way that brings it into 'encounters' with the controlled spaces of cities and suburbs. Perhaps Deleuze could not see how skateboarding could be construed as 'entering into an existing wave'?

The standing wave skateboarding enters into, I would argue, is the always-available wave of *gravity*. But there is never just a wave rising 'outside'; there is always a wave rising from 'within'. Put simply, you could never enter into any wave without *leverage and centering*. Indeed, all the most innovative skaters, Mullen tells us, even those with no training in physics, enjoy an 'intuitive sense of leverages' (Mullen cited in Lemelson Centre 2012). The point is not that skateboarding empirically contradicts the 'wave' theory offered by Deleuze but that his analysis leaves something to be thought.

Ironically, the image of the shot-putter Deleuze evokes to exemplify the old paradigm strongly recalls the freestyle trick with which this essay began: 'spinning 360s'. Both the shot-putter and the skater generate a wave of rotational momentum *within* their own bodies. In this sense, there is already a wave to ride in shot-putting and levers to pull in surfing or skateboarding. There is no need to pose an exclusive choice between 'entering a wave' and acting as a 'lever' or center of energetic origin. The most basic moves in both skateboarding and surfing – a skater's 'kick turns' or 'carves', a surfer's 'cutbacks' or 're-entries' – are acts of leverage that take the rider even further *into* the wave. The decisive

No one standing above you 27

difference between traditional sports and the new mode is that the skater or surfer, unlike the shot-putter, wants to *ride* the wave all the way: to *go with it*.

To skate or surf, then, you need to throw yourself into a wave generated within your own body at the same time as 'getting into' a wave rising from 'outside'. If you need to worry about centering, it is because you are riding in a zone of risk, because you do not occupy a stable or fixed center, because you are going outside the support of your base. Centering isn't fixed, but provisional, interactive, and fluid. Centering is what allows singularities, flipping, and spinning moves, without breaking the body. Deleuze's rhetoric, however, is consistently averse to any notion of 'centering'. In *A Thousand Plateaus*, Gilles Deleuze and Félix Guattari (2004, p. 442) explicitly address 'centering' in the context of another form of athletic activity that does not conform to Western models of sport: the martial arts.

> It is true that the martial arts continually invoke the center of gravity and the rules for its displacement. That is because these ways are not the ultimate ones. However far they go, they are still in the domain of Being, and only translate absolute movements of another nature into the common space – those effectuated in the Void, not in nothingness, but in the smooth of the void where there is no longer any goal: attacks, counterattacks, and headlong plunges.

In an accompanying footnote quoting Heinrich von Kleist's famous short story about infinitely graceful puppets, Deleuze and Guattari (p. 561) tell us that

> Treatises on martial arts remind us that the Ways, which are still subject to the laws of gravity, must be transcended in the void. Kleist's *About Marionettes . . .* without question one of the most spontaneously oriental texts in Western literature, presents a similar movement: the linear displacement of the center of gravity is still 'mechanical' and relates to something more 'mysterious' that concerns the soul and knows nothing of weight.

The 'void' evoked here, with reference to martial arts, seems a very different affair than the plural 'voids' Mullen encounters when working on new tricks. Indeed, it is hard to see how this 'void' has not become a transcendent term, posited outside any relation, neither affected nor affecting. Kleist's story is open, however, to another reading than offered by Deleuze. Since there will not be room to offer more than a few brief comments, I must ask the reader to consult a translation of Kleist's text in order to follow the implications of these remarks.

The figure of the puppet or marionette resonates among Mullen, Deleuze, and Kleist; among skateboarding, philosophy, and literature. It is true that the infinitely graceful puppets envisaged by Kleist's aspiring designer will be 'effectively weightless'. Nonetheless, they are also explicitly said to possess 'a more natural arrangement of the centers of gravity' (von Kleist, n.d.). Moreover, they are still connected to a human, whose body also dances and who is never said to be free of gravity. Indeed, in Kleist's story, it is precisely the availability of centers of gravity

28   Bill Schaffer

that allows a living connection between puppet and human in a relationship that is not simply mastered or controlled by the human. Human operators, the designer insists, have to *transpose themselves* into the puppet's center of gravity, thereby effectively decentering themselves *and* the puppet. It seems impossible, once again, to say whether the human controls the puppet or the puppet controls the human. Both are simultaneously God and puppet. The whole *assemblage*, which is made possible by the connection of two centers of gravity, is decentered *by* centering. In this reading, Kleist's impossible blueprint for infinite grace becomes uncannily reminiscent of Mullen relating both to the sophisticated puppet that is his very own body and to his board.

If deterritorialization can be a function of power, however, as the model of control suggests, then why should centering not in some circumstances be a function of resistance or creativity? The concept suggested by the encounter between Deleuze and Mullen, the implications of which may go much further than skateboarding or surfing, is a distinction between the *position of center* and the *process of centering*. From this perspective, skateboarding may be a form of *counter-discipline* that resists control. The ethic of skateboarding hybridizes the models of discipline and control. It says: "relate to yourself as dividual, but constitute yourself as an individual. Individuate through total devotion to a particular task (as in the disciplinary model), but a task that ceaselessly mutates itself, and which is done for its own sake, for 'nothing'. Become a 'source of movement', but movement of a very specific kind, experimental movement without rules or fixed forms".

Conclusion

Skateboarding today is a global culture, fully integrated with communications networks and digital imaging, inextricably connected to the vast, enveloping operations of the market. The hype of 'extreme sports' represents the commodification of skateboarding and other forms of expression as a form of spectacle. Images of tricks and the image of doing tricks can be marketed, yet they have a value that cannot be alienated or exchanged, insofar as they express a mode of belonging to a community of innovation. Skateboarding is thus both the perfect globalized commodity form for a society of control (a signifier of 'lifestyle' in the display windows of a million fashion stores) and a form of creativity that escapes the rule of money. It is both at once. A similar double bind applies to the community of hackers with which Mullen allies skate culture. Hacking is both resistance to control and an extension of control. The ease with which it 'switches' is manifest in the frequent phenomenon of hackers becoming corporate security experts. Mullen, who also happens to have made a very large amount of money from his own involvement in the marketing of skateboards, has bemoaned the way in which marketing hype corrupts the process of innovation that is intrinsic to skateboarding: 'I have a bad taste in my mouth where sometimes certain qualities are optimized and marketed, in a way that's "we are different" or "we're more extreme", and to me none of that is innovation' (Mullen, cited in Lemelson Centre, 2012).

The global culture of skateboarding is inevitably connected to the world in which it exists, but it may also offer a 'source of movement' that escapes the 'society of control'. As skaters, we may be puppets, but at least we can say there is no puppet master standing above us.

References

Andrews, E 2010, 'Rodney Mullen: another dimension', *Huck Magazine*. Available from: www.huckmagazine.com/ride/skate/rodney-mullen/. [1 March 2014].

Deleuze, G 1988, *Spinoza, practical philosophy*, trans. R Hurley, City Lights Books, San Francisco.

Deleuze, G, 1992, 'Postscript on the societies of control', *October*, vol. 59, pp. 3–7.

Deleuze, G 1995, *Negotiations*, trans. M Joughin, Columbia University Press, New York.

Deleuze, G & Guattari, F 2004, *A thousand plateaus*, trans. B Massumi, Continuum, New York/London.

European Graduate School 2012, *Manuel De Landa. Assemblage theory, society, and Deleuze*. Available from: www.youtube.com/watch?v=J-I5e7ixw78. [1 March 2014].

Foucault, M 1977, *Discipline and punish*, trans. A. Sheridan, Pantheon Books, New York.

Foucault, M 1978, *The history of sexuality*, trans. R Hurley, Pantheon Books, New York.

Gibson, J 1986, *The ecological approach to visual perception*, Lawrence Erlbaum, Hillsdale.

Kleist, H von n.d., *On the marionette theatre*, trans. I Parry, Southerncross Review. Available from: http://southerncrossreview.org/9/kleist.html. [March 1 2014].

Lemelson Centre, National Museum of American History, Smithsonian Institute 2012, *Rodney Mullen on innovation*. Available from: www.youtube.com/watch?v=umZ2Bsr0usI. [1 March 2014].

Louison, C 2011, *The impossible: Rodney Mullen, Ryan Sheckler, and the fantastic history of skateboarding*. Kindle version, Available from: Amazon.com. [1 March 2014].

Mr1hmm1 2013, *Rodney Mullen: pop an ollie and innovate (TED talk)*. Available from: www.youtube.com/watch?v=uEm-wjPkegE. [1 March 2014].

On Spinoza 2007, *Lectures by Gilles Deleuze: Blog*. Available from: http://deleuzelectures. blogspot.com.au/2007/02/on-spinoza.html. [1 March 2014].

O'Reilly 2014, *Rodney Mullen, 'The art of good practice' – Strata 2014*. Available from: http://strataconf.com/strata2014/public/schedule/detail/33736. [1 March 2014].

Peralta, S (director) 2001, *Dogtown and Z-Boys* (DVD). Sony Pictures Classics, Culver City.

Rodney Mullen: from the ground up 2013. Available from: www.youtube.com/watch? v=ieC_5foElVk. [1 March 2014].

Skaters for Public Skateparks 2006, *Freedom of space*. Available from: www.youtube.com/ watch?v=eq5aLeLPakc. [March 1 2014].

TEDx Talks 2013, *On getting up again: Rodney Mullen at TEDxOrangeCoast*. Available from: www.youtube.com/watch?v=DBbmNAZWq-E. [1 March 2014].

3 Skateboard philanthropy
Inclusion and prefigurative politics

Paul O'Connor

Introduction

Fanling Skatepark is located in an industrial park in one of Hong Kong's 'new towns' in the eastern New Territories. It is one of Hong Kong's largest designated spaces for skateboarding, a concrete park that has street obstacles and bowls. On an October night, a group of young men in their twenties skate the smaller bowl. They are experts at their craft and confident, 'carving' the transitions and 'grinding' the coping of the bowl. In observing the efforts of a novice skateboarder in his mid-teens, one of the men takes time to explain to the novice the process of pumping the transitions, a technique that allows the skateboarder to gain momentum. He checks out the novice's board and tests to see how loose his trucks are. He shares his knowledge, he demonstrates the technique, and he encourages the novice to practice, then returns to his friends and continues skateboarding.

This vignette captures informal sharing, an element of the inclusion that manifests in skateboard culture. How do these dynamics of skateboard culture play out on a larger scale as 'skateboard philanthropy'? One observable factor is the growth in recent years of a series of non-profit organizations that seek to provide young people with empowerment and independence via skateboarding. Skateistan, the Tony Hawk Foundation, the A.Skate Foundation, and Board Rescue are just a few examples of how skateboarding has been used as a force for social improvement. What do such projects tell us about skateboard culture, its values, and its politics? This chapter interrogates the inclusive nature of skateboard culture as a way to understand skateboard philanthropy. It argues that skateboard philanthropy can be understood as an example of prefigurative politics in skateboard culture, where core values are transmitted and sustained in an informal and contingent way through performance, practice, and example.

The growth of skateboarding

The growth of skateboard philanthropy can in part be seen as a result of the sustained popularity and growth of skateboarding over the last twenty years. Ocean Howell (2008, p. 476) notes that between 1995 and 2005, the number of skateboarders in the United States grew 178% (rising from 4.5 million to 12 million), whilst participation in other traditional sports grew modestly. This time frame is significant as it represents the consolidation of skateboarding's mainstream popularity, which had fluctuated dramatically in the 1970s and early 1990s. However, there are also reports that utilize Google search trends indicating interest in skateboarding is currently in decline (Cuin 2013). Such indications are ambiguous, tell us little about participation in skateboarding, and only infer Internet search habits. Reliable statistics on skateboarding are hard to provide as, if regarded as a sport, its participants eschew the organizational structure of teams, clubs, and associations typical of other sports. Some estimates have indicated that the global number of skateboarders could be as high as 50 million (Human Kinetics & Hanlon 2009, p. 198). One of the leading skateboard magazines, *Transworld Skateboarding*, estimates its global brand audience to be 13 million people, of which they cite a monthly readership of 619,886 alongside a confirmed and paid circulation to 87,308 readers (*Transworld Skateboarding* 2013). The commercialization of skateboarding in ESPN's X Games, Nike SB apparel, and the Activision line of Tony Hawk computer games speaks to the mainstream popularity of skateboarding in both entertainment and fashion. However, much of the research published on skateboarding deals with themes of resistance, either in terms of the use of public space (Borden 2001) or the counter- and sub-cultural ethos of skateboarding (Beal & Weidman 2003). Such representations appear to contradict the mainstream and commercial popularity of skateboarding.

Contradictions in skate culture

There is therefore a need to qualify some of the contradictions that exist in skate culture. Emily Chivers Yochim (2013) diligently identifies a number of these ambiguities. First, she argues that skateboarding 'has occupied a liminal space in which it has been defined as decidedly American and decidedly countercultural' (p. 177). As a result, and quite remarkably, skateboarding is able to be both a mainstream and a fringe pursuit. Complimenting this point, she notes that skateboarding has an entrepreneurial legacy and has never had a 'precapitalist moment' (p. 55). The business side of skateboarding is therefore a legitimate part of skate culture. However, businesses are scrutinized by skateboarders to the extent to which they support and include the efforts, ideas, and participation of skateboarders. Such is the importance of this authentic engagement in skate culture that it is essential for skateboard companies to continually maintain and demonstrate these ties. Such dynamics portray skateboarding as more than simply a sport or hobby. Yochim speaks consistently of skateboarding as a culture and highlights how skateboarders themselves reject the label of skateboarding as a sport as both limited and misleading. With reference to these points, we can also recognize that skate culture has its own politics, a politics that becomes distinct with reference to skateboard media. Sports researchers Becky Beal and Lisa Weidman (2003), in their research on skateboarders and analysis of skate media, present 'authenticity' as one of the most salient aspects of inclusion in skateboard culture. They note that skateboarders prioritize individuality, creativity, and 'participant control' and

32   *Paul O'Connor*

are critical when these elements are threatened. The authors note that the hallmark of inclusion as a skateboarder is quite simply premised on participation, that is, being someone who commits to skateboarding regularly. Distinguishing the issue of participant control, Yochim (2013, p. 88) notes that 'Skateboarders frequently communicate to instruct one another in skateboarding's core principles and values. However, such instruction is contingent in form, for were it too direct or formal it might begin to resemble the restrictions skateboarders see in traditional sports'. Yochim and others have shown that in various ways, skateboarders make continuous and subtle manoeuvres to preserve and transmit skateboard culture to one another.

In this chapter, I explore how skateboard philanthropy can be understood as part of this transmission and how it corresponds to a particular type of politics. First, I shall present a methodological overview of the research, followed by a discussion of inclusion in skateboard cultures. I then explore examples of skateboard philanthropy and argue the relevance of prefigurative politics.

Methodology: a confessional

The method of this ongoing research is misleading without the recognition of my emic perspective as a skateboarder for twenty-eight years. From an anthropological perspective, my 'insider' position suggests a predisposition to cloud certain objectivities. By another measure, as an academic I also possess a peculiar interest in skateboarding that is not necessarily shared by other skateboarders. My desire to explore the social construction, politics, and embodiment of skate culture can be seen to run counter to the primary importance of physical participation in skateboarding. Whilst skateboarding as a practice is arguably best understood through experience, skate culture demands greater academic attention. In adopting an academic and intellectual interest in skateboarding, I have also developed an etic perspective on skateboarding. This chapter therefore comes from a third space, a liminal position between quite different worlds.

Through observation and participation in skate culture and engagement with media materials, I have focused on developing a nuanced picture of skate culture around the theme of inclusion. I have also conducted, by way of online correspondence, interviews with a former volunteer at one skateboarding non-governmental organization (NGO) and the founder of another. This research includes my own ethnographic work with veteran skateboarders in Hong Kong and the UK and observation at a collection of 'skate spots' in Hong Kong. Analysing skateboard media and academic works on skateboarding also provides an important contrast to ethnographic observations.

Skateboard culture and inclusion

In my research and analysis of skateboard media, I have noted the increasing number of charitable groups that work with skateboarding as a force for social good. At the same time, in my ethnographic observations of skateboarders, I have also witnessed spontaneous sharing and cooperation in the informal ways skateboarders assist one another. This includes, but is not limited to mentoring and the sharing or passing down of tips, old boards, and tools. These practices, both the large-scale philanthropy and the informal sharing, mirror each other and can be described as examples of social inclusion.

Before looking at some examples of skateboard philanthropy, let me unpack the idea of inclusion and present some examples of how it manifests in skate culture. First, the idea of social inclusion has become popular in academic work on education and on the rights and activities of individuals with disabilities (Bossaert et al. 2013). In this realm, inclusion becomes part of education policy and curriculum design. Broader notions of inclusion pursue issues of identity, representation, technology, and peace studies (McCrone & Bechhofer 2008; Parker & Song 2007, Piatelli 2009). In much of the literature notions of inclusion are seldom defined, often being presented as self-evident. Frederick Miller and Judy Katz (2002, p. 17) state that 'inclusion creates a sense of belonging and when each person realizes a sense of belonging to the organizational community, motivation and morale soar'. Inclusion is therefore recognized as a force for good, a way to have people engaged in their communities and with one another. However, the positive representation of inclusion often betrays its ambiguities. Inclusion tends to exist alongside exclusion. A point Deborah Piatelli (2009, pp. 3–4) argues is that inclusion can also be regarded as assimilationist, even culturally imperialist, thus effacing and exclusionary. What we may posit is that inclusion, in order to be truly inclusive of other ways of being, must not include people in one singular and generic way but include people in the manner in which they are able to participate (Young cited in Piatelli 2009, p. 4). This requires acceptance of individuality, ability, and social conditions.

Exclusion

Here I must address a key point: skate culture also has tendencies and patterns of exclusion. Nowhere is this more prominent than in terms of its unconventional trope of masculinity that celebrates creativity but reinforces a dominant heterosexuality. By this measure, female skateboarders and LGBT skateboarders are regarded as peripheral in core skate culture (McGuire 2013; Pappalardo 2013; Welch 2011; Yochim 2013). Whilst this is an important debate with growing recognition, it deserves its own space to be explored more fully on a separate occasion.

The individual/the group/the community

In skate culture, we see that there is a very open acceptance of individuality and ability. This is demonstrated in Beal and Weidman's work and also in Yochim's analysis of niche skate videos. It is here that Yochim highlights that skateboarders are presented as valued team members but also as individuals. Their performance in the videos, their choice of fashion, the style of their skateboarding, and the

34   *Paul O'Connor*

music that accompanies their segment are demonstrations of individuality that are seen as an integral part of skate culture. She argues that 'Skateboarding is a culture that highly values individuality while at the same time promising the benefits of cooperation and inclusion in a larger group' (2013, p. 143). She goes on to clarify this message through the words of one of her respondents: 'you do it together and everyone just does it their own way' (p. 179). These comments here dovetail with those of Piatelli earlier and provide an argument that skate culture is politically oriented for inclusion.

Another inclusive dynamic is the enduring feature of fraternity in skateboard culture. Friendship is a salient aspect of the everyday nature of navigating the city and finding places to skateboard (Jenson, Swords, & Jeffries 2012). The act of skateboarding itself is often enough for two strangers to socially connect. An evocative example is one of Israelis and Arabs peacefully skateboarding together (Friedel 2013). Inclusion in skateboard culture is not premised on cultural or political assimilation, style, or technique. Moreover, it is participation in skateboarding, as Beal and Weidman (2003) highlight, that is a central element not just of skate culture authenticity but also of inclusion.

In a remarkable piece of research by Adam Jenson, Jon Swords, and Michael Jeffries (2012, p. 382), skateboarders are shown to be a force for wider social inclusion. Following the activities of skateboarders in the Northern English cities of Newcastle and Gateshead, the authors see a value to the social presence of skateboarders in the community. The authorities noted that in areas where skateboarders congregate, crime and anti-social behaviour had actually fallen. In one account, an elderly lady raised the issue of skateboarders with a local councillor. The councillor commented that he braced himself for a series of complaints but was surprised to hear the lady celebrate the presence of skateboarders near her home and declare that they made her feel safe (p. 382). As a result, the Gateshead Five Bridges site, which has long been used by skateboarders, has been developed by the City Council specifically for the use of skateboarders and has included their participation in the building efforts and maintenance of the space. These comments replicate the arguments of Howell (2005, p. 40) that skateboarders are the 'shock troops of gentrification'. With reference to Philadelphia's Love Park, Howell refers to professional skateboarder Ricky Oyola, who states that skateboarders 'made this place', that previously it was the haunt of drug dealers and homeless people (p. 40).

Commitment

Along with the recognition of the positive contribution of skateboarding to society and civic space is also an acknowledgement of the considerable amount of effort and dedication exacted by skateboarders in skateboarding. The commitment to participate can, at times, result in a sharing openness that is visible amongst skateboarders. It is this inclusive ethos that I highlighted in the opening vignette of this paper, and it is replicated in the charitable works and NGOs that promote skateboarding as a positive, life-altering activity for young people. In my ethnographic research performed in Hong Kong, New York, and Exeter in the UK, I have witnessed countless examples of what, building on Lefebvre's rhythmanalysis (2004), could be termed a rhythm of inclusiveness in skateboard culture. Rhythmanalysis is a critical perspective that seeks to understand interconnecting patterns of behaviour. Recognizing that the human body has overlapping rhythms such as sleep, respiration, and menstruation prefigures an argument that rhythm must be of importance in human life. Skateboard culture, and arguably all culture, has particular rhythms. Some of these are inclusive; examples include but are not limited to skateboarders catching each other's boards, rolling 'lost' boards back to owners, tacit recognition of turns on apparatus being skated, sharing of tools, praising each other's achievements (which can also mean praising simple moves for novices), introducing others to skate spots, and sharing food and drink. I note all these specifically because I have witnessed them occurring amongst individuals who do not know each other. Talking to Orson, a veteran Hong Kong skateboarder, revealed another dynamic of this inclusion. Over the years, he has given dozens of old boards and shoes to young skaters, often to marginalized ethnic minority youth, who hang around skateparks and can't necessarily afford their own boards.

The value of skateboarding

At the heart of this discussion, there is a further question about skateboarding. If, as I have argued, it can be regarded as a form of social inclusion, what does it actually offer society? Does skateboarding have a value, and does it possess a politics? The first way in which I would like to answer this is to highlight that skateboarding and skateboarders have long been subject to a stigma as outcasts and 'slackers' with 'no direction' (Malott & Peña 2004, p. 64). It is often the case that such impressions of skateboarders are used to justify their exclusion from the public spaces. This point is taken further by the idea of exchange, which has been a key interest of anthropologists and social theorists (Eriksen 2010, p. 184). Exchange speaks of the value of a commodity or practice and its presence and importance within a culture. Skateboarding, whilst never pre-capitalist, has an ambiguous exchange value. By this, I refer to the practice of skateboarding, not the commercial skateboard industry itself. Iain Borden explores this with reference to the presence of skateboarders in urban centers, the supposed locus of capitalist activity. Borden argues that, like the homeless, skateboarders use and occupy space 'without engaging in economic activity' (2001, p. 233). Skateboarders, using Zygmunt Bauman's (2007, p. 4) phrasing, are 'flawed consumers', occupying and even damaging public space but not consuming whilst doing so. Borden goes on to highlight that skateboarders desire and utilize the city whilst rejecting the rules of ownership and use. He distinguishes this by stating that 'skateboarding is a critique of ownership, but not of wealth' (p. 240). The inclusive element of skateboarding in the city is therefore not a rejection of the opulent city but an enactment to free the city and make it accessible for all types of pleasure. Street skateboarding clearly poses a challenge to the norms of the business elite that

36   *Paul O'Connor*

Saskia Sassen (2001, p. 281) sees to be determining the design and use of our contemporary cities. Reading Borden, we come to see that whilst skateboarding may be understood as apolitical, its practice is layered with participatory politics on which I shall elaborate in what follows. Rather than skateboarding being void of an exchange value, it presents a political value in its performed message.

Following Borden's (2001, p. 233) comments on the ambiguous exchange value of skateboarding in terms of its absence of production, he goes on to acknowledge that the effort put into skateboarding creates play and pleasure. It is an argument replicated in the testimony of Yochim's (2013, p. 84) informants – skateboarding involves transcendent bodily joy. Skateboarding is equated with freedom, experimentation, and creativity. A recurring theme in skateboard media is the role skateboarding has played in channelling creativity. The Hand in Hand video series from the Ride Channel on YouTube showcases the connections among the creativity of skateboarding, art, music, and visual media (Ride Channel 2012). It is here that ideas of inclusion dovetail with a pedagogy that sees heuristic play as instrumental in education (Gustavson 2007). Former professional skateboarder Matt Hensley, who now plays accordion in the Celtic punk band Flogging Molly, has described how his passion for skateboarding equipped him with the skills to become a musician: 'I wouldn't be playing an accordion in this crazy band if it wasn't for skateboarding. I know that to be the truth. Skateboarding has given me everything' (Ride Channel 2012). For Hensley, there is no separation between skateboarding and music. This is also evident in Jocko Weyland's (2002) book on skateboarding and Curry Malot and Milagros Peña's (2004) work on punk rock culture. Beyond the connection to music, Hensley draws out his passion and commitment to skateboarding as a guide instructing how to commit and succeed in his goals.

Professional skateboarder and lead singer of the punk band Black Flag Mike Vallely (cited in Jeremias 2003) states that 'skateboarding saved my life. It gave me a creative outlet and in turn self-respect and hope . . . empowering me with a very physical but productive form of self-expression'. Vallely goes on to make further powerful claims, not just of the value of skateboarding but also about the vacuous brand of commercial skateboarding that he sees as becoming dominant. The empowerment Vallely has gained from skateboarding is something he in turn espouses as a responsibility to pass on to others. This resonates with Miller and Katz's (2002, p. 17) understanding of inclusion. In other words, the fulfilment and sense of purpose achieved through skateboarding is for many people so intoxicating and empowering that it appears they simply and altruistically want to share it. This is in many senses a valid argument, but I also suggest that the ethos of inclusion in skateboarding is also about participant control, and it comes to be a way in which skateboarders maintain control over the values and mores of skate culture.

Skateboard philanthropy

Such is the popularity of skateboard philanthropy projects that it would be difficult to provide a concise list of the numerous large- and small-scale ventures that exist. What is observable is that a number of prominent charities or foundations have been set up by various professional skateboarders. In many cases, these were established in the early 2000s, this being, as mentioned, a time of rapid growth in the popularity of skateboarding. Notable charities headed by professional skateboarders include the Tony Hawk Foundation, Rob Dyrdek Foundation, and the Sheckler Foundation, established in 2002, 2003, and 2008, respectively. Each of these charities seeks to engage communities, build skateparks, or support young people through skateboarding projects. Skateboard philanthropy is also global in its reach. As I revise this chapter in January of 2015, my Instagram feed provides updates on the charitable work of professional skateboarders Tony Hawk and Nyjah Houston in Ethiopia. The Go Skateboarding Foundation, established in 2005, organizes an international Go Skateboarding Day each year and raises money to support skateboard projects and scholarships for young people. There are projects which extend beyond a focus on helping just young people or skateboarders such as the Skate for Change initiative, which advocates skateboarders making a positive impact in their community. The Skate for Change project has sought to bring water, clothing, and food to homeless people in Lincoln Nebraska, United States. In late 2014, a group of teenagers set up their own version of Skate for Change in Hong Kong. This highlights the notion of rhythmic feedback. The values of skateboarding influence the development of skateboard philanthropy. In turn, news and recognition of these projects influences skateboarders to engage in philanthropic projects in their own communities.

Skateistan

Initially the brainchild of Australian skateboarder Oliver Percovich, Skateistan has become a globally recognized NGO that uses skateboarding as a way to engage and educate Afghan children. What possible use could skateboarding be to a war-torn and unstable country such as Afghanistan? Percovich provides a simple but edifying answer: 'being a skateboarder you fall down and you have to get back up again' (Beyondsport 2013). He states that skateboarding requires a bravery to overcome adversity, that it is precisely what children in Afghanistan need (2013).

The project of introducing skateboarding in Afghanistan has been sensitive to provide the tools rather than the 'cultural imposition' of skateboarding's Western culture. This resonates with Piatelli's (2009, p. 4) comments that inclusion must be premised on the participation and incorporation of difference. Afghan children are included as participants in skateboarding and are not exposed to Western media representations of skateboard fashion and skateboard style. In short, inclusion allows for their difference and provides them with the opportunity to make skateboarding whatever they want it to be. As a result, skateboarding in Afghanistan has become very popular with girls, who ride their boards in their shalwar kameez and associate status with protective clothing. Both of these can be regarded as departures from the Western values of dress in skateboard culture (Fitzpatrick & Skateistan 2012, p. 119). However, the importance of individuality and creativity in skateboard culture has been preserved in this new setting. One of

38   *Paul O'Connor*

my respondents, Sophie Friedel (2014, pers. comm., 25 March), a previous volunteer at Skateistan, sees that skateboarding can be used as a tool for education and social connectivity and can simply be for fun:

> Let's not forget, that skateboarding has also the tendency to create conflict, on a personal as well as social sphere. However, I strongly support the idea, that the action of movement and in this case skateboarding, has a quality to transform currents of energy, to gain a peaceful state of being and a peace of mind experience.

Friedel importantly connects inclusive notions of peace with bodily affect, highlighting a need to explore skateboarding and embodiment. In her appraisal, she acknowledges that change comes not from skateboarding but from the person who partakes in the practice, and thus skateboarding is in multiple ways a vehicle for transformation but not the driving force.

Veteran skateboarder and founder of the International Association of Skateboard Companies (IASC) Jim Fitzpatrick describes Skateistan's success as being founded on the key tenets of skateboarding, 'Independence. Persistence. Self-reliance. Creativity', qualities he argues are central in education (Fitzpatrick & Skateistan 2012, p. 7). These same values are championed by skateboard philanthropists in various fields, from Stoked Mentoring in New York (which helps adolescents develop life skills through action sports) to Board Rescue (that provides free skateboards to disadvantaged youth). At a further level, they also fit seamlessly with the dominant neoliberal policies of developed Western nations. This is a point highlighted by Howell (2008) in his analysis of the popularity of skatepark projects as a way to cultivate responsible, entrepreneurial, and self-reliant youth. Skateboarding has increasingly become recognized as an activity which can build social and cultural capital.

The A.Skate Foundation

The A.Skate Foundation uses skateboarding as a form of inclusion for autistic children. The founder, Crys Worley, is a mother of two children, one of whom has autism. The A.Skate Foundation organizes skateboard clinics in which autistic children can have the opportunity to skateboard with the guidance of skateboarder volunteers. These clinics are held across the United States, and in early 2014, they also began clinics in Ireland.

The A.Skate clinics can only be held with the participation of skateboarder volunteers. Worley states that it has never been difficult getting skateboarders to help out, as they see value in participating. She says that the passion skateboarders have for skateboarding receives recognition and validation by doing good works (Crys Worley, 2014, pers. comm., 7 February). She importantly highlights that skateboarders cannot be essentialized as good or bad; they include all sorts of people, and in essence they are no different from other young people. In response to my questions on the inclusion she witnesses in A.Skate Worley responded, 'I feel that those who skateboard and have stuck to it understand the isolation that autism comes with and they are eager to have a purpose and teach and share what they have adopted into their lives' (Crys Worley, 2014, pers. comm., 7 February).

Saving lives

A further example of skateboard philanthropy also comes in the form of well-recognized 'rock star' philanthropy. Jeff Ament from the band Pearl Jam has become prominent in contributing to the creation of skateparks in under-privileged communities. Most notably, Ament has been involved in the construction of a skatepark in the Pine Ridge Native American reservation in South Dakota (Carrasco and Lessing 2012). The contribution of skateboarding is valued here amongst Native American youth and parents alike, as it is seen as an empowering tool that can work to lower the high rates of suicide within the community (Eagle 2011). Ament comments that skateboarding is of particular value to the dispossessed, as it provides a medium for them to triumph. He says, 'the poor kid is the hungrier kid. He has got one skateboard and it is all chewed up and he rides that thing all day and he's the best skateboarder in town' (Offthewalltv 2012).

Bangalore skater Abishek Enabe comments that before he skated, his life had no meaning; he was working in an office, living for the weekend. He describes a lifestyle that was a 'rat race' and in-authentic (Levi's 2013). This is a comment that again connects to the question of the exchange value of skateboarding and its place in a world of production. It also presents a political insight about the alienation of modern life, as Enabe sees skateboarding as a way to break the routines and demands of everyday life. In a telling inclusive enthusiasm about skateboarding, he states that he wants 'more people to skate' (Levi's 2013). The Holystoked Bangalore skatepark combines the local enthusiasm of skaters like Enabe with the philanthropy of professional skateboarders such as Stefan Janowski, Chet Childress, and Al Partanen with corporate sponsorship from Levi's jeans (Fleming 2013; Mehring 2013).

These examples of skateboard philanthropy represent the intersection of business interests, social responsibility, education, and the promotion of the positive benefits of skateboarding. These charities reflect the smaller-scale processes of sharing that are present in skate culture and project them onto a much larger canvas. At a fundamental level, this philanthropy is engaged with social inclusion.

Prefigurative politics

The term 'prefigurative politics' is closely aligned with the anarchist movement (Gordon 2008, p. 13). Politically, it grows from the 'principle that one's mode of resistance should embody the world one wishes to create' (Graeber 2009, p. 222). Originating in the late 1970s from Marxist thought and social movements, it is also compared to the non-violent protest and politics of Mahatma Gandhi and Martin Luther King. It has more recently been recognized as a philosophy of direct action and participatory politics. Anthropologist Marianne Maeckelbergh (2009, p. 88) explains how prefigurative politics privileges process, horizontal

40   *Paul O'Connor*

participation, and strategy. In sum, it is a politics of inclusion that refutes the linear idea of movement to a goal and instead posits that the means are as important as the ends in any political process. As a result, prefiguration has an emphasis on lifestyle, process, and participation: if these are congruent with the values of the group and their political orientation, then change shall follow. Maeckelbergh (2009, p. 66) describes prefigurative politics as an attempt 'to make the processes we use to achieve our immediate goals an embodiment of our ultimate goals, so that there is no distinction between how we fight and what we fight for'. Such values are represented in skateboard philanthropy. One overt example can be made in reference to the slogan 'be the change' that is used by the Sheckler Foundation. This highlights prefiguration in that more than moving to make change, one has to simply embody and be it.

My argument is that skateboard culture, which has not explicitly concerned itself with politics, appears to be enacting a prefigurative politics in which participation, horizontality, and inclusion combine as a strategy for moulding a world accessible and sympathetic to the lifestyle of skateboarders. I see skateboard philanthropy as a way to extend the informal and 'contingent' sharing of knowledge Yochim describes in skate culture (2013, p. 88). Skateboard philanthropy then becomes a way of managing the image and understanding of skateboarding while skateboarding itself becomes more mainstream and 'big business'. We see that many skateboarders have worked with the commercial interests of big business (see the Holystoked Levi's project mentioned early) as a way to extend the inclusive ethos and empowerment they have experienced in skateboarding. The encroachment of big business into skateboard culture is increasingly regarded in positive terms. As Kara-Jane Lombard (2010, p. 478) highlights, it provides a way to augment the impact of skateboarding and give skateboarders more opportunities to earn a wage in the pursuit they love. In contrast, Yochim (2013, 109) argues that mainstream representations of skateboarding are regarded in positive terms whilst also being seen as 'problematic'.

The problem of the mainstreaming of skateboarding and its commercialization is that skateboarders fear the loss of their participant control. So in reaction to the growth of skateboarding in mainstream popularity and commercial interests, skateboard philanthropy is arguably one way to preserve skateboard culture and a method to educate others about what skateboarding involves. Skateboard philanthropy resists notions of skateboarders as a social blight and ideologically circumvents more standard forms of charity by providing access to an activity that traditionally has had questionable exchange value. The recognition of skateboarding as a rebellious and at times stigmatized activity has not been displaced, least of all amongst skateboarders. There is suspicion and skepticism about philanthropic activities that seek to co-opt skateboarding authenticity as cultural capital. Those projects that fail to preserve the values of skateboarding will, I argue, not succeed in gaining the support of skateboarders. In this sense, I make the case that skateboard philanthropy is a form of prefigurative politics in skate culture. It is a politics that makes action directly through activities which promote and serve to preserve skateboarding.

Conclusion

Returning now to Fanling Skatepark, the rather banal example of inclusion I presented in the introduction to this chapter can be understood as a microcosm of dynamics that have far greater reach. Understanding inclusion in skateboarding as prefigurative politics, particularly at the large scale of skateboard philanthropy, enables us to make sense of a confluence of key issues. Skateboard philanthropy is a macro version of a micro practice in skate culture. That is, the inclusion that manifests itself at the skatepark or in conversation at the local skate shop is premised on participation, and this is replicated in the larger-scale philanthropy of the Tony Hawk Foundation and Skateistan. Skateboard philanthropy can be seen as an extension of participant control. It can also be understood as part of skateboard entrepreneurialism, which Yochim (2013, p. 30) argues has always been a feature of skate culture. It also allows us to read skateboarding as strategically political. This politics, I stress, is not focused on the appropriation of urban space alone, but as prefiguration, it contains a transformative edge, a rhythm that seeks to preserve not just places to skate but also the values, attitudes, and knowledge required to skate. Lefebvre's rhythmanalysis is relevant here again; skateboarders are constantly responding to the daily rhythm in which their pursuit is positioned. Carefully they strive to control skateboarding as it becomes too mainstream, to enact protectionist policies of consumption when brands lose their authenticity. Like any culture, it must preserve its rituals and traditions if it is to survive; it must police its boundaries but also remain in dialogue with the outside world on which it so poignantly relies. Whilst earnestly not wishing to be cynical about a culture in which I am also embedded, it is important to question the altruism of skateboard inclusion and philanthropy. If they are understood through prefigurative politics, such actions can be read primarily and positively as attempts to preserve an authentic skate culture.

Acknowledgments

I am very grateful to Kara-Jane Lombard for allowing me to contribute to this project on skate culture and humbled by her diligent care and advice throughout. I would like to express my thanks to Crys Worley from the A.Skate foundation and also Sophie Friedel, former Skateistan employee. Both gave their time to answer my questions and provide valuable feedback. My thanks also to Warren Stuart of the Hong Kong X-Fed and Tim Ruck from the Boarding House Exeter.

References

Bauman, Z 2007, *Consuming life*, Polity, Cambridge.

Beal, B & Weidman, L 2003, 'Skateboarding and authenticity', in RE Rinehart & S Snyder (eds), *To the extreme*, State University of New York Press, New York, pp. 337–352.

42 *Paul O'Connor*

Borden, I 2001, *Skateboarding, space and the city: architecture and the body*, Berg, New York.

Bossaert, G, Colpin, H, Pijl, SJ & Petry, K 2013. 'Truly included? A literature study focusing on the social dimension of inclusion in education', *International Journal of Inclusive Education*, vol. 17, no. 1, pp. 60–79.

Beyondsport 2013, *Beyond Sport Summit 2013: Sport on the edge*. Available from: www.youtube.com/watch?v=0MbBv9HiDWs. [14 October 2014].

Carrasco, S & Lessing, C 2012, 'Skateboard philanthropists use skate parks to empower native youth', *JVA Consulting*. Available from: http://jvaconsulting.com/skateboard-philanthropists-use-skate-parks-to-empower-native-youth/#.UzO9BtwxGlI. [14 October 2014].

Cuin, A 2013, 'The death of skateboarding – is skateboarding declining', *LoveExtremeSports*. Available from: www.loveextremesports.com/the-death-of-skate-skateboarding-declines-globally. [10 April 2014].

Eagle, K 2011, ' "Skateboarding saves lives" theme for Pine Ridge Skate-Park', *Native American Times*. Available from: www.nativetimes.com/life/people/6218-skating-saves-lives-theme-for-pine-ridge-skate-park. [21 June 2014].

Eriksen, TH 2010, *Ethnicity and nationalism: anthropological perspectives*, Pluto Press, London.

Fitzpatrick, J & Skateistan 2012, *Skateistan: the story of skateboarding in Afghanistan*, Skateistan, Berlin.

Fleming, R 2013, 'India's DIY Skatepark', *X Games ESPN*. Available from: http://xgames.espn.go.com/skateboarding/article/9489456/holy-stoked-collective-bangalore-india-builds-free-skatepark. [14 October 2014].

Friedel, S 2013, *Get naked! A transformative approach to peace research on the example of the art of living sideways and the aesthetic of transrational peace(s)*, MA thesis, University of Innsbruck.

Gordon, U 2008, *Anarchy alive: anti-authoritarian politics from practice to theory*, Pluto Press, London.

Graeber, D 2009, *Direct action: an ethnography*, AK Press, Edinburgh.

Gustavson, L 2007, *Youth learning on their own terms: creative practices and classroom teaching*, Routledge, New York.

Howell, O 2005, 'The "creative class" and the gentrifying city: skateboarding in Philadelphia's Love Park', *Journal of Architectural Education*, vol. 59, no. 2, pp. 33–42.

Howell, O 2008, 'Skatepark as neoliberal playground: urban governance, recreation space, and the cultivation of personal responsibility', *Space and Culture*, vol. 11, no. 4, pp. 475–496.

Human Kinetics & Hanlon, T 2009, *The sports rule book*, Human Kinetics, Champaign, IL.

Jenson, A, Swords, J & Jeffries, M 2012, 'The accidental youth club: skateboarding in Newcastle-Gateshead', *Journal of Urban Design*, vol. 17, no. 3, pp. 371–388.

Jeremias, M 2003, *Drive: my life in skateboarding* (DVD), Vid Canada, Canada.

Lefebvre, H 2004, *Rhythmanalysis*, Continuum, London.

Levi's 2013, *Skateboarding in India full length documentary (uncensored)*. Available from: www.youtube.com/watch?v=l0C0A9vCInc. [14 October 2014].

Lombard, K-J 2010, 'Skate and create/skate and destroy: the commercial and governmental incorporation of skateboarding', *Continuum: Journal of Media and Cultural Studies*, vol. 24, no. 4, pp. 475–488.

Malot, C & Peña, M 2004, *Punk rockers revolution*, Peter Lang, New York.

Maeckelbergh, M 2009, *The will of the many*, Pluto Press, London.

McCrone, D & Bechhofer, F 2008, 'National identity and social inclusion', *Ethnic and Racial Studies*, vol. 31, no. 7, pp. 1245–1266.

McGuire, S 2013, 'Is skateboarding ready to openly embrace a transgender skater?', *Jenkem Magazine*. Available from: www.jenkemmag.com/home/2013/03/18/is-skateboarding-ready-to-openly-embrace-a-transgender-skater/. [23 December 2014].

Mehring, J 2013, 'Levi's Holy Stoked Skatepark build in Bangalore, India', *Skateboarder Magazine*. Available from: www.skateboardermag.com/event/levis-holy-stoked-india-skatepark-build/. [15 June 2014].

Miller, FA & Katz, JH 2002, *The inclusion breakthrough*, Berrett-Koehler, San Francisco.

Offthewalltv 2012, *Pass the bucket with Jeff Ament*. Available from: www.youtube.com/watch?v=FF4GPQyH1A0. [12 May 2014].

Pappalardo, A 2013, 'Thoughts on Nyjah Houston's comments: "skateboarding is not for girls"', *Jenkem Magazine*. Available from: www.jenkemmag.com/home/2013/06/10/thoughts-on-nyjah-hustons-comment-skateboarding-is-not-for-girls/. [1 July 2013].

Parker, D & Song, M 2007, 'Inclusion, participation and the emergence of British Chinese Websites', *Journal of Ethnic and Migration Studies*, vol. 33, no. 7, pp. 1043–1061.

Piatelli, DA 2009, *Stories of inclusion?: power, privilege, and difference in a peace and justice network*, Lexington Books, Lanham.

Ride Channel 2012, *Matt Hensley on skateboarding and joining Flogging Molly – hand in hand (Part 2 of 2)*. Available from: www.youtube.com/watch?v=RU0gZ410Kp4. [17 March 2014].

Sassen, S 2001, *The global city: New York, London, Tokyo*, Princeton University Press, Princeton.

Transworld Skateboarding 2013, *Media portfolio: version 31*. Available from: http://users.grindnetworks.com/grindmedia/mediakits/twskate-portfolio.pdf. [9August 2014].

Welch, P 2011, 'Gay skaters: the last taboo', *Huck Magazine*. Available from: www.huckmagazine.com/perspectives/reportage-2/gay-skaters/. [10 March2013].

Weyland, J 2002, *The answer is never*, Century, London.

Yochim, EC 2013, *Skate life: re-imagining white masculinity*, University of Michigan Press, Ann Arbor.

4 Skateboarding activism
Exploring diverse voices and community support

Indigo Willing and Scott Shearer

This chapter aims to shed light on lesser-known populations involved with and supportive of skateboarding to move beyond narrow assumptions of those who participate in and appreciate this subculture and identify how this can benefit skateboarding activism. We argue for broadening the common (mis)understandings of skateboarding as a subculture of young males to allow for recognition of more diverse populations at the periphery, examining instances in which a broader range of people, particularly females, mature-aged skaters, parents, and individuals from the general public express support for skateboarding. Our focus addresses a gap in studies of subcultures in which the participation of females and older generations are overlooked – particularly in scenes that are practiced beyond private, indoor, and domestic spaces (Taylor 2012). Highlighting diversity within the skateboarding community adds a more inclusive and realistic representation of the fluidity and diversity in this subculture and arms skateboarding advocates with ammunition to lobby authorities for greater consideration of skate facilities and skateboarding in public spaces.

Our research takes an interdisciplinary approach that reflects our backgrounds in sociology and urban studies and as skaters within the Brisbane skateboarding community in Australia, where our study is based. Our study involves content analysis of a Brisbane-based petition and film, both focused on skate activism that includes lobbying for an upgrade of Paddington Skate Park. The petition and film emphasize the need for better funding and support for more skate facilities and freedom to skateboard in public spaces. Taking a qualitative approach, text and interviews from the petition and documentary are analysed, exploring the themes that 'unheard' populations express in terms of supporting skateboarding, how they contribute to a broader understanding of skateboarding, and the role such themes can have in further informing skate-related policies and planning as well as community initiatives.

Using examples from both sources of data, we outline how skateboarding activism can mobilize and give a platform to voices in the community obscured from mainstream representations of skating.

According to a study by the Commonwealth Scientific and Industrial Research Organization (CSIRO) on the future of Australian sport, skateboarding is 'experiencing a rapid surge in popularity' (Hajkowicz et al. 2013, p. 13). Insights gained from exploring the diverse voices that participate in and support skateboarding in Australia have relevance beyond our local community and city. Skateboarding is indeed a truly global phenomenon, and with surprisingly shifting demographics. In addition to gender, skateboarders are diversifying in age and ethnicity – from what began as a largely white, male youth subculture in the United States to being a highly visible, global subculture with broader appeal and participants of varying ages and ethnicities. Despite these changes, the dominant perception and representation of skateboarding lacks representation of diversity in terms of its members and supporters (Yochim 2009).

Why those on the periphery of skateboarding matter

The core members of skateboarding are typically considered to be young males. According to Becky Beal (1996), it is a subculture founded upon cultures and performances of masculinity. In popular culture, too, skateboarding is imagined and represented in media such as skate magazines, videos, fictional films, and advertisements as a subculture made up almost exclusively of young males. Rare exceptions do include, for example, *Jenkem Magazine* and *Manual Magazine*. Our interest is not in core skaters such as young males and pro skaters but the voices of those on the periphery of the subculture. There is a range of people on the periphery whose participation and contributions lag in visibility compared to those at the core. The wider range of people who skate includes older generations of either continuing or new skaters, skaters who become parents, and females.

Evidence of older skaters includes blogs like the United States–based *The Middle-Age Shred* (www.middle-age-shred.com) and the 'Masters' division in skate competitions such as Australia's Bowl-A-Rama for people over forty. Barbara Odanaka (2014), an author and skateboarder in her fifties who also runs a group called *Skate Moms/Sisters of Shred*, points to the rising popularity of middle-aged skateboarders:

> Some are lifelong skateboarders who never gave up the sport; others are digging out their boards after decades. They skate for fun, fitness and a feeling of freedom . . . The fact that they are three to four times older than the average skateboarder? No matter. They're proud to be the elder skatesmen (and women).

In contrast to an abundance of images of young male skaters in magazines, social media videos, documentaries and fictional films, and even in comparison to 'elder skatesmen', the presence and status of female skaters is particularly marginal (Nolan 2003). Confirming their peripheral presence while highlighting the importance of studies that acknowledge females in subcultures beyond those practiced in private, Lia Karsten and Eva Pel (2000, p. 327) state, 'the skateboarding scene is not very different from other forms of urban public play where men predominate'. Susie Weller (2007, p. 565) highlights one of the problems is that for skaters, the 'social capital within their communities, the networks, which they develop

46 *Indigo Willing and Scott Shearer*

around and through, are often bonded by gender and can be exclusive'. Beal (1996, p. 216) also argues that one of the assumptions that can hinder gender inclusivity is that some male skaters believe females do not 'fully engage in the values of the subculture'. We challenge these assumptions and argue for more close inspection and acknowledgement of females as not only participating in skateboarding but also expanding its values to be more inclusive.

Despite their lower numbers, female skaters globally have been proactive in pushing for more recognition of their engagement in skateboarding, as evident by the emergence of girl skate groups, networks, competitions, and films. Strategies include female skaters using media such as blogs on the Internet (MacKay & Dallaire 2013) and documentaries such as *Underexposed: A Women's Skateboarding Documentary* (Brodka 2013). Facebook has also been utilized as an avenue by female skaters such as the Girls Skate Australia (www.facebook.com/girlsskateoz) and Girl Skate Network (http://girlsskatenetwork.com/). Additionally, lesbian, gay, bisexual, and transgender (LGBT) people who are on the periphery rather than represented as core members of skateboarding gain more visibility and inclusion within female skateboarding groups. While not a primary focus in our discussion, clearly female representation contributes to various positive transformations of skateboarding that risk being overlooked (Atencio, Beal, & Wilson 2009).

As the discussion so far suggests, a more varied and colourful mosaic of people and outlooks exists in skateboarding that is rarely represented in dominant narratives and coverage. The ramifications of making such diversity more visible in skateboarding activism go beyond just goodwill to be inclusive by reflecting a more heterogeneous membership and set of values involved in promoting skateboarding. Skateboarders regularly have to reach and persuade individuals and groups beyond the core of the subculture, as it is more likely to be non-skaters who have decision-making power in determining funds and planning for things such as skate facilities. The more diversity skate activism reflects, the easier it is for governments and funding bodies to identify the wider benefits of skateboarding facilities and skate-friendly policies and the greater pressure they face by not taking action.

Skate activism and dilemmas skaters face in our city

Although skateboarders do not intend to damage public and private property, their activities are often perceived as vandalism, and there exists considerable hostility by authorities towards skating within the city (Chiu 2009). A major issue that arises for Brisbane and other city councils is the challenge of how to find ways for the non-skating public and skaters to co-exist, since skaters are attracted to using the urban environment in unintended ways (Németh 2006). Describing the special relationship between skating and the city, Craig Stecyk, a pivotal figure in Californian skate history, is quoted in the documentary *Dogtown and Z-Boys* (Peralta 2001) as saying that for skaters, 'Two hundred years of technology has unwittingly created a massive cement playground of unlimited potential'.

Street skating is such a quintessential part of the subculture that one solution has been for skateparks to typically have skate obstacles such as stairs, handrails, benbches, and ledges resembling those found routinely in urban spaces. But despite this, skateboarders also continue to seek out city spaces and skateable landscapes (Chiu 2009). Indeed, streetscapes and skaters' construction of identity have been described as involving 'a contesting spatial practice creating a mental, social, and body space, embodying a skater's self-identity and cultural expression' (p. 25). We therefore argue it is important not to pit the construction of skateparks and the incorporation of skateboarding into shared city spaces against each other but rather to see the need for more inclusive attitudes towards designing, planning, and funding for both.

As a case study, Brisbane skate activism provides insights into diverse community voices that support both skateparks and inclusive spaces for skating in the city. In Brisbane, Paddington Skate Park or 'Paddo', as it is colloquially known, is the only inner-city skatepark. Built in 1994, it has been left largely unmaintained, except when local skaters have done minor repairs themselves. At the time of writing this chapter, Brisbane City Council (BCC) had held community consultations on Paddo Skate Park's proposed upgrade, yet no official budget amount or final design had been released. Skateboarding in public spaces in Brisbane is highly restrictive, including in places such as King George Square, a central plaza in the city, where skateboarders face AUD$500 fines. Metal skate stoppers also adorn the majority of concrete structures that skaters might gravitate towards. Aside from Paddo Skate Park, there are no designated inner-city public spaces for skateboarders in Brisbane City. In terms of local skate activism, in 2010, the Brisbane Skateboarding Association (BSA) was established by local skaters, including Scott Shearer, one of the authors of this chapter, to advocate for the rights, needs, and interests of Brisbane skateboarders. In particular, the BSA lobbied BCC to improve skate facility provision. An online petition was created in 2013 to put pressure on BCC to develop a skate facility strategy, with additional posts on BSA's Facebook page illustrating the poor state of skate facility provisions in Brisbane.

In addition, an independent filmmaker, Kane Stewart, created *Affirmative Action: A Brisbane Skateboarding Documentary* in 2013. The purpose of this documentary was to highlight Brisbane's inadequate skate facility provision from various perspectives and outline positive ways of incorporating skateboarding into city spaces. Comments from an online petition and interviews in the documentary are qualitatively explored in this chapter, with a focus on the types of voices and themes, to show the diversity of people and views that support the Brisbane skateboarding community's calls for safe and well-designed skateparks and opportunities to skate in the city.

Skate petition discussion

The BSA online petition 'Provide a skate facility strategy for Brisbane skateparks' was signed by 1,501 people (at the time of writing). Comments made by signatories on the BSA petition are public, but we chose not to use the names of individuals and instead highlight the demographic profile of participants and common themes of interest. Our aim was to identify dominant concerns raised by different people such as females, mature-aged skaters, and parents. This is not to suggest one demographic is more or less important than others, but rather our aim is to shed light on voices in skateboarding not ordinarily given attention. We approached the petition not as a representative sample but as providing qualitative insight which illustrates diverse populations and perspectives that skateboarding activism can utilize. Guided by names on the petition, we separated all comments left by people with female- and male-sounding names. There are limitations to this approach, such as misgendering participants with more ambiguous names and dividing gender into a binary of male and female, even though social categories of gender include a much larger spectrum. However, we were careful to exclude ambiguous-sounding names as a precaution and pay close attention to comments that signified the respondents' gender. The petition also did not ask signers to reveal specific demographics such as age, whether people skate, and at what level. Our insights are drawn from what the respondents' comments reveal about themselves and their concerns.

As critiques of subcultural theory include that the presence of females is overlooked, particular attention was paid to female commenters in the petition, and examples of these are presented first. However, we provide examples of both females and males who value qualities about skateboarding connected to notions of social, physical, and mental well-being, and pride for their city, which they believe stands in contrast with the lack of quality skate facilities and spaces. Such comments challenge the hegemonic masculinity and 'antisocial' attitudes typically associated with skateboarding, which we argue are conflated and too rigidly applied. Our analysis began by identifying five main themes in female respondents' comments. These were around (1) safety, (2) multigenerational participation, (3) health, (4) social benefits, and (5) an emphasis on the need for high-quality, regularly maintained, contemporary skate facilities in Brisbane. Weller (2007, p. 570) argues that skateboarding and other lifestyles are 'more fluid than conventional understandings of (youth) subcultures'. The petition comments highlighted in this section support this.

To begin, the theme of safety is illustrated by a female who states skaters need to 'have a proper place to skate and practise [sic] with friends' (*Provide a skate facility strategy for Brisbane skateparks* 2015). Similarly, a grandmother makes the appeal that 'I want my grandsons to have a safe place to be able to skate' (2015). Given the emphasis on an ability to accept injuries as part of doing tricks, safety can sometimes be overshadowed, particularly if it clashes with performances of masculinity. Nicholas Nolan (2003, p. 324) states that females have to fight 'a peripheral role in the subculture' due to notions that skateboarding demands skaters have 'male attributes', such as not being afraid of getting hurt. We argue female perspectives on issues such as safety can play an important role in skate activism, and not because of any gendered assumptions about their ability to physically commit to skate 'like the boys'. Rather, female perspectives may be less bounded to performing particular kinds of masculinity that devalue or obscure concerns for safety.

Skateboarding activism 49

Another limitation in skateboarding studies is the overwhelming focus on youth, which reflects a broader oversight in studies of subcultures in general that ignores ageing and mature-aged members (Bennett 2011). Skateboarding is traditionally conceptualized as 'practiced by people 8–18 year old' (Borden 2001, p. 139), but demographics are broadening, including in terms of gender. Countering these assumptions, supportive comments about skateboarding being a multigenerational activity observed in the skate petition include from one mother who states, 'I skated at this park as a teenager and would like to see my son or daughter also skate here in years to come' (*Provide a skate facility strategy for Brisbane skateparks* 2015). Another comment by a female, which challenges the idea that skating only interests and concerns young males, maintains, 'skateparks are for all ages' (2015). This highlights how catering for skaters' needs in Brisbane does not just benefit young people but people of all ages. This is supported by another female commenter, who declares, 'I love going to Brisbane and seeing my middle-aged friend learning skateboarding'. A comment by a female skater highlights the cumulative neglect she has witnessed over the years across her own life course stating, 'I used to go to "Paddo" when I was 14 & nothing's really changed, it's sad' (2015).

The physical benefits of skating are another main theme raised in comments by females signing the petition. For example, one female writes that skating is 'Better than sitting indoors on screens', and similarly, another writes, 'These activities keep them active and outdoors' (2015). One female likewise points out that 'Obesity is a major problem, encourage outdoor physical activity' (2015). These females' emphasis and valuing of how skateboarding gets people 'outdoors' is not only important from a health perspective but also because subcultural studies tend to focus on the voices and experiences of females in domestic spaces such as bedrooms and in private, 'indoor' spaces (Taylor 2012). Skateboarding offers a particularly rich but underexplored realm to gain insight into the attitudes of females towards a subculture that is largely dependent on outdoor and public spaces.

The social benefits females argued in the petition's comments include that 'skate parks are vital pieces of recreation infrastructure not just for skating . . . but for young people to legitimately gather to socialize and exercise' (*Provide a skate facility strategy for Brisbane skateparks* 2015). Another female suggests better skate facilities can 'develop their communication skills while using the facilities and gives them a non-judgemental space for self-expression' (2015). Lisa Wood, May Carter, and Karen Martin (2014) and Graham Bradley (2010) echo these sentiments from their respective research. Despite the popular belief they generate antisocial behaviour, they identified skateparks as positive places for young people to socialize, build self-esteem, learn how to cooperate, and express themselves.

In relation to the theme of Brisbane's image, a female commenter raised an interesting question stating that it is 'one of the biggest cities in Australia and no skate park strategy' (*Provide a skate facility strategy for Brisbane skateparks* 2015). She felt because of Brisbane's size, it should have a strategy for developing skate spaces and facilities. We assume one reason she made this comment is that smaller cities in South East Queensland, for instance Gold Coast and Redland,

50   *Indigo Willing and Scott Shearer*

have such a strategy. Another female stated, 'Brisbane skaters deserve the right to have facilities on par with the rest of the world' (2015). High-quality skateparks of varying sizes, types, and scales are available in cities throughout the world. With access to social media, such as YouTube and Instagram, and the national and international mobility of the skateboarding community, there are now greater expectations of skate facility standards.

The perspectives by females we highlight all point to critical themes and interests that would support skate activists and those developing skate facilities and policies. We also found evidence that the concerns of females do not conflict with and are often shared by males who signed the petition. In terms of comparing Brisbane's lack of quality skate facilities with those of other major cities, for instance, one male states, 'Brisbane skate parks are of a poor standard compared to similar facilities in Europe' (2015). Another male points to both the issue of safety and the idea that other cities are superior to Brisbane. He states:

> This is extremely important to me because newer skaters like myself need good skate facilities to make it easier for us and have less injuries. It's really sad to see skaters break bones because they slipped from a crack or some fault in the skatepark. It's also annoying to see other Australian cities like Melbourne that have world class skate facilities all over the place. Brisbane needs better parks. It's the only solution.
>
> (2015)

Additionally, there are comments by males in the petition that highlight the multi-generational side of skateboarding, which challenges the dominant image of skating as only a youthful and masculine endeavour. For example, one male explains, 'As a skateboarder and a family man, I want the opportunity to take my son to modern, safe facilities. Brisbane Skate parks are out dated, run down, and not safe' (2015).

Also notable are comments by males that challenge the idea that antisocial attitudes dominate the culture and lifestyle. Males in the petition we studied included ones who voiced that skateboarding needs to be seen as a creative activity that can enrich the social life of city spaces but is marginalized compared to traditional sports. For example, one commenter argued, 'Everyone deserves a good skate park. We have many basketball courts, soccer and baseball fields why can't your town have a decent safe place to enjoy skateboarding?' (2015). A similar argument can be observed in the comment that 'Skateboarding is part of urban life. It is not going away so let's support it like other forms of recreation and commuting' (2015). Reflections about skateboarding improving society rather than being set against it are also found in the comment of a mature-aged skater who states:

> Been a skateboarder for 20 years. It's given me many life skills beyond that of the sport. Name another sport where Children, Adults, Women and Male [sic] can all play together happily, regardless of race or religion. Its creative

and produces creative and forward thinking people. Having skated all over
the UK and Australia, I would agree that Brisbane is a little behind the times.
(2015)

Iain Borden (2001, p. 151) argues that one of the key aspects of performances
of masculinity in skateboarding subculture is a projection of their 'rejection of
society as a whole'. Yet Kara-Jane Lombard (2010, p. 475) warns that while a
'consistent theme in the examination of skateboarding culture has been that of
resistance', there is also evidence that 'contemporary skaters are not necessarily attracted to resistance' (p. 465). We agree more nuanced understanding of
the subculture of skateboarding is required, which builds on broader calls for a
rethinking of subcultures as having more flexible memberships based on lifestyles
and activities (Bennett 1999, 2011) than rigid identities and belongings and as
encompassing various ages rather than anchored to youth alone. As highlighted
at the beginning of this section, the comments from the skate petition also challenge the notion that skateboarding is tightly woven to underlying associations to
deviancy, antisocial behaviour (Brayton 2005; Karsten & Pel 2000), and social
resistance (Beal 1995). The links petition commenters make between skateboarding and positive lifestyles, including social and health benefits, strongly contrast
with such conceptualizations of the subculture.

Skateboarding documentary discussion

Skateboarding is regularly documented in visual media, which are able to generate an appreciation for skating in an audience wider than just skaters themselves.
Some 'classic' examples include fictional films such as *Gleaming the Cube* (Clifford 1989) and *Street Dreams* (Zamoscianyk 2009), and documentaries such as
Dogtown and Z-Boys (Peralta 2001). Variations include historical approaches,
such as *The Bones Brigade* (Peralta 2012), which focuses on male skaters in their
forties, looking back on their involvement in skateboarding as youth. There are
also recent efforts to focus on female skateboarders in film, such as in the documentary *Underexposed: A Women's Skateboarding Documentary* (Brodka 2013).
YouTube and smartphone sharing of skate related content is a recent evolution
in documenting skating. The film *Affirmative Action: A Brisbane Skate Documentary* (Stewart 2013) is unique in that it highlights not only advanced skaters
but also the voices of participants considered to be on the periphery of the subculture, such as older skaters and parents of skaters, and also people outside the
subculture, such as members of the general public who express an appreciation
for seeing skating as a part of the city. We explore some of the themes that emerge
from this diverse range of voices and, in the process, further illustrate not only the
broad range of ages and people who skate but also those who support skating, as
is reflected in the petition.

Skater and filmmaker Kane Stewart directed and produced the documentary
Affirmative Action: A Brisbane Skate Documentary (Stewart 2013) to raise awareness about the poor conditions of skating facilities in Brisbane. Stewart has lived

52 *Indigo Willing and Scott Shearer*

in Brisbane all his life, was a sponsored skater, and, through his filmmaking and involvement in the skateboard industry, keeps connected to the city's skateboarding scene. The film informs audiences that Paddington Skate Park is Brisbane's only inner-city facility, was built in 1994, and has largely been left to neglect ever since. Although Paddo Skate Park is popular and regularly used by both locals and travellers, it is outdated and in disrepair.

While not a high-profile skateboarding film, since its release in August 2013, Stewart's independently funded film, at the time of writing, had been viewed on The Bay's YouTube channel more than 8,000 times. Interviews were conducted with high-profile skaters such as Dennis Durrant, who is based in Brisbane and is part of adidas's international team; a mix of veteran skaters such as Ben Ventress, owner of skateboard company Project Distribution; as well as younger skaters and parents of skaters. Interviews with both authors of this chapter also feature in the documentary, one in her role as a sociologist and the other in his role as president of the BSA and facilitator of a skate demo at the 2013 U.R{BNE} Festival held in the center of the city. Some members of the general public who attended the festival are also interviewed in the film. We will discuss examples that reflect diversity and interesting themes. Most interviewees' names are not presented in the documentary, so we describe their general traits and themes conveyed.

A main part of the documentary focuses on a free learn-to-skate workshop at Paddo run by Skateboarding Australia and Nike. Combined, the footage and interviews portray skateboarding as having a broad base of appreciation, participation, and benefits beyond just its core members. This includes footage of people of all ages, levels, and genders enjoying themselves skating and interviews with some of the parents of skaters. An interesting theme that arises from the comments of a father of two boys at the workshop challenges the stereotype of skateboarding conflicting with young people's ability to study. He explains that after skating, his children both 'study harder, because their bodies are all excited, they've just done something they enjoy and they're usually really positive about their homework' (cited in Stewart 2013). He continues, 'It's definitely positive, in fact, I'm so impressed by what the kids have been able to enjoy and get out of it that I went to the effort of making a ramp for them at home. I've seen my boys just gain so much confidence' (2013). These comments provide further support and reflect a study by Richard Stead and Mary Nevill (2010) on the influence of physical education and sport on education, which identified a number of benefits, including improved cognitive function, enhanced perceptual skills, and positive effect on anxiety and depression, which may improve academic achievement. The educational benefits physical activity such as skateboarding offers are not just contained to young people in the West but is also one of the motivating factors behind Skateistan, which uses skateboarding as a tool for empowering young people (Fitzpatrick 2012; Skateistan 2015).

An interesting demographic highlighted in the petition and documentary that challenges the dominant focus on youth in skateboarding and other subcultures is that of skaters past their twenties, some of whom were young when Paddo Skate Park first opened. Norm Higgins, for example, well known in the Brisbane skate scene and a member of the BSA, was at the clinic, as his daughter was attending. He states, 'Look at all these little kids here, they're loving it, but councils don't seem to recognize it [Paddo] as somewhere that really needs that injection. We've been asking for years to do something serious here and they just sort of flatly refused' (cited in Stewart 2013). Ben Ventress, in his early thirties, also a long-time Brisbane skater, voices similar concerns. He emphasizes how 'Brisbane use to be one of the leading cities in the world for skate parks in the nineties. We're still riding those same parks . . . skateboarding is a big part of youth culture, and you know, for them to not put, you know, any money or recognition into it is terrible, it's a crime' (cited in Stewart 2013). Because of skateboarding's longevity, it is no longer only participated in by children and young people. Those who skated in the 1970s and 1980s have either continued to skate or taken it up again, often with their own children. As a result, skateboarding is an intergenerational activity with increased numbers of users and varying needs.

Indigo Willing, one of the authors of this chapter, highlights in an interview in the film that Brisbane City could take inspiration from other capital cities like Sydney, with its skate park at Bondi Beach, a major attraction for skaters, nationally and internationally. The documentary later highlights a street skating demonstration held as part of the U.R{BNE} Festival in the city in 2013. Scott Shearer, also an author of this chapter, was one of the organizers and is also interviewed. He emphasizes one of the reasons for the demonstration is that it 'will be good to show people that wouldn't normally get to see skating or be exposed to skating to check it out, what it's all about and hopefully begin to start changing minds and views and opinions about how good skateboarding is' (cited in Stewart, 2013). Shearer has been a long-time advocate for integrating skate spaces into the urban environment, and the event is an example of how the city can be inclusive of skateboarding.

The film highlights that while skateparks are an important community recreation facility, they are not the only solution for meeting the skateboarding community's needs and should not be the only option to providing skaters with access to public space (Whitzman & Mizrachi cited in Shearer & Walters 2014). Innovative approaches outside Brisbane certainly exist, and increasingly, authorities are either incorporating skate elements into the urban environment and streetscapes or liberating existing skate spots as a result of skate activism. For example, the London skateboarding community, with the supportive voices of many non-skaters, from academics to local arts identities, successfully overturned a planning decision to transform Southbank Undercroft skate spot (regarded as the birthplace of British skateboarding) into retail units, therefore retaining it as a legitimate place for skateboarding. Moreover, such bringing together of differing voices for skate activism in the Southbank Undercroft instance challenges the notion that skaters and non-skaters are only antagonistic towards each other rather than able to be collaborative (Stratford 2010).

In the local context of our own case study, the documentary on Brisbane skateboarding also makes use of a variety of voices through its vox pops with various onlookers who watch the demonstration. A man who owns a nearby barber store

54   *Indigo Willing and Scott Shearer*

who is watching comments that everyone is 'having a good time . . . even the old-ies' (cited in Stewart 2013). A group of three women interviewed together observe that it is great to see skaters in the city 'not get in trouble by the cops' (cited in Stewart 2013). One also reveals that her brother skates and the other woman in the group reveals that she does not get to see skating often, so it is great the festival offers that opportunity. Another onlooker, who appears to be a young male work-ing in the city on a break, says, 'You kind of expect to see skateboarders cruise by on the sidewalk you know in the city and you just don't see it that much anymore. It's a shame . . . They're trying to skate proof everything' (cited in Stewart 2013). The final onlooker to comment is a male post-graduate university student, who states,

> [you] not only have the benefits as a sport but also it's engaging this city and it's transforming how people see the city. You have to balance it out right. You don't want a lot of skaters in the area fine but maybe you can release some other spaces and let them engage the city and other people.
>
> (cited in Stewart 2013)

Interviews with the public audience at the festival highlight how non-skaters can have positive attitudes towards skateboarding in the city and regret that it is not permitted there. The documentary ends as it starts, with footage of some of Bris-bane's skaters skating in various parts of the urban landscape. Sometimes there are scenes of the general public applauding the skaters, such as an elderly female tourist taking a photo of Dennis Durrant, clearly admiring what he is doing despite not being a skater herself. Here we might note that the role of onlookers and bystanders who appreciate skateboarding appears to be under-utilized by activists elsewhere. Additionally, while peripheral to skateboarding, such populations are ripe for research that has so far overlooked how their voices may positively impact lobbying for inclusion of skateboarding in public spaces.

In summary, the dominant themes of the documentary are that not only should the city repair and invest in its skate facilities but also consider integrated spaces in the city for both skaters and non-skaters who appreciate their presence to enjoy and engage. Skateboarding activists could further harness support by incorporat-ing the attitudes of bystanders and the general public who see the positives skating can bring to a city. Furthermore, as conveyed by various people in the documen-tary we have highlighted, skateboarding adds social and cultural value to cities, which counters its more negative image held more commonly by authorities, town planners, and some media.

Conclusion

As this chapter has highlighted, various people are involved in, appreciate, and bring different meanings and concerns to the subculture of skateboarding. At the core are individuals for whom being a skater is a significant part of their identity and for whom skateboarding is not just about skating but also living the 'skate life'. Because of the longevity and increasingly wider appeal of skateboarding, several generations of skaters now exist, and the subculture encompasses people of varying ages, genders, and social backgrounds. The attention to the diversity in skateboarding we explored in this chapter broadens the subculture to include people such as females, older generations, those either continuing or new to skating, and others who lack visibility. Our research in this chapter also aims to challenge stereotypes and narrow views about skateboarding. As our discussion reveals, a range of people see skateboarding as having a positive influence on people's physical health and social well-being, as well as for the city's reputation in terms of its skate facilities compared with those of other cities.

There are numerous ways government and council efforts and related policies for skateboarding can be more inclusive. This includes designated hours for skaters to use public plazas, commissioned skateable architecture and public art, and other forms of acceptance of skating as part of the city center, such as skate-friendly zones. Furthermore, governments can be more committed to upgrading and maintaining skate facilities, which can be done, for instance, by producing and implementing a skate facility strategy, as is the main goal of the petition we explored. Council involvement with lesser-represented figures in skateboarding such as female skaters also remains critical for the increased growth, understanding, and accessibility of skating for broader populations. Last, the documentary, as we discussed, conveys non-skaters are open to seeing skateboarding as part of the city's cultural fabric rather than relegated to the margins.

References

Atencio, M, Beal, B & Wilson, C 2009, 'The distinction of risk: urban skateboarding, street habitus and the construction of hierarchical gender relations', *Qualitative Research in Sport and Exercise*, vol. 1, no. 1, pp. 3–20.

Beal, B 1995, 'Disqualifying the official – an exploration of social resistance through the subculture of skateboarding', *Sociology of Sport Journal*, vol. 12, no. 3, pp. 252–267.

Beal, B 1996, 'Alternative masculinity and its effects on gender relations in the subculture of skateboarding', *Journal of Sport Behaviour*, vol. 19, no. 3, pp. 204–220.

Bennett, A 1999, 'Subcultures of neo-tribes? Rethinking the relationship between youth, style and musical taste', *Sociology*, vol. 33, no. 3, pp. 559–617.

Bennett, A 2011, 'The post-subcultural turn: some reflections ten years on', *Journal of Youth Studies*, vol. 14, no. 5, pp. 493–506.

Borden, I 2001, *Skateboarding, space and the city: architecture and the body*, Oxford, Berg, UK.

Bradley, GL 2010, 'Skate parks as a context for adolescent development', *Journal of Adolescent Research*, vol. 25, no. 2, pp. 288–323.

Brayton, S 2005, "Black-lash': revisiting the "White Negro" through skateboarding', *Sociology of Sport Journal*, vol. 22, no. 3, pp. 356–372.

Brodka, A 2013, *Underexposed: a women's skateboarding documentary*, Indie Rights, USA.

Chiu, C 2009, 'Contestation and conformity: street and park skateboarding in New York City public space', *Space and Culture*, vol. 12, no. 1, pp. 25–42.

Clifford, G 1989, *Gleaming the cube*, David Foster Productions, Gladden Entertainment, USA.

Hajkowicz, SA, Cook, H, Wilhelmseder, L & Boughen, N 2013, *The future of Australian sport: megatrends shaping the sports sector over coming decades*, CSIRO Australian Sports Commission Report. Available from: www.ausport.gov.au/__data/assets/pdf_file/0019/523450/The_Future_of_Australian_Sport_-_Full_Report.pdf. [20 April 2015].

Fitzpatrick, J 2012, *The tale of skateboarding in Afghanistan*, Skateistan, London.

Karsten, L & Pel, E 2000, 'Skateboarders exploring urban public space: ollies, obstacles and conflicts', *Journal of Housing and the Built Environment*, vol. 15, no. 4, pp. 327–340.

Lombard, K-J 2010, 'Skate and create/skate and destroy: The commercial and governmental incorporation of skateboarding', *Continuum: Journal of Media and Cultural Studies*, vol. 24, no. 4, pp. 475–488.

Németh, J 2006, 'Conflict, exclusion, relocation: skateboarding and public space', *Journal of Urban Design*, vol. 11, no. 3, pp. 297–318.

Nolan, N 2003, 'The ins and outs of skateboarding and transgression in public space in Newcastle, Australia', *Australian Geographer*, vol. 34, no. 3, pp. 311–327.

MacKay, S & Dallaire, C 2013, 'Skirtboarder net-a-narratives: young women creating their own skateboarding (re)presentations', *International Review for the Sociology of Sport*, vol. 48, no. 2, pp. 171–195.

Odanaka, B 2014, *Middle-aged skateboarders defy family skeptics, and falls*. Available from: http://articles.latimes.com/2014/jan/17/health/la-he-old-skaters20140118. [12 March 2014].

Peralta, S 2001, *Dogtown and Z-Boys* (DVD), Agi Orsi Productions, VANS Off the Wall and Sony, USA.

Peralta, S 2012, *Bones Brigade: an autobiography*, Nonfiction Unlimited, USA.

Provide a skate facility strategy for Brisbane skateparks 2015, change.org. Available from: www.change.org/p/provide-a-skate-facility-strategy-for-brisbane-skateparks. [20 April 2015].

Shearer, S & Walters, P 2014, 'Young people's lived experience of the "street" in North Lakes master planned estate', *Children's Geographies*, DOI: 10.1080/14733285.2014.939835

Skateistan 2015, *About us*. Available from: www.skateistan.org/content/our-story. [19 April 2015].

Stead, R & Nevill, M 2010, *The impact of physical education and sport on education outcomes: a review of literature*, Loughborough University, Leicestershire, UK.

Stewart, K 2013, *Affirmative action: a Brisbane skate documentary* (DVD), The Bay Skate, Australia.

Stratford, E 2010, 'On the edge: a tale of skaters and urban governance', *Social and Cultural Geography*, vol. 3, no. 2, pp. 193–206.

Taylor, J 2012, *Playing it queer: popular music, identity and queer world-making*, Peter Lang, Bern, Switzerland.

Weller, S 2007, 'Skateboarding alone? Making social capital discourse relevant to teenagers' lives', *Journal of Youth Studies*, vol. 9, no. 5, pp. 557–574.

Wood, L, Carter, M & Walker, K 2014, 'Dispelling stereotypes . . . skate parks as a setting for pro-social behavior among young people', *Current Urban Studies*, vol. 2, pp. 62–73.

Yochim, EC 2009, *Skate life: re-imagining white masculinity*, University of Michigan Press, USA.

Zamoscianyk, C 2009 *Street dreams*, Scissor Farm Entertainment, USA.

5 He catches things in flight

Scopic regimes, visuality, and skateboarding in Tyneside, England

Michael Jeffries, Sebastian Messer, and Jon Swords

Skateboarding is often explicitly credited with being creative (Beal 1995; Borden 2001; Howell 2005). However, the specific nature of this creativity and its importance for individual skaters goes largely unexplored. Robert Rinehart (2008, p. 77) specifically highlighted the 'self-expression, artistic, and non-conformist' subcultures as core to its attraction. For individual skateboarders, the very act of skating provides a creative outlet. Skaters commonly describe their own way of skating, or that of their friends, as a personal style, defining their own place in the lore of a local skate scene. This is one reason the presence of a strong visual culture in skateboarding, expressed both through graphics on products such as boards and via commercial and DIY photography and video, results in claims to creativity, but these assertions are seldom followed up in any detail other than describing the material.

Iain Borden (2001, p. 152) provides a more detailed analysis of skateboarding's 'graphic attitude', identifying an eclectic use of imagery drawing upon comic books, music genres such as rap or heavy metal, and sophisticated typography. He characterizes the resulting visual confusion, incomprehensible outside skateboarding, as a form of romantic resistance to social norms, especially to family. But skateboarding is also mainstream and is visualized by multinational corporations in advertisements designed to sell branded products to middle-class children and teenagers who have played skateboarding games on consoles or watched the brand-intensive coverage of the X Games.

Given the often vague and general assertions that skateboarding is inherently creative, coupled with the representations of skateboarding which often inadvertently undermine the claims that it is alternative and transgressive, our purpose here is to explore the practice and motivation of skaters who also create photography, video, and zines. We identify the opportunities that skateboarding has provided for creativity and how this varies among individual skaters. In addition, we explore the extent to which their work reproduces the clichés of skate imagery. Therefore our primary focus was on their personal visual practice in its widest sense, not just the content and style of their photography and video, but also and just as importantly, the purpose, means of display, possible audiences, and position within the local scene. The next section outlines the idea of scopic regimes, which we use as an explanatory framework to understand the production of our

58 *Michael Jeffries, Sebastian Messer, and Jon Swords*

participants' work. We also trace the emergence of what we characterize as skateboarding's dominant scopic regime. Section three presents our findings before we draw together our conclusions in section four.

Scopic regimes

The conceptual framework we use to understand the visualization of skateboarding comes from work on scopic regimes. This term refers not only to what we see but also to how it is produced, who it is produced by, and where it is reproduced (Rose 2012). The concept has its origins in Christian Metz's (1982) work on cinema, in which he differentiates between the different visualities of cinema and theatre. Metz argues that although both art forms are similar in performance and staging, they offer different ways of seeing. Cinema presents actors, music, sound, and special effects in an unobtainable way. Theatre presents the same, but you experience them 'really'. Metz suggests you could reach out and touch them in the theatre, but cinema denies this and distances the viewer physically and metaphorically from what they are seeing.

Martin Jay (1988) extends the concept of scopic regimes to include different ways of seeing in art, highlighting three dominant regimes in Western painting: Cartesian perspectivalism, the 'art of describing' (associated with seventeenth-century Dutch art), and the Baroque. Each presents a distinct worldview through both an artist's eyes and critic's interpretation, each separating the viewer from the depicted in different ways. Importantly, however, he argues single scopic regimes are not as hegemonic as they may seem and offer us many possible ways of seeing as we interpret them. Antonio Somaini (2008) reiterates this point, arguing we should be careful not to oversimplify visualities and instead appreciate how scopic regimes come into being through the subjects we capture in images, the media we use, and the context through which we interpret them.

For Allen Feldman (1997, p. 30), scopic regimes are infused with power, understanding them as forms of political visualization: 'the regimens that prescribe modes of seeing and objects of perception. A scopic regime is an ensemble of practices and discourses that establish truth claims, typicality and credibility of visual acts and objects and politically correct modes of seeing'. Using Feldman and Somaini, then, we have a methodology to unpick the formation and reproduction of scopic regimes that goes beyond analysis of individual photographs and photographers. Understanding scopic regimes requires us to understand the discourses and processes which create them (for examples, see Feldman 1997; Gregory 2011). In the following section, we begin this process by tracing the emergence of skateboarding's dominant scopic regime.

The emergence of skateboarding's scopic regime

Skateboarding can be traced back to at least the late 1950s (Borden 2001; Mortimer 2008; see Emery 2015 for even earlier proto skateboards), but the contemporary scene grew out of late 1970s West Coast surf culture in the United States.

Skateboarding therefore had an antecedent visuality upon which to draw from surfing. Fundamental to the evolution of the portrayal of skateboarding and popularizing its appeal were the Z-Boys of Dogtown (Santa Monica), California. It was the spatial tactics of the Dogtown skaters – reconnaissance for 'new' found spaces which could be appropriated for skateboarding – and their adoption of some of the visual and behavioral characteristics of gang culture, borrowing the style of tags from Los Angeles Chicano gangs for their deck graphics, which marked out the Z-Boys (Borden 2001).

Sean Mortimer (2008) and Craig Stecyk and Glen Friedman (2000) provide a substantial collection of historical articles and photographs from the early days of skating, and here we can see early signs of a particular vision of skateboarding emerging. The pictures and text conjure a culture concerned with the immediate, the personal, and the experiential. Risk taking, injuries, and expertise are eulogized. Interviewers commonly explain the subject is a person of few words, does not have much to say, who lives for the moment. Stecyk and Friedman's (2000, p. vii) introduction is telling: 'it is through . . . original articles that the standard was set for generations of rebellious individuals to follow and what is known today as the archetype skater was first brought to light'. The content of imagery from this time is recognizable today with the focus on individuals and their tricks. The wider skate scene is also captured in those images, with insiders recording the emergence of a new subculture, archiving the lives of young people in a particular place at a particular time.

Borden (2001) examines the reasons photography, both still and moving images, is so important in skateboarding. First, skate photography has an instructional and archival function – recording and preserving places, people, and tricks (p. 6); tracking an individual's progress; enabling the image's user to analyse and correct their performances; capturing and disseminating new, innovative tricks; and enabling other people to learn these from having seen them performed (pp. 114–119). Second, photography has a social function. It is a medium of exchange, providing evidence of tricks performed with kudos for 'firsts'. New tricks are rapidly disseminated, initially through friends but today via the Web, and bragging rights are contested for the novelty of being the first to recreate the move in a particular locale (pp. 119–135), each repetition seen as a new creation (p. 262). Finally, Borden suggests photography can have a spatial function, identifying a particular space and, implicitly or explicitly, an emotional connection to place (p. 123–125). Skate photography can be both documentary and also an aesthetic object.

Borden (2001, pp. 114–119, 127) also discusses the impact of equipment such as motor drives, flashes, wide angles, and stroboscopes on the ways in which skateboarding has been captured at different points in time. With each advance in technology, new possibilities were opened to photographers to capture tricks in new and interesting ways. Moving images were first captured on film, then video, and most recently digital cameras. Post-production techniques have also advanced, making it easier to edit still and moving images. The advent of digital technology has been significant, enabling more photographs to be taken and in some ways democratizing skate photography as digital cameras become cheaper.

Indeed, it was difficult for most skateboarders to afford the kind of equipment available to professional photographers, but over time, the technology has become cheaper, allowing the subculture of creative skaters we're examining to use photography as part of their skateboarding.

Photographers and filmmakers help foster individual skateboarders' profiles in the industry by documenting their tricks and publishing the resultant images. There was a skateboard industry as soon as there was skateboarding, but board manufacturers initially were small scale and their markets local. By the 1980s, the top professional skaters were attracting endorsements from clothing and skateboard manufacturers, who paid thousands of dollars a month to riders to use their equipment (Mortimer 2008). Today the top riders make millions of dollars a year in sponsorships, endorsements, and competition fees. Photography and film play a crucial role in getting to this level. Gregory Snyder (2011, p. 320) outlines the initial steps: '[f]or skateboarders the process of building a career starts when you begin to amass a portfolio of documented tricks'.

As skaters become better known and more in demand, they attract financial backing and sponsorships. Images of them must display the brands they promote. Both imagery for magazine features and for advertisements in magazines require skateboarders to look spectacular. Publishers need this to sell magazines; equipment and clothing manufacturers need to sell their products. The net result is that magazines' features are almost indistinguishable from advertisements in their style and content. The symbiotic relationships between magazines and advertisers, sponsors and skaters, skaters and photographers have produced (and reproduced) a scopic regime or genre of images of the individual skateboarder caught mid-trick with sponsors' logos pointed towards the camera lens.

But there is a tension here. The branding of skateboarding and the involvement of massive corporations have mainstreamed what was once seen as something for outsiders. Indeed, as we mentioned in the introduction, Borden (2001) highlights the resistance of skate culture to social norms. Skateboarding's dominant visual imagery and text create a powerful masculine identity, an 'outlaw image' (Atencio, Beal, & Wilson 2009; Brayton 2005; Wheaton 2003), perhaps in opposition to other youth masculinities, for example, 'jocks', 'lads', and aspirational alternatives (Giesler 2014). This is counter to this mainstream image and what made skateboarding appear 'cool', which in turn attracted companies such as Nike.

But this cool image is also undermined from another angle. Much of skateboarding's visualizations add to the sport's pervasive sexism (Atencio, Beal, & Wilson 2009; Borden 2001; MacKay & Dallaire 2013), homophobia (Borden 2001; Petrone 2010), and exclusion by class and ethnicity (Jenson, Swords, & Jeffries 2012; Karsten & Pell 2000). Atencio and Beal (2011) made a direct link between skateboard visuals and romanticized, DIY, outsider art. Matthew Atencio and Becky Beal were specifically concerned with a skate-inspired art exhibition, titled *Beautiful Losers*, which toured widely around North America in 2004, but their critique explores the problems within skate culture that undermine its claims to be anti-establishment and transgressive.

He catches things in flight   61

In the following sections, we explore the production of skate visuals from the perspective of local photographers in Tyneside, North East England. From our previous work on the skate scene in and around Newcastle-upon-Tyne, we knew several skateboarders who were active photographers, bloggers, and video and zine makers who had sustained their individual creativity hand in hand with their skateboarding. We worked with them to identify the roots of their practice, their role, and the role of their work within the local skateboard scene and to understand how, by their creative practice, they might reproduce or contest the scopic regime of skateboarding.

Methodology

For the past five years, we have worked with skaters in Tyneside and, more recently, Norwich to understand the ways they conceptualize the city (Jeffries, Messer, & Swords 2013; Jenson, Swords, & Jeffries 2012). Through our interaction with them, we have come to know the local scenes well; their histories, myths, legends, and the role of visuals for particular skaters. This was important, as we adopted a visual methodology to understand the geographies of the local scene. As part of this research, we have exhibited the visual work of participants, including that of Tyneside's skate photographers and video makers. It is through this sustained, participatory approach that we have met and built strong links to the skateboarding creatives in this study.

For this chapter, we interviewed six of those skaters. All six are in their early to mid-twenties; all started skating aged between ten and fifteen and have continued to skate to the present day. All six are creatively active, with skateboarding as a major focus of that creativity, and five have skate-related blogs or websites. We have known five of them through our previous work for periods of between six months and five years. One risk of this familiarity is that they might be aware of any views we had on the visualization of skate culture, although our previous work has primarily focused on spatial mapping and the social value of urban sports rather than on imagery. The sixth person we had not met until a premier of their recent skate DVD, although he knew of our work. Four have done or are doing university-level arts subjects (photography, graphics, or architecture) and a fifth intends to. The sixth has a business degree. All interviews lasted around one hour, the participants having been given an outline of the questions in advance. The questions focused on how and when they started skateboarding, their creative practice in relation to skateboarding, and skateboarding culture in general. Interviews were transcribed and coded for analysis.

Creativity and Tyneside's skate scene

This section outlines three distinct visualities that emerged from our analysis. The interviews revealed how skateboarding had facilitated and fostered the creativity of all six participants. It has provided a subject for their work and extended their enjoyment of skateboarding. The participants were all aware of the dominant visual representation of skateboarding and, to a greater or lesser extent, they all positioned their creative outputs in relation to that scopic regime, sometimes positively. For example the dominant, perhaps clichéd use of certain lenses and flash photography was readily acknowledged, but the reasons for their use were also clearly articulated:

> [The use of a fish eye lens to photograph skateboarding] is a cliché, but it's a cliché for a reason, it's one of the best ways to capture the movement, the experience of the skateboarder.
>
> (Interviewee 2, pers. comm., 13 February 2015)

The repetitive stylistic content of skate photography and video was highlighted more negatively:

> I don't like a lot of skateboard videos anymore . . . There is that intro, really fast music, all falling over or bailing hard, then there's a bit of down time where the guy's smoking a cigarette . . . then maybe in the middle a montage of something a bit different . . . It's just the same over and over.
>
> (Interviewee 3, pers. comm., 4 February 2015)

From the coding of the interviews, we identified three distinct conceptual approaches to the visualization of skateboarding. Two of the participants can be understood as 'skate photographers', which we define as re-producing the dominant visuality of skateboarding as seen in adverts and magazines. The approach of three further participants had more in common with reportage than mainstream skate industry photography, and their creative practice extended beyond just photography to include other visual outputs. Finally, the sixth participant's visual work is a form of critique of skateboarding culture and uses skateboarding as a lens through which to consider the built environment. We use these conceptual approaches to structure the rest of this section. We examine what each group captures and their motivations for doing so; how they capture Tyneside's skate world through their practice and choice of equipment; and finally how they are positioned in relation to others in the local scene.

Skate photography: 'documenting the trick'

Interviewees 1 and 2 identified themselves and were identified by the other participants as 'Skate Photographers', whose aim it is to document an individual's tricks at their most spectacular and exact. As Interviewee 1 (pers. comm., 10 February 2015) explained, 'The whole point of shooting skateboarding is you're documenting the trick. Document[ing] as accurately as possible. I don't want to change it. Not supposed to. The number one rule'. For Interviewee 2 (pers. comm., 13 February 2015), it was about doing justice to the subject, capturing the skill and expertise of the skater: 'I don't want to take a photograph that downplays what the skater's doing. I don't want to take a photograph that makes the skater's trick look not as good as it is'.

He catches things in flight 63

Their photographs are typically of a single skater – no other people or extraneous content are in view – often in mid-air, dramatically framed by the built environment. They concentrate on shooting difficult or unusual tricks to capture the moment when the trick is at its most extreme in terms of skill and visual impact, thus reproducing the dominant scopic regime outlined earlier. They are able to do this for three interconnected reasons.

First, like all the participants, Interviewees 1 and 2 are skaters themselves. Each explained that a trick has a perfect moment, an instant in time when board and skater are at their most spectacular, and knowing – or sensing – that moment was second nature from their years of skateboarding. Their intimate knowledge of the physicality, skill, and technique of tricks was essential to capture their essence on camera.

Second, both own the same high-specification equipment used by professional photographers working for magazines and advertisers. Each has a range of lenses of different focal lengths, a variety of flashes and lighting equipment, and more than one camera. Neither participant went out with a camera on the off chance of getting a shot or, if they did, this was not mentioned as part of their core creative practice. Considered choices were made when they went out to shoot: 'You get to the point of where you're going out, "what do I need?" and you have to decide. Right, that lens, that lens, now everything fits in the bag' (Interviewee 1, pers. comm., 10 February 2015).

Third, both photographers have learnt about photography through their educations (one did a commercial photography degree; the other is studying architecture). Both took time and pride in planning photographic sessions, which included setting up lighting equipment, arranging times to go out, and building trust with the skaters. Both tricks and shots would be practiced, often repeatedly, until a trick was successfully landed and the image framed perfectly to capture the right moment. Their training in photographic techniques allowed them to capture precise shots but also enabled them to explore the ways in which their subjects were photographed. A dominant theme was an explicit desire to highlight their expertise and understanding both of photography and of skateboarding, to differentiate their images from those that a casual observer could take:

> [I] try to find the most obscure, interesting angle to shoot it from so it doesn't look like someone from the general public literally just walked along and clicked away. Everyone has a camera these days. Everyone can take a photo. You want to [show the] thought [that] went into it: you've composed the image, set up the lights, set the camera up perfectly. No Photoshop required. That's what we were taught; do as much in camera as possible.
>
> (Interviewee 1, pers. comm., 10 February 2015)

This was particularly the case for the participant whose degree in photography concentrated on a commercial, professional context, emphasizing the need for technical excellence, planning the shoot, and the use of appropriate equipment.

These comments hint at how Interviewees 1 and 2 see and position themselves as the expert photographer and expert filmmaker, respectively. They are proud

Figure 5.1a & 5.1b Typical photographs by Interviewees 1 and 2. Their images consist of single skaters, shot at the high point of a trick, often with a fish-eye lens with flash to freeze the movement. Extraneous background is minimized. These images closely reproduce the style of advertisement photography from skateboard magazines. Figure 5.1a courtesy of Adam Todhunter ©. Figure 5.1b courtesy of Johnny Haynes ©.

of their expertise, and it is also recognized by others in the demand for their services from local skaters. As the quotes show, explanations of their practice often contained explicit criticism of photographs by non-skaters, which are perceived to have a different sensibility and lesser purpose. This is in part because skate photography is also a display of the photographer's insider knowledge. It shows their dual identity as both skater and photographer. The image proves their skater credentials, which in turn demonstrates the 'authenticity' and perceived objectivity of the photographic image. They are the professional photographers of the local skate scene.

This identity is important for their futures, with both wanting a career in skate photography. The outcome of their practice is photography and video that reproduces the dominant scopic regime. Both have had photographs in national skate magazines, and both have links to the skate industry. However, working within the constraints of the scopic regime also creates a tension between trying to appeal to the photo editors whilst also developing a distinctive and recognizable visual identity. As Interviewee 1 (pers. comm., 10 February 2015) explained,

> You want your peers to look at it, other skate photographers, the way you looked at skateboard photography when you were first getting into it . . . you want people to be able to see it and not look at the names . . . [to recognise] that's one of [my] photos.

Reportage: 'what else was going on'

The Reportage Photographers were much more concerned about the wider context: less interested in tricks, more alert to the wider culture of skating. As Interviewee 3 (pers. comm., 4 February 2015) put it, 'I like seeing what else was going on at the time that was happening. A little bit of a cultural side to it as well as just what's happening in the photograph'. There are clear differences in attitude between those interviewees who were identified as Skate Photographers and those who took a reportage approach. All three publish blogs as their main platform, but their content is diverse, the photography and the skate scene only one of several themes such as lifestyle, portraits, or graphic illustration. The reportage photography, while still recognizably about skating, places a strong emphasis on spontaneity and 'grittiness' rather than technique and planning to compose the shot.

The Reportage Photographers were openly critical of photographs and videos reproducing the dominant scopic regime, especially those associated with commercial magazines. These participants criticized them for their repetitive content and structure, sentiments which were absent from the interviews with the Skate Photographers:

> [The genre of skate photography] doesn't really interest me that much. I like looking at it but at the same time it doesn't interest me. I don't feel it evokes

Figure 5.2a & 5.2b Interviewees 3, 4, and 5. Their photography covers a wide range of subject matter. Images of skating typically show skateboarders as peripheral to the image and not doing complex tricks or even skating at all. Instead, the skaters are commonly placed in a wider spatial context, blurred by movement or natural lighting conditions. Figure 5.2a courtesy of Lewis Ellenden ©. Figure 5.2b courtesy of Ben Armson ©. Figure 5.2c courtesy of Adam Thirtle ©.

He catches things in flight 67

Figure 5.2c

the . . . I like the emotional side to it a bit more. At the end of the day, it's just another trick, down at whatever location.
(Interviewee 3, pers. comm., 4 February 2015)

Interviewees 3, 4, and 5 do not have the same educational training in photography as the Skate Photographers (although one had done a foundation year in photography and another a degree in graphic design), which goes some way to explaining their different approach to both content and planning. The influences on this group were also different to that of the Skate Photographers. Instead, they are producing a hybrid of street photography, portraiture, and skate photography with their lifestyle and culture as their primary subject. Younger magazines, such as *North Skate Mag* (dedicated to skateboarding and 35mm film photography) and *Dank* (which uses editorial photo shoots influenced by fashion and lifestyle photography to develop narratives) were cited as inspirational. Consequently, a range of high-specification equipment isn't as crucial for them: 'Sometimes it's only my camera; I don't bring out a flash or anything like that. I don't like carrying things around' (Interviewee 5, pers. comm., 12 February 2015). These participants are not performing roles as recorders of tricks but as recorders of the local scene and the people in it. This is illustrated in the content of their blogs, one of which has been maintained by Interviewees 4 and 5 for seven years. This has become a site of nostalgia and heritage, and a curatorial role has also developed with a new Instagram site specifically intended for archiving and disseminating images and posts from 'back in the day'.

Despite their very different focus, skateboarding was still fundamental to their identity, so their relative disinterest in the genre of skate photography and the influence of the skateboarding industry does not represent a lesser engagement with skating. The practice of all three photographers documents the Tyneside skate scene, which helps maintain a cohesive community largely based around Native Skate Store. The reportage includes some technically excellent photographs, but the content is social: the people, days out with friends, and who got up to what.

The Analyst

The sixth participant expressed a different visuality. Through his practice, the Analyst explores skateboarding as a form of spatial expression as well as the politics of wider skate culture. His practice is rooted in DIY culture, linked to a lo-fi, almost punk aesthetic and expressed in photography, sculpture, painting, music, and zines. He captures skating (himself and others), but from a more artistic perspective that allows him to analyse the interaction of skateboarding and architecture: 'When I'm just by myself I just set up the camera to capture what I'm doing. Skateboarding is ephemeral. You preserve space, that activity, it only exists when it's being performed. By documenting it you preserve that' (Interviewee 6, pers. comm., 5 February 2015). He begins discussing imitating elements of skateboarding's dominant scopic regime through style and equipment:

> There is an aesthetic, an aesthetic a lot of skate photographers, myself included, adhere to . . . the fish eye distorts the photo, makes if look more dramatic, look spectacular. Whoa! Kinda warped, giving a real sense of motion through that.
>
> (Interviewee 6, pers. comm., 5 February 2015)

He then switches to sharing the attitude to equipment and the happenstance of production of the Reportage Photographers: 'I just bring a camera along with me when I'm gonna go out skateboarding then capture things that happen, rather than plan' (Interviewee 6, pers. comm., 5 February 2015). But at the same time, he likes to depersonalize depictions to focus on the action rather than on the skater. In his photography, this involves more close ups that focus on the relationship between board and object. This more experimental approach reflects his education as an art student on a contemporary photography degree.

His exploration of space in his artistic practice is also explicitly political. It isn't political in the sense of rejecting a particularly way of seeing; rather, he explores the place of skateboarding in wider society. His work features the conflicts between skaters and those seeking to privatize space. It deliberately challenges the sexism and homophobia of the mainstream skate representation, and yet being a skater is essential to his identity.

His work is situated in an artistic paradigm which would not be recognized by mainstream skate publishers, but neither is his audience primarily skaters; it may

He catches things in flight 69

Figure 5.3 Interviewee 6. The front covers of two of his zines exploring Newcastle's cityscape, architecture, and exclusion of skateboarders. The zines are made on standard photocopiers and distributed via local skate and comic book shops. Note they are also free, an explicit choice by the skater as part of his practice. Photo by Mike Jeffries, used with permission from Euan Lynn ©.

be few local skaters are aware of his work. The commonality with the five other participants is that skating has provided the foundation in which his individual practice and creativity are rooted.

The Tyneside skate scene has evolved an ecology in which diverse and complimentary specialisms have created roles for our six participants: the expert Skate Photographer and Filmmaker; the Lifestyle Photographer and the aspiring Street Photographer; the Curator; and the Analyst, although the participants might not recognize themselves in those terms.

Conclusion: 'the way you shoot skateboarding is how you'd like skateboarding to appear'

Our interviews provided a highly nuanced account of the practices of six of Tyneside's skateboarders. All of them invest considerable time and resources in their activity. For all of them, creativity was central to their identity, although none are yet able to pursue this as a main career. All the participants define their creative practices in relation to the scopic regime of skate photography. Those who identify themselves as Skate Photographers reproduce the regime's tropes but seek to establish a visual language which was recognizably their own within the genre. This seems to be a trade-off, to some extent, to enable them to pursue their ambition of a commercial career. Technical knowledge and perfection of execution are most highly valued. For them, authenticity is about the objectivity of the photograph. The Reportage Photographers have a more critical attitude to the dominant scopic regime. They move among genres, including lifestyle and street photography, and their subject is social. Their approach to photography is markedly different. Authenticity is in spontaneity and capturing the moment. Equipment is chosen to be light and mobile rather than for superior image quality.

The Analyst uses the techniques of both the Skate and Reportage Photographers. He is even more promiscuous than the Reportage Photographers in his choice of equipment and media: digital, 35mm film, Polaroid, and photocopier. Increasingly, he resists the scopic regime through subject matter, which challenges stereotypes and prejudices within skate culture, and through the framing of his photographs, which 'depersonalize' the subject and have an almost macroscopic focus. He does not seek authenticity but cultivates the distortion and 'warp' of the images inherent in the limitations of the technology used.

Skateboarding has provided our participants the opportunities and motive to develop significant and sustained creative practices. As well as the symbiosis of skate and photography as activities, there are parallels between being a skateboarder and being a photographer. Skills and techniques are learnt from the close reading of the photograph – trying to work out what happened before and after the moment frozen by the shutter – followed by their re-enactment until perfected. The equipment becomes an extension of the body and, at least for some, there is equivalence in their attachment to their particular camera and skateboard. Both skateboarding and photography are central to our participants' identities and to their perceptions of the world. One participant, for whom photography has taken on a greater significance, said he continued to skate because of the photography. Another stated he would always feel like a skater even if he no longer skated.

In mobilizing the concept of scopic regimes, we have sought to illustrate the important intersubjectivities among space, skater, photographer, and regime. We have sought to avoid privileging the image in this analysis, to highlight the social, personal, and economic factors influencing the recreation of skateboard visuals and their position vis-à-vis the dominant scopic regime. The personal is particularly important and the influence of newer, less mainstream media (e.g. *Dank* and *North Skate Mag*) and has allowed some participants to explore new genres. These sources are more local than imagery associated with transnational skate brands originated in the United States and offer more authenticity in their depiction of skateboarding. It appears, for those participants at least, positioning themselves outside mainstream skateboarding through their visualities is important and has echoes of the original outlaws who invented skateboarding.

Acknowledgements

We are very grateful to the six interviewees for taking part and their supportive interest in this work and to Jackie in Native Skate Store for his continued help and insights.

Examples of creative practice from the Tyneside skate scene can be found on several blogs: www.adamtodhunter.co.uk, www.4-sightskateboardzine.com, http://euanlynn.tumblr.com/, http://barmson.tumblr.com/, http://lewisellenden.com/, www.digitaldeekies.com/.

References

Atencio, M & Beal, B 2011, 'Beautiful losers: the symbolic exhibition and legitimization of outside masculinity', *Sport in Society*, vol. 14, no. 1, pp. 1–16.

Atencio, M, Beal, B & Wilson, C 2009, 'The distinction of risk: urban skateboarding, street habitus and the construction of hierarchical gender relations', *Qualitative Research in Sport and Exercise*, vol. 1, no. 1, pp. 3–20.

Beal, B 1995, 'Disqualifying the official: an exploration of social resistance of skateboarding', *Sociology of Sport Journal*, vol. 12, no. 3, pp. 252–267.

Borden, I 2001, *Skateboarding, space and the city: architecture and the body*, Berg, Oxford.

Brayton, S 2005, ' "Black-lash": revisiting the white negro through skateboarding', *Sociology of Sport Journal*, vol. 22, no. 3, pp. 356–372.

Emery, B 2015, 'The prehistoric skateboard?', *Jenkem Magazine*. Available from: www.jenkemmag.com/home/2015/02/11/the-prehistoric-skateboard/. [25 February 2015].

Feldman, A 1997, 'Violence and vision: the prosthetics and aesthetics of terror', *Public Culture*, vol. 10, no. 1, pp. 24–60.

Giesler, CM 2014, 'Pranking Peter Pans: performing playground masculinities in extreme sports', *Text and Performance Quarterly*, vol. 34, no. 4, pp. 334–353.

Gregory, D 2011, 'From a view to a kill: drones and late modern war', *Theory, Culture and Society*, vol. 28, no. 7, pp. 188–215.

Howell, O 2005, 'The "creative class" and the gentrifying city: skateboarding in Philadelphia's Love Park', *Journal of Architectural Education*, vol. 59, no. 2, pp. 32–42.

Jay, M 1988, 'Scopic regimes of modernity', in Foster (ed), *Vision and visuality*, Bay Press, Seattle, pp. 3–23.

Jeffries, MJ, Messer, S & Swords, J 2013, 'Playing out. The importance of the city as a playground for skateboarding and parkour', in J Teitle (ed), *The other 17 hours: valuing out-of-school time, Bank Street occasional papers*, vol. 30, Bank Street College, New York, pp. 1–14.

Jenson, A, Swords, J & Jeffries, MJ 2012, 'The accidental youth club: skateboarding in Newcastle Gateshead', *Journal of Urban Design*, vol. 17, no. 3, pp. 371–388.

Karsten, L & Pell, E 2000, 'Skateboarders exploring urban public space: ollies, obstacles and conflicts', *Journal of Housing and the Built Environment*, vol. 15, no. 4, pp. 327–340.

MacKay, S & Dallaire, C 2013, 'Skirtboarder net-a-narrative: young women creating their own skateboarding (re)presentations', *International Revue of the Sociology of Sport*, vol. 48, no. 2, pp. 171–195.

Metz, C 1982, *The imaginary signifier: psychoanalysis and the cinema*, Indiana University Press, Bloomington.

Mortimer, S 2008, *Stalefish: skateboard culture from the rejects who made it*, Chronicle Books, San Francisco.

Petrone, R 2010, ' "You have to get hit a couple of times": the role of conflict in learning "how" to be a skateboarder', *Teaching and Teacher Education*, vol. 26, no. 1, pp. 119–127.

Rinehart, RE 2008, 'Exploiting a new generation: corporate branding and the co-optation of action sport', in Giardina, MD & Donnelly MK (eds), *Youth culture and sport: identity, power and politics*, Routledge, New York, pp. 71–89.

Rose, G 2012, *Visual methodologies*, Sage, London.

Snyder, GJ 2011, 'The city and the subcultural career: professional street skateboarding in LA', *Ethnography*, vol. 13, no. 3, pp. 306–329.

Somaini, A 2008, 'On the scopic regime', *Leitmotiv*, 5, 2005–6, pp. 25–38.

Steckyk III, CR & Friedman, GE 2000, *Dogtown: The legend of the Z-Boys*, Burning Flags Press, New York.

Wheaton, B 2003, 'Lifestyle sport magazines and the discourses of sporting masculinity', *The Editorial Board of the Sociological Review*, vol. 51, no. S1, pp. 193–211.

6 Posing LA, performing Tokyo

Photography and race in skateboarding's global imaginary

Dwayne Dixon

'Ok, can you go around again but get higher?' The photographer is crouched in the center of the forbidding concrete bowl, his face nearly invisible behind an imposing digital camera, the lens pointed up towards the lip of the nine foot wall. We were in Chiba Prefecture, a few hours' drive east of Tokyo, at a concrete skatepark and resort hotel complex adjacent to some of Japan's best surfing beaches. Facing the California coast from along the Pacific Rim, the bowl uncannily echoed back the grand concrete skateparks of 1970s SoCal and in that echo reverberated skateboarding's globalized history and collapsing cultural distance. As an East Coast American street skater, I felt out of place in the big, smooth transitions as I attempted to mimic the light, flowing technique of skateboarding's fabled West Coast ancestors who first recognized the empty pool as an endless wave. I dropped in from the shallow end, accelerating left and arcing upwards as the wall went to vertical. I struggled to control my skateboard's velocity as I hurtled vertiginously across the smooth surface. Feeling myself going out of control, I bailed, flinging myself away from the wall towards the flat bottom as my board went skittering wildly around the bowl like a missile dangerously off target. My feet ached with the impact. My body throbbed with the aftereffects of the near-chaos I'd just escaped. But when I sheepishly turned to apologize to the photographer for ruining the shot with my panicked dismount, he was beaming. 'That was great! So high!' With the photographer's pleasure, I felt the disorienting shape of different expectations dissipate my embarrassment: for him, it wasn't important that I couldn't carve a simple line through the deep end but only that I appear for an instant to fulfil his idealized image of a skater. And not just any skater but one conjured from across three decades and an ocean away and refracted through the lens of Hollywood.

I had been recruited, along with my friend Dan – another 'white boy' skater – through a network of Tokyo skateboard friends, to serve as an animated prop for this photo shoot featuring one of Japan's hottest heartthrobs, Takahiro, the newly anointed lead singer for Japan's enormously popular fourteen-member pop sensation/boy band, Exile. The concept for the shoot was to recreate key scenes from *Lords of Dogtown*, the 2005 Hollywood film mythologizing the Los Angeles origins of contemporary skateboard culture. Takahiro was 'playing' the role of actor Victor Rasuk, who in turn portrayed Tony Alva, the most renowned and celebrated

74 *Dwayne Dixon*

skater of the late 1970s, while Dan and I were cast as generic white kids. The photo essay was to appear in the second issue of a newly launched magazine entirely devoted to showcasing the band and their lifestyles under the English tagline 'Culture and Fashion'. The magazine, entitled *Gekkan EXILE* (*Monthly Exile*), was another commodity-vehicle of the band's already formidable presence in the Japanese pop media landscape, enhancing their particular brand of cosmopolitan, masculine celebrity aimed at young consumers.

Before Takahiro arrived with his manager in their own exclusive car from Tokyo, Dan and I were expected to skate around the park to provide a range of action photos that could be used to supplement the main images featuring the star. Neither of us had ever skated anything like this before, and as we talked about how to approach the curved, vertical walls, we had to remind ourselves we weren't actually skaters in this instant but stunt doubles in specifically raced bodies, imitating actors who portrayed other (mostly) white skaters from a different time and space. For the photographer and art director, we were perfectly convincing props in this respect, combining the requisite whiteness, youthful masculinity, and skateboard appendages sufficient to capture the *fūniki*, the aura or atmosphere of the film, rather than simply re-enact it. Put to work in this way, the materiality of the park and the actual skill required to ride it were subordinated to uncanny historical, spatial, and cultural displacements refracted through lenses on both sides of the Pacific.

Skateboarding's perceived authenticity as a (American) youth practice ricocheted wildly through the aperture of this media event in which Japanese pop celebrity was overlaid on Hollywood celluloid fantasy was extruded from the mythology circulated globally through skateboard media. Thus, the shoot's entire concept was a fantastic and globalized tangle of trans-Pacific imitation, nostalgia, appropriated style, and mimetic performance anchored in the physical space of the park itself and in our fleshy presence on camera. This globalized mimesis of skateboard history was especially visible in the perfect copy of a 1970s suburban SoCal swimming pool – bone dry, of course – complete with blue tile border, built adjacent to the concrete bowl. Dan and I marvelled at this architectural replica symbolizing skateboarding's raw, improvisational ethos. We laughed at how ironic it was, as North American skaters, that we'd had to travel to Japan to actually ride skateboarding's most fetishized site of authenticity, the drained backyard swimming pool, but only as a simulacrum of itself.

Takahiro had since arrived and been briefed by the art director, costumed appropriately, and handed a vintage late 1970s skateboard from the stylist's own personal collection. He joined Dan and me down in the white-walled pool, where we looked up at the photographer expectantly, awaiting direction. He stood with an assistant, carefully scrutinizing still photographs of a key scene in which Victor Rasuk (as Tony Alva) trespasses in the deep end of a bone-dry but majestic pool, with board raised overhead, proclaiming his profound discovery to his friends on the patio above: 'This wave breaks twenty-four hours a day, every day!' (Hardwicke 2005). It was a difficult shot to deconstruct. Without the suburban house and manicured lawn, the pool we stood in, yards from the wrong side of the

Pacific Ocean, was nothing more than a displaced architectural gimmick. So the photo assistant herded us closer together in the shallow end with the pool's white walls and blue-tiled lip framing us. Dan and I faced towards Takahiro, who stood facing the camera with arms raised, imitating Rasuk-as-Alva's actorly enthusiasm. 'Am I believable?' he joked. Then, unleashing a heartthrob smile, he gestured with the old 1970s board, and the camera whirred away above our tableaux. A lighting technician adjusted his reflector to transform the Japanese sun into a Hollywood glow.

The photo shoot illuminates skateboarding as a rich intersection of architecture, youthful bodies, and images – a triangulation structured through the commodification and circulation of information within globalizing capitalism. This commodified image refracts the ethnographic moment and the larger questions it contains: how does skateboarding come to life as a media object and as a global sign powerfully congealing the elusive aura of 'youth' as a compelling commodity in its own right? How do race, (sub)cultural meanings, and mythologies of youthful authenticity enliven skateboarding as a transcultural media commodity? These questions propel us into the fast transitions between concepts of globalization, cross-Pacific history, and youth culture and finally bring us to a skateboard/media encounter on Tokyo's streets.

Skateboarding and the global youth imaginary

From Los Angeles to London, Osaka to Sao Paulo, representations of skateboarding abound, whether in advertising photos, televised competitions, video games, or affiliated with clothes and shoe fashions. Skateboarding's increased global visibility is concomitant with the rise of heavily promoted and mediated youth-oriented 'action' sports in the late 1990s, and it has become both catalyst and reference for current global waves of street fashion, extreme sports, and broad marketing vocabularies aimed at young demographics. By ethnographically approaching the construction of the skateboard image itself, the global cultural and capitalist networks animating images of youth become more visible in the social relations and creative work happening at the site of the photo shoot. What is especially apparent is how these global, commodified images of youth intersect bodies, spaces, and media histories, metabolizing simultaneously the Americanized vision of the teenager with the contemporary cultural cool of the global city. This relationship between youth and urban space, solidified through image production, is a crucial feature of what I term the 'global youth imaginary'.[1] Skateboarding effectively signifies youth and urban space while also drawing on a strong subcultural history and thus becomes a powerful, enlivening component in the creation of this imaginary.

It is unsurprising that skateboarding has become a valuable commodity-sign within global capitalism. Because skateboarding confers a perceived authenticity derived from underground youth styles, it serves to link sites of desires and elusive cool. Former pro skateboarder and architectural historian Ocean Howell (2003) critically links skateboarding's frequent commercialized media appearance with

76 *Dwayne Dixon*

the rise of urban cool, stating that in the mid 1990s when urban culture became 'cool' again,

> Advertisers wanted to celebrate all things edgy, and skateboarding looked like the newest, edgiest, most urban thing happening. In 1995 ESPN launched the 'Extreme Games' (later renamed 'X-Games), with skateboarding as the flagship event, and with televised adverts for Mountain Dew and Doritos and, a few years later, the Marines.

Projected on screens across the world in spectacular displays of the youth imaginary, skateboarding had become globally legible, far removed from its faddish origins as a Californian plaything epitomizing the widely exported vision of the American lifestyle. This mass-mediated commodification of skateboarding was another instance in which 'youthful bodies became the festive sites where mass culture modeled "youth" as a consumable substance, as a style . . . Virtually every aesthetic formation in popular culture has been complicit with this mass-market fetishization of youth' (Latham 2002, p. 16). This mass fetishization of youthful bodies is visible within the *Gekkan EXILE* photo shoot, produced under the historical sign of American rebel cool.[2]

The global imaginary of skateboarding, given substance as a Tokyo-produced media artifact, overlays the American-Japanese axis of politics, economics, and cultures irradiating a crucial genealogy of globalization beginning before World War II and echoing out along the Pacific Rim. The global youth imaginary is refracted here through the densely tangled histories of American pop culture, raced male bodies, and fantasies of an urban 'anywhere'. Despite its diffuse allure, the imaginary is nonetheless contingent upon skaters living and exploring in the global city.

In framing the skateboard image, we must situate skateboarding's place in a broad narrative of globalization in which the waves of popular youth culture wash outwards on a mass scale but eddy into highly localized currents of youth identities. Marketed massively but circulated with local specificity, skateboarding does not necessarily saturate every market or social world equally, even if it is widely recognizable as a sign of (risky) youth (sub)culture.

Skateboarding, as a youth practice made widely legible and meaningful through its spectacular and spectacularized media forms, requires a schematic of globalization that accounts for the diachronic hegemonic cultural force exerted by the United States after WWII and continued as major capitalist economies transitioned towards information and service industries in the 1970s. Specifically, we must attend to American cultural power so as to trace skateboarding's erratic lines across the Pacific Rim and into Japan. For this sense of historical continuity, Stuart Hall gives us his concept of 'global mass culture', a form of globalization emerging in the aftermath of colonial empires and becoming especially 'Americanized' after WWII. Mass culture is defined by the mediated character of globalized capitalism and 'dominated by the modern means of cultural production, dominated by the image which crosses and re-crosses linguistic frontiers much more rapidly

Posing LA, performing Tokyo   77

and more easily, and which speaks across languages in a much more immediate way' (Hall 1991, p. 27). It is this attention to the image that is of primary interest here, particularly how 'the visual and graphic arts have entered directly into the reconstitution of popular life, of entertainment and of leisure' (p. 27). The image, travelling through media networks far more sophisticated than when Hall located its globalizing power, crosses over national boundaries with great speed while carrying cultural residue. With its obvious mobile power, the image crucially constitutes the shape-shifting contours of the global youth imaginary.

Over the twenty-five years following Hall's early assessment of global mass culture after the Cold War, sophisticated and nuanced accounts have followed. Arjun Appadurai's (1996) salient argument for transnational flows and Kōichi Iwabuchi's (2002) necessary challenge to theories based on hegemonic American cultural power both elaborate on 'the new forms of global economic and cultural power which are apparently paradoxical: multi-national but de-centered' (Hall 1991, p. 30). This is the hallmark of a mode of capitalism Felix Guattari termed 'World-Wide Integrated Capitalism' which, despite its comically sinister description, is one not interested in the flat delivery of a uniform commodity or in cultural homogenization but in the extraction and valuation of difference (Guattari 1996, p. 216). Semiotized capital transmogrifies differences, using them to 'connect heterogeneous domains and asymmetrical potencies and powers' and control desire from the broad expanse of the social down to 'the modes of sensibility, tastes, and choices of each individual' (p. 251). In this form of globalized capitalism, images technologically domesticate and transmit alluring forms of difference endlessly through time and space. Correspondingly, 'youth' has become a mutable, heterogeneous, and highly mediated figure. As a potent vector for the desires of and for youth, the image within semiotized capitalism is able to traverse national and cultural boundaries, gaining new momentum as differences of meaning and value multiply across its surfaces as it passes among interconnected viewerships. 'The life of images is not a private or individual matter. It is a social life,' argues W.J.T. Mitchell, 'reproducing themselves over time, migrating from one culture to another' (2013, p. 93). This form of 'multi-national and de-centered' semiotized capitalism, with its hunger for difference and its logic of commodified heterogeneity, intensifies the flow and increases the social force of images moving across 'national boundaries', producing what Karatani Kôjin (cited in Ching 2000, p. 240) terms an 'imagined transnational community'.

Given the photo shoot is inspired by the nostalgic fantasy of SoCal youth culture, the question arises: what to do with America? Clearly this is not an 'imagined transnational community' coming into a mediated existence untouched by the powerful resonances of American pop culture. Indeed, skateboarding itself is operating here as a sign synonymous with America and youth. In the 'de-centred' context of Hall's vision of globalization, how does a youth imaginary map itself through American skateboarding across national borders? While American cultural hegemony has been de-centred, we are faced with an uncanny Japanese reflection of commodified American youth culture, demonstrating how the transnational fetishization of youth has been re-imagined and re-framed.

Posing LA

Despite skateboarding's value within visual lexicons of youthful 'cool', choosing *Lords of Dogtown* (Hardwicke 2005) as the inspiration for the newly anointed star Takahiro's photographic debut in Exile's expansionist adventure in publishing seems a curious choice for the editors of the magazine. The film itself was a financial misadventure for Sony/Columbia, only recouping $13 million of its $25 million production budget, and only a fraction of those dollars came from foreign box offices. From this, one would assume a global disinterest in the unruly exploits of some Venice Beach teens decades prior. Rather than mimetically reflecting a widely popular film to Exile's audience, the goal of the photo essay in the magazine more broadly is to introduce Exile's fans to curated cultural objects such as food, styles, and places and to make these cultural objects desirable by overlaying them with the Exile brand and vice versa. Exile's members would serve as arbiters of taste, 'sharing' their seemingly personal favourite pieces chosen from the rich global streams of cultural commodities they, as celebrities, are imagined to drift among. Takahiro, as the latest and youngest figure inserted into the pop construction of the band Exile, has become a crucial branding tool: his boyish visage was central to the band's continued visibility in the J-pop landscape.

Exile is a popular boy band with remarkable longevity, as it has refashioned itself under its putative leader, Hiro, who was born in 1969. Keeping the 'boy' in 'boy band', Takahiro is fifteen years younger than Hiro and at the time of the shoot was twenty-four. Having become the young, fresh face of an aging pop band, Takahiro is among Japan's celebrity performers or *tarentô* and serves as a beautiful figure scripted to intrigue even non-fans with lifestyle narratives as his image is projected across multiple media platforms. In her analysis of the production of 'trendy dramas' in Japan where *tarentô* feature as the putative stars, Gabriella Lukacs (2010, p. 203) has termed *tarentô* 'intangible commodities'. They are disposable, with their popularity being of limited durability; they circulate through media and thus commodified are infinitely reproducible, they are created through 'the social labor' of agents, producers, script-writers, stylists, and media executives, and most importantly to their value, their media personae are crafted around affect with its ability to inflect and nuance the feeling and sense of commodities (p. 203).

At the resort skatepark, Takahiro's task was to generate a feeling of youthful, global cool by performing a version of himself enacting scenes from his purported favourite film. As the domesticating agent of difference, Takahiro interpreted a spectacular form of American youth culture. Like the television dramas in Lukacs's account, the photo shoot was another among many 'vehicles for the transmission of information about the tarento' (p. 31). This creation of a youthful imaginary persona inhabiting a global cultural space communicated at the level of intimate 'sharing' gives consuming viewers 'a sense of comfort and familiarity that effectively compensated for the erosion of older forms of solidarity and community' in the continued long economic malaise drastically reshaping the lives of Japan's youth (p. 31).

Posing LA, performing Tokyo 79

Takahiro shares an exotic lifestyle narrative of rebellious California teenagers with his audience by inserting himself into this melodramatic filmic story. Thus he demonstrates his own transnational mobility and, more importantly, blurs the film's American fantasy into a legible cultural proximity with his own appealing, youthful presence. Takahiro is enlisted as an actor in his own media image narrative: by simultaneously serving as celebrity model advertising contemporary fashion brands and as star in his own re-enactment of a movie mythologizing SoCal skateboard culture, he appears to be transported out of Japan into a floating imaginary costumed with a fantasy of American youth rebellion. Within the media space, he transposes himself into the place of another actor through stylish appropriation. Takahiro's performance does not simply present another carefully harvested piece of American pop culture but invites the viewer to share with him the wondrous plasticity of a fluid lifestyle, a lifestyle never contingent on actually being in America or, moreover, becoming a skater ripping empty pools in Los Angeles. Takahiro's photographic mimesis positions young skateboarders as embodiments of an 'America' rendered as 'an object of consumption, whether through material goods or as media images' and effectively shapes 'America' into a borderless, dehistoricized figure, severed from the violence of war and continued U.S. military presence marking American-Japanese national relations (Yoshimi 2003, p. 441). The very title of the photo essay, 'The Origins of West Coast Style in 1975' (2009), calls on a valorized spatial/temporal site in skateboarding parlayed into current cool. That is, the youth imaginary gains volume and substance from an authenticating history in 'America,' or, more specifically, a Southern California youth fantasy, made comfortably available through media images. And of course, these images in turn are made desirable through the intangible, commodifying labor of Takahiro's visualized body.

Takahiro's performing persona works to domesticate skateboarding into a fetish object able to conjure a dream of California displaced from the concrete specificity of the United States. The photographer and art director of the photo essay intentionally strove not to reproduce America but instead to create a fantastic copy of the 'America' depicted in *Lords of Dogtown* (Hardwicke 2005) as a youthful mythological site. The pool and other, less nationally specific features like a chain-link fence and a palm-lined roadway, generate a Hollywood vision of American space, much in the way Tokyo Disneyland (TDL) famously creates a fantasy of 'America' by intentionally copying the original site in Anaheim, California. What visitors to Tokyo Disneyland expect is transport to an imaginative space 'outside' Japan – an exotic daytrip into a fantasy of America. Similarly, Takahiro's labor was intended to bring the viewer's own desires and imagination into fantastic proximity with a mobile media space of 'American' youthfulness. The camera framing the three of us young men playing at play – dressed like cosplayers imitating a favourite imaginary character – refracted the concrete referents of SoCal swimming pools and streets. Takahiro's play-performance is enhanced by these sites that mark skateboarding as authentic; the performance is an invitation to get 'outside' the national frame of subjectivity and join Takahiro within the floating, global space of youth culture. The images are then released

80 *Dwayne Dixon*

into the media semiotics of capitalism, condensing the elusive traces of urban energy, teenage vitality, and (masculine) rebellion.

It was this effervescent alchemy the stylist, Takahashi, hoped to evince as he went through his racks of clothes, pulling together an outfit for the next shot. He talked to me about the different kinds of skateboards he'd brought to the shoot from his personal collection, just in case they needed a retro prop for a shot. 'Do you ever ride them?' I asked as I sat patiently in the shade cast by the crew's van. 'Oh, no, they are way too expensive!' he laughed. 'I just collect them because they are part of such a cool history'. Pausing, he added thoughtfully, 'And I guess they are kind of like my tools for work'. Dan had already changed into black board shorts, a white button-up shirt over a grey, long-sleeve t-shirt, and a tan fedora. He sat in a folding chair next to me, looking uncomfortable. Now it was my turn: black button-up short-sleeve shirt over a white T-shirt featuring a psychedelic skull design, black jeans, and the finishing accessory, a bandana Takashi folded wide and then tied low around my forehead. He buttoned the top button on the shirt and stepped back. 'Yes, perfect. You look like Suicidal Tendencies', he said, referencing the infamous hardcore punk/thrash metal band from Venice Beach. With my tattooed arms exposed and my ensemble of bandana and shirt carefully composed, I had been styled into a deracinated approximation of a Venice Beach gangster flavoured with some East Los Angeles 'cholo' style. Dan smirked. We both felt like posers, but my costuming felt more comical and racially egregious as all three of us sat in a row, Takahiro in the center, outside a beachfront ice cream shop painted innocently in tropical colours. 'Look like you're celebrating after a good session in the bowl', a production assistant directed us. 'I'm not sure I know what that feels like', Takahiro joked self-deprecatingly, undoing the pretence of the scene and slyly reminding all of us of the fiction we were improbably re-creating. Takahiro's joke also reasserted his own performance as the newly anointed star of Exile, offset by Dan and me on either side, since he still looked basically like himself, despite the styling; we, by contrast, found our raced, foreign identities disciplined into flat legibility *because* of the styling. Takahiro's outfit was fashionable but yet more neutral than our exaggerated outfits, and therefore his image was already more mobile, as if he could step off set into a different fantasy with barely a wardrobe adjustment.

Race and rendering the pose real

Apart from our abilities to actually ride skateboards, we brought one legitimating feature with us to the shoot that articulated the fantasy to the putative center of youth culture: our whiteness. In the park, the conflation of our race with skateboarding was painfully articulated. During the morning session when Dan and I were asked to ride the big concrete bowl, several local skaters stood bemusedly watching me clumsily attempt to carve the deep end. When the photographer and art director were satisfied they had enough good action shots, I gratefully climbed out, nodding in meek embarrassment and offering small apologies to the patient skaters waiting around the lip. Tanned, in sweat-stained protective pads, one

Posing LA, performing Tokyo 81

dropped in and effortlessly raced around the lip of the deep end. As we watched, Dan said, 'Why didn't they just use these guys? They can actually ride this thing'. The answer was clear to both of us: skateboarding was only a superficial accessory for Takahiro – an exotic accoutrement to enhance the flexibility of his image, valuable precisely because of its very intangibility. For Dan and me, on the other hand, skateboarding defined our identities and was now essentially connected to our whiteness and masculinity. In this (West Coast) origin fantasy, our skateboarding was native to our whiteness because from whiteness emerges the skateboard as crucial object and sign of youth culture. To use local Japanese skaters in Takahiro's *tableaux vivant* would have undone the fragile racial alchemy upon which the entire concept depended. Takahiro was the cosmopolitan superstar with the beautifully coiffed and dyed hair and heart-breaking boyish smile commodified for circulation throughout Japanese popular culture and outwards across East Asia, the Pacific Rim, and beyond. In translating (and arguably inflating) the cool of *Lords of Dogtown* (Hardwicke 2005), Takahiro's posing needed to be authentically anchored, not only in the mimetic architecture, as argued earlier, but in the racial legitimacy our white skater bodies offered.

This process echoes how race appears at Tokyo Disneyland (TDL) within the (re)presentation of 'America' and its production of a global imaginary. The *gaijin* or foreign ('white') workers at TDL 'function as "authentic artifacts" with whom the Japanese guests can have their pictures taken to legitimate the experience of the foreign vacation' (Brannen 1992, p. 230). Much like these gaijin employees at TDL, Dan and I appear as 'authentic artifacts' legitimizing Takahiro's fictional positioning between cultural spaces demarcated by racialized desire and distinctions. It is our raced bodies performing the action of skateboarding that brings the re-enactment of the imaginary to life. This is the difference with the (white) foreign workers in Tokyo Disneyland: their labor continues to perpetuate an 'American' exotic fantasy while Dan and I are put to work authenticating a global youth imaginary by standing in for the historically real white and brown skaters fictionally represented in a Hollywood drama. In short, we serve as 'authentic artifacts' for Takahiro's domesticating performance of skateboarding as sign of transnational youthful cool. Takahiro enacts a re-visioning of the global youth imaginary wherein Japanese bodies conditionally displace normative whiteness and take center stage. But it is a contingent performance: to use actual Japanese skaters over white ones would unmoor the image from the racialized referents of the fantastic (and fantastically white) SoCal zone of origin.

Takahiro is an intangible commodity hard at work, drifting deeply within layered media texts of *Gekkan EXILE* and *Lords of Dogtown* in a kind of conceptual house of mirrors. Dan and I too become perversely recursive objects: skaters imitating actors imitating skaters. This is the crucial tension: the entire performance depends on a conflation of America, youth, and white masculinity condensed onto Dan and me as referents. This conflation however requires the catalyst of Takahiro's sensual cool to reshape this 'America' into a media production that fits Japan and the contours of the Pacific Rim beyond a bit more comfortably.

82 *Dwayne Dixon*

In this sense, skateboarding becomes a powerful vector in cultural flows, able to carve freely across the global youth imaginary.

Performing Tokyo

With the sun setting, the best light of the day was reserved for solo shots of Takahiro. An assistant carefully tilted a reflector upwards to gather the last glimmers of the sun. Takahiro's face was cast in a warm glow. His body softened by the blue shadows pooling behind the dunes, Takahiro posed on a fallen log and looked patiently out across the Pacific. The camera shutter whirred gently, capturing a few final frames.

Takahiro's last, pensive gaze back toward the invisible California coastline reflects, none too subtly, the familiar trajectories of popular culture: America persists as a site of fantasy, perhaps not as hegemonically as it once did, but now, unfettered within semiotic capitalism, its arcane youth histories are given new, mediated value. But this metaphoric reading is a bit too convenient and cannot account for the uncanny mirroring of the careful assemblage of Takahiro's posturing within the mimetic space of the pool and alongside the authentic(ating) white, skateboarding bodies Dan and I inhabit. The entire day's work, with so much creative and physical energy expended, produced another small media artifact sent adrift among the countless images detailing the micro-fetishization of youth. Takahiro's gaze is not metaphorically cast outwards from Japan towards some youth utopia. Why should he have to look anywhere when he is actively creating the very object of longing right there on that beach in Chiba? If his gaze uncannily reflects anything, it is a fragmented *mise en abyme* of globalized youth fantasy given flesh and history through the carefully posed and performed cultural embodiments of skateboarding.

This anthropological account about a curious photo shoot replicating stills from a mediocre Hollywood film is also a story about Takahiro's malleability into a useful 'intangible commodity' which in turn is nested within Exile's own brand story. Exile's saga is a chapter in the long narrative of Japan's pop culture, which folds back into a story of globalization: how a nation like Japan or South Korea might invest in its national soft power even as these cultural borders dissolve into regions like East Asia or the Pacific Rim, with their many surging, sleepless cities sparkling in the theorist's eye. The youth imaginary I've described here flourishes precisely at the confluence of mass culture celebrity and Japan's sophisticated media industries collaging American media and spectacular youth practices like skateboarding. Skateboarding, represented in the mimetic props of fashion and architecture, orients desire towards a mythic SoCal dream-time laced with Hollywood glitter and counter-culture 'realness'. Dan and I are incorporated into Takahiro's sensual labor before the camera, together projecting a proximate fantasy from an exotic, youthful past.

This account analyses the social life of the *production* of images, seeking to understand skateboarding figures amidst the de-centring drift of images precipitated through semiotized capital. It demonstrates how, despite decades of

Posing LA, performing Tokyo 83

increasingly regionalized and de-centred globalization, the expansive concept 'youth culture' is still linked to 'America' and an assumed whiteness. Takahiro's 'intangible' cosmopolitan image is enhanced when local Japanese skaters are kept well out of the frame. While this historical reservoir of white youth rebellion, signified here by skateboarding, continues to be overlaid onto new cultural logics of a youth imaginary arising around the Pacific Rim, it is critical to remember skateboarding remains a local practice as much as a commodified, global sign. Across Japan, skaters are collaborating to make images of themselves skating local architecture and thus contribute to another, less visible layer of skateboarding's global imaginary.

A few weeks after the photo shoot with Takahiro, I was in the backseat of a small car crammed with professional photo gear, heading towards one of Tokyo's major intersections, where Harajuku flows into Shibuya for a different kind of media production. Ryo, who works by day as a photo assistant, and Itoshin, a pro skater who rides for the underground company Lesque, were heading to one last spot to get some photos: a fashion boutique with its windows carefully adorned in high-priced accessories. We parked and checked for security. It had gotten very late. A few people passed, some stumbling as they emerged from the garish throb of bars and clubs nearby. One of the night's last trains ran towards Shibuya station, thrumming through Miyashita Park and the orderly homeless encampment erected there by displaced day labourers after the economic crash in the early 1990s. Ryo began to assemble his lights at the shadowy perimeter of the broad three-stair entrance to the boutique. Itoshin pulled a small block of wax from his bag and meticulously rubbed tight circles along the face of the top stair to make it smooth and fast.

The two of them were temporarily appropriating this small corner of Tokyo's sprawl to go to work making photographs of street skateboarding. The images they'd been shooting together all evening were careful compositions of Itoshin's skateboarding skill displayed across thoughtfully chosen pieces of Tokyo's architecture. The photographs would then be edited by Ryo and Itoshin before being possibly used for Lesque brand advertisements, featured on Lesque's website, or run alongside interviews in Japanese skate magazines. To this end, the photographs needed to capture the *fūniki* – the aura – of Tokyo as a global city, where its built surfaces emit raw possibilities and improvisational pleasures through the surface of the image. The photos needed to combine meaningful, urban specificity with Itoshin's skaterly performance.

Ryo arranged his lights carefully across the empty sidewalk. His insurgent media apparatus was an unlikely counterpoint to the glaring billboards, screens, and illuminated advertising of this highly mediated capitalist space. While Ryo attempted to frame Itoshin's skating such that the image conveyed concrete, localized realness, Shibuya's screens are bright with 'images of multiple other places within Japan, from around the globe, and from the fantasy worlds of advertising' (Morris 2010, p. 293). Screens proliferate on smartphones in nearly every hand as well. All these screens only increase the sense of being in the midst of multiple worlds converging and wheeling off again, as if standing within an endless cloud

84 *Dwayne Dixon*

of shifting images and sounds. It is no wonder Shibuya's intersections appear in media representations of Tokyo again and again: the huge screens beam in other worlds only to turn the crowded streets below into an endless tableaux of techno-future Japan and, by extension, an Orientalist youth imaginary of soft cute-power.

It was against this depiction of Japan's urban spaces that Ryo and Itoshin prepared to create their own visual texts grounded in the specificity of Tokyo's streets. Their use of global city-space was also unlike the celebrity photo shoot in which the performance of Japanese stardom posed within a nostalgic fantasy of LA skateboarders. The exclusive boutique, closed for the night, was 'opened' for new business as a stage for Ito's skateboarding action. Rather than attempting to create a feeling of a fantasy 'elsewhere' laced with cosmopolitan cool as in the *Dogtown*/Takahiro shoot, Ryo's cameras framed Tokyo within a visual lexicon of authenticity calibrated against other skating photographs made in the world's urban environments. Ryo's composition of the boutique emphasized Tokyo's fragments and detritus: the garbage in the alley, the chips in the stairs, the worn surfaces, such that Tokyo's edges blurred into other cities.

Ryo's lights cast a bright circle and, together with the camera, altered the ordinary space into a space of performance and media production. Itoshin began skating the top stair. He popped up and onto the edge of the third stair, landing 'backside,' with only the metal of the rear axle impacting, and then smoothly grinding down the stair's length. He abruptly snapped up with a clean 'ollie' over the sidewalk and into the alley beyond. Ryo shot a few quick test frames, capturing both the (mis)use of the shop's architecture and the grime of Tokyo's peripheral spaces, normally just out of view. Together, skater and photographer work hard to produce new meanings and values, and in the process, they amplify the contestation of space epitomized by the homeless encampment up along the train tracks struggling to maintain in the face of Shibuya's corporate hegemony.[3] This scene emphasizes the improbable micro-transformation of the global city, with its layered signs of youthful consumption, into a skate spot where immediate physical pleasure is extracted and valuable photographs, laden with embodied and architectural authenticity, are produced. In this small moment of light and movement, all other screens are forgotten, their fantasies dimmed. The world condenses into this fierce locus of energy.

There is no gazing back across the Pacific through a Hollywood haze. Ito skates across the mundane architecture of the global city. He performs Tokyo's streets as part of a larger transnational urban space where youthful energy is conjured and unleashed into media circuits. The performance of the city's architectural possibilities is encoded into Ryo's photographs, but the specificity of Tokyo is enveloped within the youth imaginary, where it is the authentic trace of the global city that persists. Much like the global appeal of other media products such as 'trendy dramas', '(t)he emphasis of the urban facilitates culture-border crossing . . . the urban increasingly lacks specificity, it is "anywhere", "anyplace" and "anyone", the urban thus passes through cultural boundaries through its insistence on "sameness"' (Chua 2007, p. 133). The urban staging crucially intersects Ryo's artfully

Posing LA, performing Tokyo   85

composed photos with global vocabularies of youthful space and performance. Yet the image is not flattened out into absolute 'sameness': it possesses a powerful residue of authenticity conferred through Ito's skilful skating.

Under semiotized capitalism, skateboarding's varied depictions 'connect heterogeneous domains' shaping 'the modes of sensibility, tastes, and choices' (Guattari 1996, p. 251) of culturally and geographically dispersed consumers. Architectural and white-boy props metonymically articulate Takahiro's celebrity with a sensually nostalgic embodiment of youthful American cool, authenticating Takahiro's pose. His 'intangible commodity' is a youthful surface enhanced and enlivened with the cool aura of mythologized, West Coast skateboard history. Skateboarding, seen through Ryo's viewfinder, is de-centred from an American cultural narrative, refocused so other (Japanese) bodies, in other spaces, come into alluring view. At the same time, skateboarding's imaginary is still haunted by an 'America' populated by visions of whiteness but shifted into new semiotic registers produced across the Pacific. This glimpse of skateboarding posed and performed within Japan demonstrates the conflicted shape-shifting of a de-centred globalization, populated by conflated racial and national spectres of ('American') legitimacy challenged by skaters on the streets of Tokyo. Ryo and Ito's photos re-imagine the global city as a site and surface where skateboarders work out new media codes of spatial and embodied meaning and, through their collective labor, incite the pleasure of beholding the youth imaginary come radically to life.

Notes

1. Leerom Medovoi (2005, p. 296) uses the term 'suburban counterimaginary' to describe the 'beaches of the Pacific' in relation to the young male surfers in the quintessential teen film, *Gidget*, and their desire for a space wherein to self-fashion a resistant alternative to the Fordist teleology of post-war American adulthood, an adulthood signified in the stultifying tract housing of the burgeoning suburbs. The term can be applied to skate culture and its reassignment of a zone of youthful independence from the 'beaches of the Pacific' to North American backyard pools and streets. I recognize Medovoi's use of the term is loosely applied to spatial sites represented in popular media. My reassignment recognizes the immediate line of descent from surfing to skateboarding as linked body practices with shared (or mutated!) counter-cultural aura. This aura gives critical realness to the youth imaginary and is evident in the first cinematic depiction of a skateboard lifestyle. Noel Black's 1965 film *Skaterdater* features a gang of young male skaters whose daredevil, disorderly exploits come to an end when they ultimately lose their leader because he 'grows up' by falling in love with a girl. This cinematic genealogy helps to situate *Lords of Dogtown* within established stylistic codes of youthful rebellion inscribed in the sub-genre of skateboard films.

2. While the image serves as the condensed site of this youth fetishization, it is important to briefly trace how skateboarding is transposed from the level of bodily action into images. As individual practice, skateboarding operates as a phenomenological relationship among body, board, and surface, what Iain Borden (2001, p. 98) has framed (through Heidegger's theorizations of the tool-object) as a 'primordial relationship . . . rendered spatial and dynamic'. Put simply, skateboarding acts on the self in the unfolding, improvisational pleasure of the body exploring (built) space and motion through the extension

86 *Dwayne Dixon*

of the board. Thinking of skateboarding in this way is to already encounter it as expression of 'the symbolic semiotics of the body' – the pre-verbal energies and desires of skateboarding's movements through space – then appropriated and commodified 'to make them function like components or cogs in the semiotic machine of capital' (Lazzarato 2006). Skateboarding's intense physiological feelings generated in fleshy contact with the built environment distill into signs of 'realness'. The 'realness' of bodily vitality that skateboarding represents is amplified by its 'realness' at the macro-level of youth culture histories, specifically its enshrinement within the utopic mythologies surrounding the experience of youth in Southern California: the cultural and spatial ingredients with which the global youth imaginary takes its ambivalent shape. The potent fusion of youth and skateboarding's realness at the level of individual and cultural experiences are central to skateboarding's signifying power, incorporating the fetishized body of youthful experience within the global vocabularies of the youth imaginary.

3. By the end of the summer of 2008, the park would become a flashpoint of homeless, artist, and activist resistance against corporate-sponsored gentrification. It would be revealed that the Shibuya Ward government and Nike had been in secret negotiations resulting in a multi–million-yen agreement for Nike to pay for the transformation of the government-neglected, narrow strip of park into a Nike-branded sports area, subsequently erasing a longtime homeless refuge amid some of Tokyo's most expensive real estate. Central among its promoted features was a skateboard park, coinciding with Nike's successful efforts to legitimate itself as a brand within the global skateboarding subcultural market after numerous failed attempts. The protests against this deal recalled Miyashita Park's long history as a site of political resistance, most recently in the 2003 demo-rave against the U.S. invasion of Iraq. The park was occupied this time for nearly six months – from March to September 2010 – as activists and the remaining homeless residents fought against the privatizing 'Nikefication' of public space. The park, in part, was designed to attract skaters as a means to enclose their energies, perceived as a 'nuisance'. The government ultimately seized the park, and its enclosure was completed as Nike held the naming rights to the park. Those opposed to this corporate colonization of public space thought 'the park's "Nikefication" would transform it into an "ad for Nike", into a place for consumers rather than citizens, and that entrance fees and evictions were inconsistent with the idea of "public gardens" (the literal translation of *koen*, park)' (Cassegård 2011, p. 415). 'As a youth-centered consumer-oriented space, Shibuya was frequently positioned in . . . media discourses both as a literal location where this "[youth] problem" was concentrated as well as a metonym for broader social anxieties about contemporary Japanese life' (Morris 2010, p. 298). The park, usurped by Nike, illustrates the corporate gentrification of city space made newly desirable under the sign of the global youth imaginary. This gentrifying process of enclosure displaces the homeless with an increasingly policed youth population, withdrawing a public resource and producing instead a corporate preserve.

References

Appadurai, A 1996, *Modernity at large: cultural dimensions of globalization*, University of Minnesota Press, Minneapolis.

Borden, I 2001, *Skateboarding, space and the city: architecture and the body*, Berg, Oxford.

Brannen, MY 1992, ' "Bwana Mickey": constructing cultural consumption at Tokyo Disneyland", in JJ Tobin (ed) *Re-made in Japan: everyday life and consumer taste in a changing society*, Yale University Press, New Haven, CT, pp. 216–234.

Posing LA, performing Tokyo   87

Cassegård, C 2011, 'Public space in recent Japanese political thought and activism: from the rivers and lakes to Miyashita Park', *Japanese Studies*, vol. 31, no. 3, pp. 405–422.

Ching, LT 2000, 'Globalizing the regional, regionalizing the global: mass culture and Asianism in the age of late capital', *Public Culture*, vol. 12, no. 1, pp. 233–257.

Chua, BH 2007, 'Conceptualizing an East Asian popular culture', in K-H Cheng & BH Chua (eds), *The inter-Asia cultural studies reader*, Routledge, Oxon, pp. 115–139.

Guattari, F 1996, *Soft subversions*, Semiotext(e), New York.

Hall, S 1991, 'The local and the global: globalization and ethnicity', in AD King (ed), *Culture, globalization and the world system: contemporary conditions for the representation of identity*, University of Minnesota Press, Minneapolis, pp. 19–31.

Hardwicke, C 2005, *Lords of Dogtown* (DVD), Columbia Pictures/Tri-Star Pictures, USA.

Howell, O 2003, *Extreme market research*. Available from: www.webdelsol.com/Topic/articles/04/howell.html. [28 April 2015].

Iwabuchi, Ki 2002, *Recentering globalization: popular culture and Japanese transnationalism*, Duke University Press, Durham, NC.

Latham, R 2002, *Consuming youth: vampires, cyborgs, and the culture of consumption*, University of Chicago Press, Chicago.

Lazzarato, M 2006, *'Semiotic pluralism' and the new government of signs: homage to Félix Guattari*. Available from: http://eipcp.net/transversal/0107/lazzarato/en. [28 April 2015].

Lukás, G 2010, *Scripted affects, branded selves: television, subjectivity, and capitalism in 1990s Japan*, Duke University Press, Durham, NC.

Medovoi, L 2005, *Rebels: youth and the Cold War origins of identity*, Duke University Press, Durham, NC.

Mitchell, WJT 2013, *What do pictures want?: the lives and loves of images*, University of Chicago Press, Chicago.

Morris, B 2010, 'Un/wrapping Shibuya: place, media, and punctualization', *Space and Culture*, vol. 13, no. 3, pp. 285–303.

'The origins of West Coast style in 1975' 2009, 月刊 *EXILE (Gekkan EXILE)*, vol. 2, September.

Yoshimi, S 2003, '"America" as desire and violence: Americanization in postwar Japan and Asia during the Cold War', *Inter-Asia Cultural Studies*, vol. 4, no. 3, pp. 433–450.

Part 2
Sites and space

7 Southbank skateboarding, London, and urban culture

The Undercroft, Hungerford Bridge, and House of Vans

Iain Borden

Over the last few years, skateboarding spaces in London have been subject to considerable controversy and development, with widespread media attention and fiercely expressed opinions. Issues raised include democracy, public space, cultural value, historic preservation, commerce, and urban design. This chapter takes an overview of three different but closely adjacent skateboarding spaces and explores their connection with wider urban culture: the Undercroft at the Southbank Centre (SBC) and how a skate space can intensify debates over architectural, historical, usage, and legal aspects of public space; the proposed Hungerford Bridge skate space, also at the SBC, and how skate spaces might be designed differently to conventional skateparks and skate plazas; and the nearby House of Vans, and how skateboarding is integrated within wider design, artistic, and commercial operations.

The Undercroft

When the Hayward Gallery, Queen Elizabeth Hall, and Purcell Room (Festival Wing) complex opened at the SBC in 1967, three of its architects belonged to the radical architectural group Archigram. According to their architectural ideas, the Festival Wing's meandering walkways and ground-level spaces – the latter commonly referred to today as the Undercroft – were left open for unpredictable and unknown uses (SBC 2013a). Consequently, when skateboarding first came along in 1973 (LLSB 2014a), it provided exactly the unexpected eruption of creativity for which these architects had hoped. Where the designers had produced flat spaces surrounded by apparently uselessly angled banks, the skateboarders saw these same slopes as providing a freely accessible version of the commercial skateparks then being constructed across the world, including London's Skate City along the River Thames. The Undercroft roof was another bonus, under which – up and down tangled banks and between curious Doric-mushroom columns – up to a thousand skateboarders at a time freely emulated the surf-style skateboarding being promoted in magazines like *Skateboard!* and *Skateboarder* (Borden 2001).

As this suggests, architecture here is far more than a building as concrete structure and is also comprised of what people do there. As philosopher Henri Lefebvre (1991) has argued, architectural and urban space is made up of the physical

92 Iain Borden

places we use (the Festival Wing's Brutalist concrete spaces), the conscious ideas we have (the architects' designs), and also people's actual, everyday experiences (skateboarders and other users).

Skateboarding, therefore, is absolutely part of the SBC, not as a history of architecture as a physical monument, design invention, or national symbol but as a place where people – skateboarders and others – have made an extraordinary expression of youthful energy and joy. Nor has skateboarding been a short-lived moment in the history of the SBC; having been in the Undercroft for nigh on forty years, this is very probably the oldest place in the world which has been subjected to skateboarding in a continuous and intensive manner.

Figure 7.1 Ben Jobe, 'backside tailside' at the Undercroft's seven-stair in 1996. Courtesy of Wig Worland ©.

Skateboarders' determined usage of the Undercroft was particularly evident during the 1980s and 1990s. After many skateparks had closed by the early 1980s, a new street-based skateboarding emerged, with skateboarders using the 'ollie' move to ride over the ledges, handrails, and other paraphernalia of everyday spaces. The Undercroft changed, too, becoming less like a free skatepark and more like a city street, appropriated by both skateboarders and the homeless, whose 2,000 or more shelters constituted Southbank's Cardboard City; according to *The Spectator*, amid this otherwise 'godforsaken waste-land', the skateboarders provided 'one of the few rational purposes' and 'some small evidence of human life' (Wheatcroft 1979, p. 28).

The Undercroft changed again in 2004 and in 2006, when several skateable concrete and stone blocks were installed by Richard 'Badger' Holland and skateboard-arts group The Side Effects of Urethane, with financial support from Sony Playstation, Nike, Casio G-shock, Olympus and others (Holland 2015, pers. comm., 30 January). This initiative rendered the space particularly suited to street skateboarding. 'At a time when a good ledge spot was the holy grail', enthused Jake Sawyer, 'this really was a godsend' (cited in LLSB 2014b). At the same time, the SBC organized other niceties, such as lighting, CCTV, and a benign police presence to reduce petty crime. Railings and yellow lines demarcated a

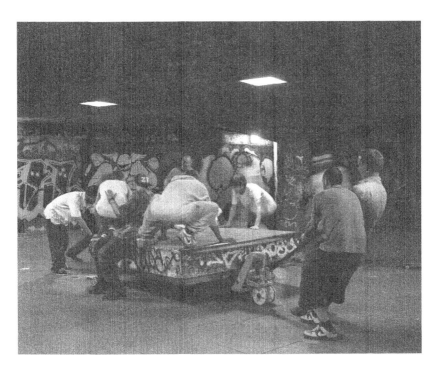

Figure 7.2 Richard Holland (second from right) and others installing skateable blocks at the Undercroft in 2006. Courtesy of Wig Worland ©.

94 *Iain Borden*

skateboardable space for the SBC's liability insurance and so legally allowed skateboarding to occur.

Murals and graffiti also started to appear in the Undercroft (again with SBC permission), marking it as a center for varied urban arts. BMX riders, photographers, filmmakers, poets, dancers, and musicians were now being increasingly drawn to the spot. As photographer Wig Worland (cited in LLSB 2014b) noted, the 'complete no-mans land' Undercroft facilitated a 'studio in the street' where 'no one would bother you', while skater Nick Jensen (cited in LLSB 2014b) has similarly commented on how the attitude at Southbank has informed the style and aesthetics of his artwork. For Karim Bakthouai (cited in LLSB 2014b), the social space mattered most, the Undercroft allowing an escape from gangland crime and other council estate constraints: 'All the people I know like, they all fucking in jail, I didn't want that, I ain't about that, I'd rather be skating'.

Despite these positive attributes and the SBC's own improvements to the Undercroft, and while recognizing it was, according to Mike McCart (then SBC Commercial Director), 'the Mecca of skating in the world', over 2004 to 2005 the SBC still reduced by two-thirds the amount of skate space available. This assertive action recalled past episodes when skateboarding had been discouraged, such as the mid-1980s, when SBC security teams scattered stones, prized up paving slabs, and generally made skaters' lives uncomfortable. Alternative SBC tactics in other years have included turning off evening lighting, hosing down the floors, drilling grooves, and adding rails to some of the banks (LLSB 2014a, 2014b).

Despite this history, skateboarding at the Undercroft has continued to prosper, the Undercroft achieving near mythic status as the epicentre of UK skateboarding, where tens of thousands have learned their craft, from novices to professionals, and from hard-core locals to occasional visitors. The Undercroft lays strong claim to being UK skateboarding's most precious home, its original Garden of Eden, oldest sparring partner, and most famous Wembley arena – all rolled into one. It is also a place of pilgrimage for skateboarders worldwide, coming long distances to roll across one of skateboarding's most hallowed grounds.

Given all this, it is unsurprising that large numbers of skaters and the general public alike reacted extremely unfavourably to the SBC's suggestion in March 2013 that, to help fund a massive £100+ million package of improvements to the Festival Wing, the Undercroft should be turned into retail units, with skaters being relocated to the adjacent Hungerford Bridge site (SBC 2013c). United mostly under the 'Long Live Southbank' (LLSB) banner, carefully orchestrated by Paul Richards and others, and possibly also enjoying oft-rumoured substantial financial backing from the father of Undercroft skater Tom 'Blondey' McCoy (Butter 2014), these objectors mounted a skilful oppositional campaign under the headings of 'You Can't Move History', 'Preservation and Not Relocation', and 'Construction Without Destruction'. Significantly, in contrast to the SBC's press releases and marketing statements, LLSB eschewed any formal PR representation in favor of a highly effective amalgam of the physical (on-site presence, marches, and events) and the digital (online petitions, Web site, YouTube, Twitter,

Facebook, etc.) – a strategy which later won 'engagement campaign of the year' at the annual Change Opinion Awards.

Widespread backing came from the skateboard community, musicians, artists, general public, and British MPs Kate Hoey and Ben Bradshaw. Most importantly, after 150,000 people had signed a petition supporting LLSB and more than 27,000 had opposed the SBC planning application, the Conservative Party Mayor of London, Boris Johnson (cited in LLSB 2014a), seized the political opportunity to back the LLSB, calling the Undercroft 'the epicentre of UK skateboarding' and 'part of the cultural fabric of London'. As Johnson (cited in Brown 2014) saw it, this 'much-loved community space' also 'attracts tourists from across the world and undoubtedly adds to the vibrancy of the area'. Effectively vetoing the SBC's planning application, Johnson's declaration was a decisive moment in LLSB's eventual victory (SBC 2014a).

Moreover, legal factors were at play. Simon Ricketts, partner at King & Wood Mallesons SJ Berwin and the UK's most highly rated planning lawyer, worked with LLSB to have the Undercroft designated an 'Asset of Community Value' (ACV) under the Localism Act 2011 and also sought to have it designated as a 'Town or Village Green' under the Commons Act 2006 (Butter 2014; LLSB 2014a, 2014b). While the ACV was a political success for LLSB, it actually did little to secure skateboarding's future at the site. However, the possibility of the Undercroft being classified as a town or village green was much more threatening to the SBC, both in case any decision went against them and because of mounting legal costs. Faced with this public, political, and legal turmoil, the SBC leadership – Artistic Director Jude Kelly, Chief Executive Alan Bishop, and Governing Board Chairman Rick Haythornthwaite – finally capitulated in January 2014, signing a section 106 planning agreement with Lambeth Borough Council, and so effectively securing the Undercroft for skateboarding in perpetuity (Brown 2014).

Stepping away from this LLSB victory, however significant it may be for skateboarding, it is worth remembering why so many non-skateboarders have also come to the Undercroft and supported the LLSB. People from all over London and the world enjoy seeing the Undercroft's unique combination of skateboarding-against-concrete, of unruly disorder amidst increasing sanitization, and so witnessing a truly public space in action. Skateboarding at the Undercroft is 'inspiring and uplifting', commented one member of the public. 'It promotes all kind of values that we need in this society' (cited in LLSB 2014a). Or, as another noted, 'take away the diversity of the Southbank and you will kill the charm' (cited in LLSB 2014a). Even conservative newspaper *The Times* proclaimed that destroying the skate space to provide retail outlets would amount to 'cultural vandalism' (Purves 2013).

This is important stuff and transcends the immediate needs of skateboarding to speak to a larger question as to the kinds of public spaces we desire today. As David Harvey (2003, p. 941) has noted, the

> right to the city . . . is not merely a right of access to what the property speculators and state planners define, but an active right to make the city different,

96   *Iain Borden*

to shape it more in accord with our heart's desire, and to re-make ourselves thereby in a different image.

In concert with Harvey, skateboarding at the Undercroft suggests that public spaces can be richer than typical shopping malls or high streets, where coffee outlets, branded shops, and chain restaurants abound. It suggests that different people doing different things perceive and enjoy city spaces in different ways. It suggests that we would like our cities to be similarly varied, at once loud and quiet, rough and smooth, colourful and monochrome, flat and angled. And, above all, it suggests that we most enjoy cities and buildings when they both comfort and challenge us, when they provide us with things which we both expect and cannot anticipate. Skateboarding at the Undercroft and SBC is, then, one small yet vital part of this process.

Hungerford Bridge

When the SBC proposed moving skateboarding 125m from the Undercroft – to a comparably sized 1,200m^2 and visible site beneath the railway Hungerford Bridge – many found this very suggestion disclosed a lack of understanding of what street-based skateboarding was about. Equally serious design challenges were also therefore implicated. How could this new Hungerford Bridge space avoid institutionalizing street-based skateboarding within a skatepark-like environment? What might it look, feel, and operate like? Who could design it? And how might it relate to the Undercroft?

To pursue these questions, during 2013, Richard Holland, Søren Nordal Enevoldsen of SNE Architects, and I worked with the SBC to develop the new facility's brief and design (Borden & Holland 2013a). In doing so, we continued to argue vehemently that skateboarding should remain at the Undercroft, and we supported the LLSB via publications, videos, and other contributions (Borden 2013, 2014a; LLSB 2013a). I had also contributed to previous campaigns supporting the Undercroft, including the *Save Southbank* documentary (Whitter & Shuall 2008). But we also felt that Hungerford Bridge might offer some benefits as a temporary or permanent Undercroft replacement or possibly as an additional facility. Given that the SBC were committing more than £1 million to the new space and guaranteeing its skateboarding use for 125 years (SBC 2013d) – quite possibly the most generous gesture ever made by a public institution towards skateboarding – this was surely worth investigating.

The initial brief drawn up by Holland and me distilled the requirements of Undercroft skaters articulated at consultation meetings in April and May of 2013, such as views that the space 'doesn't get built as a standard concrete skate park' and instead should 'preserve the character of South Bank' and 'create a lively and dynamic area that everyone can enjoy' (SBC 2013b). The collaborative nature of the subsequent design development was deliberate and essential. As a long-time historian of skateboarding and urban space, I provided academic and theoretical input, as well as personal expertise as a skater since 1977. Holland, meanwhile, was producer of the Undercroft's street-style blocks – the most prominently used of its features. He was also renowned as a skateboarder for twenty-five years, creator of numerous skateboardable installations in Bermondsey, Helsinki, Lille, Peckham, and Shoreditch (Borden & Holland 2013b), and former co-owner of the local skate shop Cide, which had played a 'pivotal role' in supporting Southbank skateboarding (LLSB 2014b).

As architect for Hungerford Bridge (selected after an invited competition in mid-2013), Enevoldsen was perhaps uniquely qualified to take on the design role, having been previously responsible for Copenhagen's acclaimed 4,600m^2 Faelledparken skatepark. At another Copenhagen project at Prags Boulevard, he had overseen an installation of furniture and equipment for skateboarding and parkour, while at the mixed-use Rabalder Parken in Roskilde, a rainwater system was inventively repurposed by Enevoldsen for skateboarding and other activities, recalling the drainage ditches appropriated by American skaters in the 1960s and 1970s. In addition, Enevoldsen was a committed street skater, yielding further skateboarding experience (Borden & Holland 2013b). A Focus Design Group provided additional expert input and included Ricky Adam for BMX, Niall Neeson for skate culture, Tom Oswald for street art, and James Sutton for parkour, as well as a professional street skateboarder (a regular Undercroft user who preferred to remain anonymous). Additional support was provided by the SBC's Mike McCart (Director of Policy & Partnerships) and Mark Rushworth (Property Director), as well as by a multi-disciplinary technical team. Finally, several design workshops with skaters and other users were held during October and November 2013 to further enrich the designs (Borden & Holland 2013b; SBC 2013e).

Given the brief's origins in the desires of Undercroft skaters, the Hungerford Bridge designs unsurprisingly display many characteristics of typical street skateboarding spots such as Bercy (Paris), KulturForum (Berlin), MACBA (Barcelona), and the Undercroft: large and open flat-floor space surrounded by banks, ramps, ledges, steps, and other features. Significantly, one of Enevoldsen's design tenets, underlining the scheme's difference to skateparks and skate plazas, was that everything had to have multiple functions, and nothing was solely for skateboarding. Furthermore, and again unlike smooth skatepark finishes, the materials proposed are typical urban flagstones, stone, and brick, thus replicating the gritty textures of the Undercroft and other street spots. Besides a large brick wall for street art, several other extensive (and costly) site modifications included cutting away the underside of an existing concrete ramp to improve public visibility (about 9 million footfall per annum) and an illuminated roof to provide rain protection from the porous railway overhead (Borden & Holland 2013b; SBC 2013e).

Overall, as Enevoldsen's design meant nothing was intended purely for skateboarding, the Hungerford Bridge design assumed the character of a public space that just happened to be good for skateboarding. While some skaters perceived it as being like the Whites Grounds skate plaza at London Bridge – a smaller fenced and timetabled facility, operated under a local council's playground regime, and thus as a controlled place 'oppressing the free expressive nature of skateboarding' (LLSB 2013b), others nonetheless disagreed with these comparisons. According to

Figure 7.3 Final design for the Hungerford Bridge skate space, 2013. Courtesy of Søren Nordal Enevoldsen/SNE Architects ©.

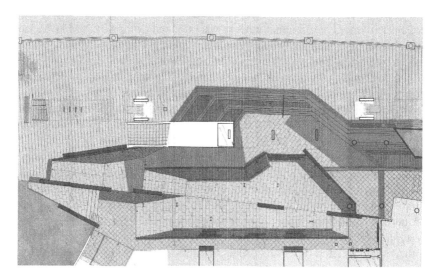

Figure 7.4 Plan of Hungerford Bridge skate space, 2013. Courtesy of Søren Nordal Enevoldsen/SNE Architects ©.

local skater Bedir Bekar, Hungerford Bridge provided 'a true street-skateboarding spot' which 'builds on the Undercroft's street heritage whilst providing the right flow and openness' (cited in Borden & Holland 2013b). Others agreed. 'What's being built is not a skatepark', stated Warwick Cairns. 'It's a space: it has typical "found space" features that can become a skate place in the minds, and through the actions, of skateboarders' (cited in Borden & Holland 2013b).

Southbank skateboarding, London, and urban culture 99

Tellingly, yet other skaters remained unconvinced, frequently rejecting Hungerford Bridge on the *a priori* grounds that, as street skaters often prefer appropriating existing architecture rather than using purpose-designed skateparks, it is impossible to *deliberately design* architecture which is directed at skateboarders yet still attractive to them. 'A found space such as this can never be recreated', remarks skater and photographer Jenna Selby of the Undercroft. 'Those who try are blind to the very essence of what skating is about' (cited in LLSB 2014b).

Recent history, however, discloses numerous places worldwide where skateboard-friendly design has been successfully implemented into urban spaces and buildings, including the stealth-skateboardable Auditoria Park (Barcelona, Foreign Office Architects) and the Phaeno Science Centre (Wolfsburg, Zaha Hadid Architects). At the US$700 million Opera House, (Oslo, 2008), architects Snøhetta even consulted skateboarders regarding textures, materials, and skateable areas. Parts of the building and surroundings are consequently arranged with marble ledges, kerbs, bench-like blocks, and railings (Blum 2008; Borden 2014b). Similarly, at the Landhausplatz (LHP) public plaza (Innsbruck, 2011), designed by LAAC Architekten and Stiefel Kramer Architecture, an undulating concrete surface of flats, banks, ledges, plateaus, and blocks accommodates 'a new mélange of urban activities' suitable for pedestrians, skateboarders, and BMX riders alike (Dezeen 2011; Ritter, Treichl, & Wedekind 2012). Consequently, German skateboarding website Playboard.de (2014) describes LHP as providing 'obstacles of all kinds which are perfectly integrated into the cityscape'.

Another example lies closer to the Undercroft. At the Buszy (Milton Keynes, 2005), designed by architect Richard Ferrington and skateboarder Rob Selley along with initial advice from me, a £100K facility beside the train station offers a simple ledge-and-block arrangement under an open-sided roof. Buszy has been acclaimed by professional skateboarders as 'the best spot they have ever skated' (Armes 2008) and by a UK skateboarding guide as 'easily one of the best block spots in the country' (Skates and Ladders 2009). Even the Undercroft itself suggests how Hungerford Bridge might attract street skaters, not least because its architects' preference for indeterminate uses may not have expressly included skateboarding but certainly allowed for its possibility. Even more tellingly, the Undercroft features used most extensively today – the skateable blocks installed by Holland and colleagues – were indeed provided expressly for skateboarding, thus turning the space into something approaching a skate plaza or skatepark street course.

Even though the Hungerford Bridge site – nicknamed 'Mellow Banks' and 'Bird Shit Banks' by local skaters (LLSB 2014a) – had previously accommodated skateboarding, another challenge has undoubtedly been its potential to counter the LLSB claim that 'you can't move history', which I myself asserted in an early LLSB video (Borden 2013). Certainly Hungerford Bridge cannot compete with the Undercroft's decades-long association with skateboarding. Here, skateboarding has created a personal, collective, mental, and sensual relationship with Brutalist architecture, a history composed of memories and events, pleasure and pain, belonging and alienation, trial and tribulation. Notable Undercroft events have

100 *Iain Borden*

included innumerable skate jams, demos, visits, videos made by professional teams, and even appearing in video games like *Thrasher: Skate and Destroy* and *Tony Hawk's Pro Skater*. As such, many Undercroft histories are composite and international, as revealed by a professional skater's description of the space being 'as well known to skateboarders around the world as Big Ben or Buckingham Palace' (LLSB 2014a). Even more telling are myriad personal histories, the product of the thousands and generations of local skaters. Typical here is Southbank Sam's (cited in LLSB 2014a, 2014b) impassioned description of the Undercroft as a place which 'means everything to me. It's my life, when this place closes my heart will break'.

Even here, however, there are counter-arguments. While a cultural practice's *previous* history cannot be moved or replicated – ontologically it always remains in the past – the *on-going and future* history can change, such that similarly embodied practices from markets to football stadia (like Borough Market, Wembley, and Arsenal's Emirates stadium in London) have all flourished after geographic transplantation and architectural transformation. Furthermore, the idea that history is intransigent runs contrary to street skateboarding's mobile and transitory nature, which involves exploiting a particular spot for months, days, or minutes and then moving quickly on. As skater Aaron Bleasdale (1996) once commented, London skaters prefer not to stay in one place but 'go and skate the streets – there's sick spots everywhere'. Indeed, the history of street skateboarding is in many ways a constant search for new skateable terrains and opportunities (Borden 2001).

Nonetheless, despite this tendency towards perpetual mobility, certain places do become skateboarded for months, years, or even decades. Even these skate spots, however, can successfully move location. At Montreal's Big O – originally constructed as an entrance tunnel for 1976 Olympics athletes – this raw concrete structure had been appropriated by skateboarders and covered in graffiti – just like the Undercroft. Faced with impending demolition in 2011, due to construction of the Montreal Impact soccer stadium, skateboarders worked with the authorities to physically move the tunnel 50 meters. Re-opened in 2013, Big O's relocation has been celebrated as a victory for skateboarders and Montreal Impact alike, confirming skateboarding's ongoing presence in the city (Ethernal Skate Films 2013; Tison & Walsh 2006).

Another variation of this theme is evident at Paine's Park. Following the controversial banning of skateboarding from the LOVE Park square in downtown Philadelphia, (Howell 2005) this US$4.5 million facility for street-based skateboarding was opened in 2013 in a nearby waterside park, next to Philadelphia Museum of Art. Designed by architect Anthony Bracali with local skateboarders and financed by the Franklin's Paine Skatepark Fund, it offers 2.5 acres with brick banks, handrails, stone ledges, stairs, blocks, and even benches rescued from LOVE Park. Bracali explains, as with Hungerford Bridge, that the main idea was for a skateboardable space that looked unlike a skatepark, 'a great public space that just happened to be a skate park', thus merging different uses and so allowing the space to be 'more usable and sustainable over time' (Clark & Hyland 2013).

Figure 7.5 Final design for the Hungerford Bridge skate space, 2013. Courtesy of Søren Nordal Enevoldsen/SNE Architects ©.

Although some skaters do view the facility as being too much like a skatepark and not enough like a real public space, Paine's Park has nonetheless been generally welcomed by skateboard blogs such as *Quartersnacks* (2013) and praised for attracting skateboarders, BMX riders, and general public alike (Owens 2014). Significantly, locals have also appreciated the varied skaters attracted to the site: 'I am a little heavier, and I still don't know how to kick flip', noted Michael Haeflinger (cited in Philly Love Notes 2013). 'But at Paine's, [e]veryone is so mellow and supportive and friendly' (2013).

Should it ever be completed, this all bodes well for Hungerford Bridge. However, following the SBC's welcome decision to retain the Undercroft for skateboarding and the subsequent impact upon SBC finances, the viability of Hungerford Bridge is currently uncertain. Although the SBC still apparently wishes to provide the Hungerford Bridge space – now as *addition to* rather than *replacement for* the Undercroft – this depends on funds being identified. Certainly, if and when created, this new skate space must fulfil the promise of Enevoldsen's collaborative design, providing the Undercroft's ledges, banks, rails, and steps while avoiding the feel of an overtly designed skatepark. It cannot have fees, fences, or rules, but must be freely open, shared by all, a place skaters can appropriate and so help create a vibrant public skate space in the full sense of those terms.

House of Vans

Given skaters' vehement rejection of any suggestion that Hungerford Bridge become like a skatepark, it would be expected that any regulated and/or commercialized space in the vicinity would be equally fiercely opposed. Yet at the House of Vans, opened in 2014 just a few hundred meters from Hungerford Bridge, exactly this kind of space has appeared, and to considerable welcome.

102 *Iain Borden*

The key element here is that the backer – clothing company Vans – has a carefully nurtured and decades-long association with skateboarding. Originally founded in California in 1966 as a direct-selling shoe operation, by the end of the 1970s, the affordable, grippy, and durable nature of Vans shoes made them the de facto choice for skaters and surfers worldwide (Palladini 2009). Subsequently during the 1980s, Vans realized that larger leisure markets could be targeted, and in 1988, it was sold to private equity investment firm McCown De Leeuw & Co. for US$74.4 million. By 1996, Vans had already reached an annual turnover of US$100 million, and by 2000 had shifted into extensive global non-skate markets, becoming a NASDAQ-traded company as a result. Sold again in 2004, this time to American conglomerate VF Corporation for around US$400 million, by 2014 Vans global revenues had reached more than US$2 billion, with a goal of US$2.9 billion by 2017 (Funding Universe 2015; *Mandatory Information* 1996; VFC 2013, 2015).

The enormous scale of these earnings could easily have generated accusations of Vans indulging in a commercial exploitation of skateboarding. Despite its occasional support for grassroots initiatives like the Undercroft's skateable blocks, Nike's skateboard-oriented sub-brand Nike SB, for example, has sometimes been vilified as a non-skateboarding multinational's attempt to muscle in on a skate scene worth around US$5 billion in 2008 (Beal 2013). In particular, independent skate company Consolidated has vented anti-Nike and anti-corporate sentiments with its 'Don't Do It' and 'Don't Do It Foundation' campaigns (Hargrove 2012), warning against skateboarding being 'hijacked by outsiders who have no passionate story in the surf, skate, and snowboard community' (Bradstreet 2011).

Given this denouncement of Nike – and Airwalk, Powell, Vision, World Industries, and others have all faced similar criticism – it might be expected that Vans, with its global chain of shops selling leisure shoes and clothing predominantly to non-skaters, would encounter comparable condemnation. Unlike Nike, however, Vans have followed the advice of their 1990s public relations firm Weber Shandwick Worldwide (Browne 2004), carefully maintaining the appearance and behaviour of an organization which, according to original family-owner Steve Van Doren (cited in Palladini 2009), 'has always been the underdog, the smaller company that scrapped and worked harder'. This is sound advice in the field of action sports, where since the early 2000s, marketing companies like Weber Shandwick and Fuse have constantly reminded corporate brands that they have to treat skateboarders as sensitively as when dealing with religious groups. Bill Carter of Fuse (cited in Browne 2004) warns that skaters 'want to see you support the sports not just on a mainstream level'. 'They don't want fanfare. They just want to *see* it. What they don't want to see is a brand coming with no grassroots support and just slapping a logo onto a high-profile event' (2004). For Vans, this has been achieved by supporting a slew of art, print, film, and other creative initiatives – from contributing $400,000 towards the acclaimed *Dogtown and the Z-Boyz* skate documentary (2001) to the recent Vans Custom Culture project to inspire art and design in high schools – all demonstrating how Vans 'gives back' to the skate community. Hence also Vans' own directly skater-focused initiatives, ranging from skateparks, DIY constructions, Vans Shop Riot, and other competitions to the Offthewall.tv channel and *Living Off the Wall* documentary series.

Particularly popular among skaters is the Vans Warped Tour, an eclectic mixture of action sports and rock, reggae, punk, and hip-hop, which every year attracts more than 600,000 North American visitors (Palladini 2009). In contrast to Nike SB's headline sponsorship of the spectacularized and arena-based Street League Skateboarding international series, Vans have been more socially innovative in these operations. For example, since 2006, the Vans Warped Tour has incorporated the progressive All Girl Skate Jam competition inaugurated by Latina skater Patty Segovia-Krause, which 'sent shock waves through the male dominated skateboard industry' (Beal 2013; I Skate Therefore I Am 2011). According to Tom Delonge of rock band Blink 182, the Warped Tour is a 'cultural circus' and 'the first cultural experiment of the post punker, alternative nation of kids' (cited in Palladini 2009); indeed, the whole Warped Tour is a 'big backyard party' where 'freedom and chaos' co-exist (Palladini 2009).

Vans have also been active in skateparks, most famously with the re-creation of the Combi-Pool – the notoriously challenging square-and-round bowl installed at California's Pipeline skatepark in 1979 and destroyed nine years later. Constructed within a skatepark in Orange County in 1999, Vans claim that its version of the Combi-Pool still 'dares even the most experienced skater' (Palladini 2009) and, since 2005, has held an annual invitational 'pool party' lasting several days, beamed live via the Internet and YouTube highlights to hundreds of thousands of skaters worldwide.

More inventive, though, is the House of Vans initiative. First opened in 2010 with a club-like, invite-only facility in Brooklyn, New York (NY Skateboarding 2011) and followed up by roving music- and skate-based events across America, the House of Vans London (HoV) version was opened in August 2014. Occupying 2,500m^2 of Victorian railway arches (previously used by The Old Vic theatre for experimental arts) and located next to London's famous Leake Street graffiti venue, HoV is a highly unusual combination of free-access skateboarding alongside art, music, and film, thus furthering Vans' association with creative producers.

As with Hungerford Bridge, this has been a collaborative production, deploying a team of marketeers, designers, and fabricators with considerable prior experience working with Vans and/or the skate scene: Kat Mackenzie and Henry Clay of Black Sparrow Presents (experiential marketeers) for event production and construction management, architect Tim Greatrex working with professional skateboarder and designer Pete Hellicar for overall design, professional skateboarder Marc Churchill of Line Skateparks for skatepark design, and Pete Warboys for skatepark construction (Greatrex, 2015, pers. comm., 19 February; *House of Vans London* 2014; Jones 2014).

Like the Hungerford Bridge open-space designs for skaters and non-skaters, HoV adopts a multi-arts approach in which five tunnels are given discrete functions: art gallery, cinema, gig venue, and skateboarding. Skate culture is symbolized through interior design features derived from concrete banks, swimming

104   *Iain Borden*

pools, drainage pipes, and other skateboardable terrains, a patterned rubber floor recalling the 'waffle' sole of Vans shoes, and vintage memorabilia. The skate spaces cater for different abilities and interests, including a street area and mini-ramp. Most challenging is a complex-shaped bowl, 'an unforgiving masterpiece that can destroy you and elate you' (Leeks 2014a) which combines varying transitions, heights, forms of coping, and – in another reference to classic Vans shoes – black-and-white checkerboard tiling. Two iconic arch cut-outs – one per side wall – additionally demand from skaters a combination of exacting trajectory, advanced technicality, and abundant bravado.

Unlike in Brooklyn, the London HoV is open to the public, including free skate, art, and film sessions. The avowed intention of allowing HoV to evolve through its visitors seemed, in the first few months at least, to be borne out by events ranging from movie screenings, drawing workshops, and book fairs to exhibitions of skate art, graphics, photography, and video. This kind of programming helps explain how, despite its global operations, Vans continues to enjoy endorsements from creative producers like Lowbrow artist Niagara, graffiti artist Neck Face, and skateboard graphic designer Wes Humpston, as well as musicians from Motorhead and Slayer to Public Enemy and Eminem (Palladini 2009). HoV skatepark users are also surprisingly diverse, with one-third more than thirty years old, and including significant numbers of similarly aged females – far more than skateparks typically attract (Holden 2014). Social media and Internet and live camera feeds have also helped connect HoV to local and international audiences. For example, the Crossfire Halloween Massacre event – a 'raucous night' of jam skate sessions, deathpunks Turbonegro, 'Massacre' art, and horror film screenings – aired via a live web feed and later appeared in innumerable online videos and blogs (Leeks 2014b).

Despite operating as continuous advertisement for its billion-dollar backer, HoV's wide artistic and social net is quite different to a typical skatepark, the carefully nuanced design and program of activities encompassing at once some of the Undercroft's authentic urbanism, Hungerford Bridge's more varied skate terrains, and the creative artistic milieu commonly associated with skateboarding today, from film and photography to music, poetry, and street art. In this context, HoV is clearly different to the corporate annexation of skateboarding and popular culture for which Nike SB and others have been criticized. It is also a step beyond the kind of corporate sponsorship (Mountain Dew, Pepsi, etc.) which, as Tony Hawk (2015) has recently commented, allows skaters to get on with skateboarding yet remains outside core skate values. HoV, then, marks a shift in the outright opposition between, on the one hand, the authentic, real, street-level, and unfunded (as many skaters commonly perceive skateboarding) and, on the other hand, the inauthentic, spectacularized, controlled, and commercial (companies, sponsors, media). Understood within the wider context of Vans and skateboarding, HoV is an example of what Lawrence Lessig (2008) has termed a 'hybrid' economy, operating simultaneously as a commercial economy for financial gain *and* as a sharing economy for collaborative and collective benefit. In short, HoV shows how the commercial, spectacular, and controlled as well as the authentic, performative, and disorderly might, in certain circumstances, exist in harmonious and even creative conjunction.

Conclusion

History will tell if this is too much to claim for HoV, which is very much in its infancy, and whose long-term future undoubtedly depends on Vans' financial success and, indeed, on HoV's own contribution to that prosperity. Having cost UK£1 million to fit out, plus an additional UK£1 million per year to operate, the HoV facility clearly has to pay its way. There are also uncertainties about the other Southbank spaces. At the Undercroft, continued spats over usage (Wainwright 2015), the relative paucity of skateable terrain, and adjacent land-owners tightening up their anti-skate measures means that the LLSB campaign success just might, in years to come, appear more like a victory for nostalgia than for skateboarding's long-term prosperity along the Southbank. At Hungerford Bridge, it is unclear how funding will be identified and whether the SBC will ever construct it. Even then, questions remain as to how well Enevoldsen's design might be translated into built form and, more importantly, how inspiring it might prove for skaters and others. Would it escape the stigma of being purposely provided for skaters, and could it become truly appropriated like a street skate spot?

But for now at least, there is much to be celebrated. Compared with the dark days of the 1980s when skateboarding all but disappeared in many neighbourhoods, and even compared with the 1970s when it was largely dismissed by public and media alike as a childish craze, skateboarding has now been accepted at some places like the Southbank as an established part of our urban, cultural, and economic well-being. These three spaces show how skateboarding is vital to thousands of skaters, is appreciated by even greater numbers of the public, and is even essential to wider artistic and commercial operations. In these three spaces, skateboarding is at once indispensable, desirable, and necessary. Here, for now, it thrives.

References

Armes, A 2008, *SKM8*. Available from: www.rudi.net/books/6911. [23 January 2015].

Beal, B 2013, *Skateboarding: the ultimate guide*, Greenwood, Santa Barbara, CA.

Bleasdale, A 1996, 'Interview', *Sidewalk Surfer*, no. 9 (August), unpaginated.

Blum, A 2008, 'New Oslo Opera House is really a stealth skate park', *Wired*, vol. 16, no. 12. Available from: www.archive.wired.com. [12 January 2015].

Borden, I 2001, *Skateboarding, space and the city: architecture and the body*, Berg, Oxford.

Borden, I 2013, *Iain Borden on the (lack of) Festival Wing consultation*, 18 September. Available from: www.youtube.com/watch?v=EMQwktfjeTA&spfreload=10. [19 September 2013].

Borden, I 2014a, 'Architecture', in *Long Live Southbank*, London: Long Live Southbank, London, pp. 68–97.

Borden, I 2014b, 'The spaces of skateboarding', *The Architects' Journal*, vol. 28, November, pp. 56–59.

106   *Iain Borden*

Borden, I & Holland, R 2013a, *Urban arts at the Hungerford Bridge site: briefing for designers*, Southbank Centre, London.

Borden, I & Holland, R 2013b, *Evaluation of the Hungerford Bridge skate space report, Southbank Centre planning application #13/05522/FUL*, London Borough Lambeth.

Bradstreet, K 2011, *Thinking small for the future of skate*, Consolidated Skateboarding. Available from: www.consolidatedskateboard.com. [16 January 2015].

Brown, M 2014, 'Southbank Skate Park must stay, says Boris Johnson', *The Guardian*, 15 January. Available from: www.theguardian.com. [15 January 2014].

Browne, D 2004, *Amped: how big air, big dollars, and a new generation took sports to the extreme*, Bloomsburg, London.

Butter, S 2014, 'Wheels of fortune', *London Evening Standard*, 14 April. Available from: www.standard.co.uk. [16 April 2014].

Clark, K & Hyland, T 2013, 'Q&A with Drexel alum Tony Bracali', *Drexel Now*, 21 May 2013. Available from: www.drexel.edu. [6 June 2013].

Dezeen 2011, *Landhausplatz by LAAC Architeken and Stiefel Kramer Architecture*. Available from: www.dezeen.com. [27 November 2012].

Ethernal Skate Films 2013, *Big-O rebirth @ The Pipe*. Available from: www.youtube.com/watch?v=feRrG34LWY4. [9 November 2013].

Funding Universe 2015, *Vans. Inc. history*. Available from: www.fundinguniverse.com. [26 January 2015].

Hargrove, K 2012, 'The Don't Do It Foundation: fighting to save speciality retailers', *TransWorld Business*, 31 July 2015. Available from: www.business.transworld.net. [16 January 2015].

Harvey, D 2003, 'The right to the city', *International Journal of Urban and Regional Research*, vol. 27, no. 4, pp. 939–941.

Hawk, T 2015, 'Tony Hawk: who you callin' a sell out?', *The Berrics*, 23 January. Available from: www.theberrics.com. [26 January 2015].

Holden, L 2014, 'Skate ramps buzz with old city rollers', *The Times*, 23 August, Available from: www.thetimes.co.uk. [24 August 2014].

House of Vans London 2014, Press release (July).

Howell, O 2005, 'The "creative class" and the gentrifying city: skateboarding in Philadelphia's Love Park', *Journal of Architectural Education*, vol. 59 no. 2, pp. 32–42.

I Skate Therefore I Am 2011, *Interview with Patty Segovia, creator of All Girl Skate Jam*. Available from: www.istia.com (2 November). [22 March 2012].

Jones, G 2014, 'House of Vans London Sneak Peak', *Sidewalk*, 14 July. Available from: www.sidewalk.mpora.com. [1 September 2014].

Leeks, Z 2014a, 'Vans X Crossfire Halloween Massacre Bowl Jam gallery', *Crossfire*, 3 November. Available from: www.caughtinthecrossfire.com. [4 November 2014].

Leeks, Z 2014b, 'Vans X Crossfire Halloween Massacre 2014', *Crossfire*, 7 October. Available from: www.caughtinthecrossfire.com. [15 November 2014].

Lefebvre, H 1991, *The production of space*, Blackwell, Oxford.

Lessig, L 2008, *Remix: making art and commerce thrive in the hybrid economy*, Penguin, New York.

Long Live Southbank (LLSB) 2013a, *A bigger picture*. Available from: www.youtube.com/watch?v=iFaKN98Xg3E&spfreload=10. [15 November 2013].

Long Live Southbank (LLSB) 2013b, *Response to the Southbank Centre's Hungerford Bridge skatepark plans*. Available from: www.youtube.com/watch?v=908Iudxi9Oo. [11 September 2013].

Long Live Southbank (LLSB) 2014a, *Southbank Undercroft: cultural & heritage assessment report*, Long Live Southbank, London.

Long Live Southbank (LLSB) 2014b, *Long Live Southbank*, Long Live Southbank, London.

Mandatory information 1996, *TransWorld Skateboarding*, vol. 14, no. 5, p. 46.

New York Skateboarding 2011, *The House of Vans – Brooklyn*. Available from: www.nyskateboarding.com. [16 January 2015].

Owens, C 2014, '"Skateboard urbanism" could change park planning,' *Next City*, 1 October. Available from: www.nextcity.org. [21 January 2015].

Palladini, D 2009, *Vans: off the wall. Stories of sole from Van's Originals*, Harry N. Abrams, New York.

Philly Love Notes 2013, *The one place Michael Haeflinger loves?* Available from: www.phillylovenotes.com. [1 December 201].

Playboard.de 2014, *City skateboarding guide – #5 Innsbruck*. Available from: www.playboard.de. [19 January 2015].

Purves, L 2013, 'Let these skaters swoop and crash and rattle', *The Times*, 13 May. Available from: www.thetimes.co.uk. [14 May 2013].

Quartersnacks 2013, *Wow, Philadelphia did something smart!* Available from: www.quartersnacks.com. [1 June 2013].

Ritter, A, Treichl, M & Wedekind, C (eds) 2012, *Auszeichnung des landes tirol für neues bauen 2012*, Culture Department, Tyrol, Innsbruck.

Skates and Ladders 2009, *Milton Keynes Buszy*. Available from: www.skatesandladders.com. [22 January 2015].

Southbank Centre (SBC) 2013a, *The Festival Wing*. Available from: www.thefestivalwing.com. [22 January 2015].

Southbank Centre (SBC) 2013b, *Assessment of communal value of the Southbank Centre and Queen Elizabeth Hall Undercroft*, Montagu Evans, London.

Southbank Centre (SBC) 2013c, *Southbank Centre unveils plans to transform Festival Wing*, press release (6 March).

Southbank Centre (SBC) 2013d, *Southbank Centre to the Mayor and Burgesses of the London Borough of Lambeth*, Unilateral Undertaking, London.

Southbank Centre (SBC) 2013e, *Statement of community involvement: Hungerford Bridge skateable space*. Submission to London Borough of Lambeth.

Southbank Centre (SBC) 2014a, *Southbank Centre withholds Festival Wing*, press release, (5 February).

Tison, Marc & Walsh, Barry 2006, *Pipe fiends: a visual overdose of Canada's most infamous skate spot*, Media MudScout, Montreal.

VFC 2013, Vans. Available from: www.reporting.vfc.com/2013/vans/index.html. [17 August 2014].

VFC 2015, *VF reports 2014 fourth quarter and full year results; announces outlook for 2015*. Available from: wow.vfc.com. [17 February 2015].

Wainwright, O 2015, 'Southbank bans street art event celebrating skate park's salvation,' *The Guardian*, 28 January 2015. Available from: www.theguardian.com. [28 January 2015].

Wheatcroft, G 1979, 'Busk off', *The Spectator*, 24 February, p. 28.

Whitter, W & Shuall, T 2008, *Save South Bank*. Available from: www.vimeo.com/32716340. [12 November 2012].

8 The 'legitimate' skateboarder
Politics of private–public skateboarding spaces

Matthew Atencio and Becky Beal

The neoliberal construction of skateparks and social identities

In our recent conversations with community skateboarding advocates in the San Francisco Bay Area, an oft-held view that emerged was that public funding and management of skateparks was considered inadequate. A volunteer coordinator in a local skatepark once commented to us about the lack of programming at their public skatepark: 'It's not that they don't want to; it's that they just don't have the capacity for all this programming. They can't manage it all, so they said "Why don't you do it, why don't you do that?"' (Jane, 2014, pers. comm., 14 March). Following on, we examine the contemporary iteration of 'public' skateboarding in relation to neoliberal realities of private agents and resources influencing the operation of skateparks that are located on city property under the purview of community agencies.

The discourse of neoliberalism has been identified as crucial to the modern iteration of skateboarding in urban locations in terms of how participants gain cultural kudos as well as individual fulfilment (Atencio & Beal 2011). Ocean Howell (2008, p. 476) notes that skateparks work as mechanisms to promote neoliberal ideals by reflecting free economies and limited state support. He outlines how urban managers promote skateboarding 'to reward and encourage' neoliberal values amongst young people, pertaining to characteristics such as 'personal responsibility, self-sufficiency, and entrepreneurialism' (p. 476). We want to extend this line of analysis by interrogating how city planners and managers, private businesses, parents, and skateboarders have distinctive interests and agendas that impact the operation and practices of community skate initiatives.

We suggest that the recent trend of skatepark development mirrors the recent proliferation of 'private–public' partnerships influencing city spaces across the United States. It has been argued by David Madden (2010) that city spaces such as parks are evolving in line with increased private oversight rather than under public administration for the sake of profit making. This means that private–public partnerships now largely operate and regulate spaces such as community parks once considered strictly public entities. Sharon Zukin (1991, p. 240) reveals in this regard that spaces exist as 'transitional', in the sense that they create fluid

The 'legitimate' skateboarder 109

and multi-faceted practices and identities; these community spaces reflect both global capitalism and local place, existing 'between public use and private value'. The private–public partnerships further reveal competing and diverse interests that shape these spaces and, in turn, impact boundaries of 'civil' behaviour. Ultimately, we argue that the interaction of these stakeholders in the name of the 'public good' demarcates certain accepted identities and ideal citizenship.

Within skateboarding, there are various social practices structured according to the community logics of public health, youths' personal development, and public safety. While skateparks can be opposed due to public distrust and the demonization of participants associated with youth crime and infrastructural damage (Howell 2008; Németh 2006; Taylor & Khan 2011), community-sanctioned skateparks are now greatly multiplying. For instance, there is a rapidly growing belief that skateparks can provide physical health and social benefits to young people (Dumas & Laforest 2009; Taylor & Khan 2011). Indeed, some of these recent skateparks have garnered funding from government agencies, city administrators, and foundations interested in promoting healthy lifestyles (Turner 2013).

These stakeholders have come together, albeit in unequal alliances, to 'develop' urban areas, as in the case of LOVE Park in Philadelphia (Howell 2005). We thus address how recent examples of private–public skateparks reflect a more integrated and sophisticated working relationship amongst these stakeholders. In regards to proliferating skateparks created through the private–public nexus, we ask questions about the types of citizenship identities and practices that are being privileged when these types of new community spaces are constructed.

In this chapter, we interrogate three specific case study examples to illustrate how community parks were constructed and used by various stakeholders. Our analysis gives insight into the variation in goals and uses of these skateparks, with implications for inclusion/exclusion as well as the construction of specific citizen-subjects. In our analysis, we investigate (1) the Rob Dyrdek Foundation's Safe Spot Skate Spot skate plazas; (2) Tha Hood Games skateboarding and youth festivals and Town Park based in Oakland; and (3) the Bay Area Skatepark. Since 2013, we have conducted semi-structured interviews with key leaders of the Bay Area Skatepark and Tha Hood Games. Observations were also conducted during skate events held at the Bay Area Skatepark, as well as Town Park. Media texts including website content, videos, and Facebook pages were also interrogated. For example, much of the data pertaining to Dyrdek and his role as a skatepark leader emanates from his own Foundation website; his voice is prominent here in both written and audio form.

Rob Dyrdek's Safe Spot Skate Spots

Becky Beal (2013, p. 79) describes Rob Dyrdek as a professional skateboarder who 'has made his mark as a consummate entrepreneur, continually developing ways to develop a broad audience for street-style skateboarding'. His synergistic entrepreneurial pursuits include creating action figures and television programs

110 *Matthew Atencio and Becky Beal*

and developing a professional skateboarding league, and he has been actively constructing 'skate plazas' in cities such as Los Angeles through his Rob Dyrdek Foundation.

According to its website, the Rob Dyrdek Foundation (2014) was founded in 2003 'to create healthy communities by promoting and providing the inherent benefits of skateboarding to all facets of society'. The foundation's vision statement suggests that it wants to 'encourage construction of legal street skating areas, be that through large urban skate plazas or single skate spots' (2014). Thus, there are key statements here pertaining to the multiple stakeholders from public and private backgrounds invoked to build skate plazas. Its stated goal is to reach out to local communities, and they list a range of potential partners including 'governments, park and recreations departments and local urban renewal and community improvement committees' (2014). The Foundation further outlines how they welcome involvement from 'major corporations and organizations sharing our support of legal street skateboarding who wish to give back to their communities through funding, land donation or other means of support' (2014).

Yet while making appeals for various forms of public support towards the aim of community enhancement, Dyrdek's more personal statements on the website reveal a more cynical view towards public citizens and institutions. Dyrdek comments that interlocutors such as city planners and law enforcement members who 'don't understand it' are interfering with his ability to skate in public urban spaces:

> There is not one place in the entire United States where I could go legally skate real street. Each day there are fewer and fewer places to street skate, period. Skateboarding is being choked by people that simply don't understand it. Skateboarders are sick of getting tickets and watching every good skate spot get skate-proofed or destroyed.
>
> (2014)

Dyrdek's entrepreneurial solution to this issue of 'skate proofing' is to make recourse to an authentic ideal of the 'real' urban street in his skate plaza design:

> Build real street parks. Recreational skateparks, which include street courses, mini-ramps, and bowls, will always be a part of skateboarding, but they will never play a part in keeping skaters off the streets of their communities. Not to mention that most of these recreational parks are built by people who don't know anything about any type of skateboarding. If 80% of skateboarding is real street, then 80% of the places built for skateboarders should duplicate real street.
>
> (2014)

The Safe Spot Skate Spot is thus a private–public skate space marked by Dyrdek's vision of 'real street' authenticity – even as his foundation purports to be most invested in building healthy community spaces for all citizens. The foundation message aligns with the view that 'skateparks should be conceived as a valuable

The 'legitimate' skateboarder 111

health-resource for youth because they provide various social, psychological and physical resources that encourage a safe and active lifestyle' (Dumas & Laforest 2009, p. 19), although Dyrdek's personal motivations appear more related to replicating authentic 'street' spaces.

Matthew Atencio, Becky Beal, and Charlene Wilson (2009) remind us that male skateboarders often align themselves with an 'authentic' urban or street distinction in order to gain currency in their social domains; being recognized in such authentic ways provides males with great currency within the realm of skateboarding culture. In this case, Dyrdek invokes the 'real street' as a means of distinguishing his skate spaces and his persona (as he is integrally linked with these spaces) from more 'recreational' and seemingly inferior community skatepark spaces. It is worth speculating here that while he attempts to add cachet to these community skateparks, this vision of 'real street' skate plazas also provides him with cultural kudos that proliferates his entrepreneurial capital. That is, in addition to promoting a persona that has been made popular by MTV, these spaces are also directly linked with his Street League Skateboarding (SLS) project that started competition in 2010. These links are made explicit in the Street League Skateboarding's website:

> Throughout the year, the SLS Foundation also aims to empower communities with the mission of helping to build free, public skate spots, as well as create new SLS Certified Skate Plazas capable of hosting future events and additional league programs.
>
> (SLS Certified Skate Plazas 2014)

The Street League is a competitive tour similar to the X Games, but focused more upon street-style skateboarding with an easy-to-follow scoring format. There is also involvement of professional skateboarders and large financial payouts during tour events (Beal 2013). So far, this competition has only consisted of professional male skateboarders and is hosted by communities that have committed to build several of his skate plazas, with top-up funding of $50,000 from his foundation.

Despite the description of 'free' skateparks advanced by Dyrdek's foundation, the skateparks ask community youth to petition and protest to community agencies in order to get these skate plazas funded and built. In order to appeal to more 'budget conscious council or board members', the Foundation website recommends that skateboarders explicitly connect skate plaza usage with other publicly funded facilities (The Rob Dyrdek Foundation 2014). The skate plazas are constructed similarly to other community-operated spaces; as a facility 'to be enjoyed by both the general public and skateboarders' (2014). Statements on the foundation website further promote a socially inclusive vision of the public in his skate plazas. He calls for a skate plaza in every community used by skaters of all levels, meaning 'everyone' from 'the most advanced pro to the youngest novice' (2014).

The Rob Dyrdek Foundation is not just framing its activities as socially inclusive but also as a recuperative activity. On his website, Dyrdek directly states that 'As Americans, we believe that sports are a positive influence in our kids' lives'

112   *Matthew Atencio and Becky Beal*

because it 'builds character . . . teaches them important lessons and keeps them out of trouble' (2014). Noting the positive influence of American sports such as basketball, baseball, and football, Dyrdek suggests that 'the 11 million kids who skateboard' also need to have safe and legal spaces to participate (2014). Dyrdek here refers to the popular narrative that sports spaces build character and prevent crime, invoking a problematic trope that has been deployed in other sports contexts (Atencio & Wright 2008; Cole & King 1998; Hartmann 2001).

However, skateboarding's promotion as a socially inclusive and recuperative activity has been severely called into question by researchers such as Beal (1996), particularly in terms of gender relations. Although women are increasingly participating in skateboarding (Kelly, Pomerantz, & Currie 2005; Porter 2003), it has been demonstrated that skateboarding for women can mostly be found within the ramp-style format during sanctioned events. When notions of the 'street' are invoked within skateparks, men are considered most closely with characteristics such as risk taking and are thus considered most marketable to consumers. As such, men remain dominant within both symbolic and real-life spaces (Atencio, Beal, & Wilson 2009). Belinda Wheaton (2013, p. 3) argues in this regard that ideals of excitement and extreme risk-taking within lifestyle sport have 'been appropriated to sell every kind of product and service imaginable' to young males. We thus question Dyrdek's approach to creating these skate plazas – overwhelmingly built through public agency funding – for the sake of public benefit when it seems that this young male demographic is actually being targeted and promoted.

Taken together, Dyrdek's statements to the public can be characterized as contradictory. Although all members of the public are being referenced quite clearly as advocates, participants, or funders, these plazas are seemingly set up to benefit advanced street skateboarders in the Street League or a select group of young males who often inhabit street skate spaces at the expense of others (Atencio, Beal, & Wilson 2009). Public servants and institutions are admonished by Dyrdek for not 'getting it' and indeed 'skate proofing' and 'destroying' skateboarding. Yet he asks for significant funding from these public agencies and workers, who are positioned as keys source of infrastructure funding.

The Foundation takes a 'build it and they will come' stance; yet this strategy arguably reproduces the privilege of the 'legitimate' male skateboarder as opposed to actively transforming the space to be more socially inclusive. We suggest that these skate plazas are not intended for the public citizen *per se* despite the inclusive rhetoric interspersed throughout his foundation's website. We contend that Dyrdek and his foundation actually have a more narrow perspective of who can legitimately claim and inhabit these spaces, in line with Dyrdek's entrepreneurial pursuits. This view follows Madden's (2010) suggestion that urban spaces in the public community work as cultural projects wherein various stakeholders work to construct prevailing visions of acceptability. In this case, the skate plazas are eventually characterized and operated as official Street League Skateboarding Certified Skate Plazas (SLS Certified Skate Plazas 2014). The skate plazas are thus designed primarily to support the Street League Skateboarding phenomenon, where only male professional skateboarders on this tour have access to promotion

The *'legitimate' skateboarder* 113

and cash prizes. From the perspective that the construction of 'urban publicity' within community spaces 'is an on-going, contested process' (Madden 2010, p. 189), we argue that the Dyrdek Foundation reproduces specific views on how skateparks should be used and by whom. In this case, males who typify 'coolness' and 'legitimacy' within street skateboarding (Atencio, Beal, & Wilson 2009) are considered most desirable within these spaces that are largely constructed through public agency funds for the sake of private gain.

Tha Hood Games and Town Park Skatepark

In 2005, Keith Williams (known locally as 'K-Dub') created Tha Hood Games, a skate and art festival with the goal of providing spaces in which inner-city ethnic minority youth could display their talents within their local neighbourhoods. Williams had previously been to an X Games event held in Los Angeles and felt that there was a lack of diversity among participants. Williams subsequently formed a partnership with a professional skateboarder named Karl Watson in the LA area. Together with Williams's mother Adjoa 'Barbara' Murden, a retired social worker, they linked the skateboarding platform with music, art, and fashion. According to their Facebook page, the stated mission of Tha Hood Games is 'to give inner-city youth a . . . positive platform for artistic creation, skateboarding and sharing talents & skills for their families in their communities' (Tha Hood Games 2014).

During interviews with us, Williams discussed how he manages Tha Hood Games and its base location, Town Park. It became apparent that he did not solely rely on traditional public agencies such as parks and recreation departments. Instead, he described how he develops meaningful personal relationships so that he can depend on these individuals to show up and be involved in developing the skatepark. Williams noted that he attempts 'to build bridges' with community members and even private sponsors. During an interview with us, he characterized his dialogue with the local parks and recreation department as 'they allow me to do my thing'; he then went on to state that 'you have like-minded people, you know, I got some pro skaters that show up for the kids. We have some companies they're like anytime I need anything' (Keith Williams, 2014. pers. comm., 21 February). Companies have donated paint for the murals in the skatepark, while another business has donated skateboards to hand out for free. Williams is thus clear and open that he works in tandem with a range of stakeholders representing both private and public interests.

While Dyrdek claims his skate plazas offer character-building benefits and reduce crime in the community, Tha Hood Games and Town Park are primarily envisioned by Williams as synergistic vehicles of role modelling and community building for local youth. Williams states that he is significantly committed to Oakland by intentionally programming competitions and festivals that provide opportunities for youth to work with adult mentors. The aim is for youth to craft their artistic and skateboarding skills. Williams thus sees street skateboarding not in terms of just reproducing 'real street' authenticity but as a platform for youth

114 *Matthew Atencio and Becky Beal*

and community development at a local level. Williams targets the participation of a more diverse demographic of skateboarder hailing from minority ethnic and lower socio-economic backgrounds. Our observations have revealed that many young men in the local community visit Town Park, while other skateboarders and their parents come from surrounding middle-class suburban areas.

Town Park is located in a broader Oakland community park where the Black Panthers used to provide free lunches to the local citizenry. Noting this historical link with the local African-American community, Williams (2014, pers. comm., 21 February) commented to us that 'this is a historic park, it just needs some love'. Because one of Williams's goals is to create opportunities for urban youth to practice skateboarding in their own neighbourhoods, he is currently fundraising for the construction of permanent concrete fixtures where the temporary Town Park skatepark is now located. Town Park was initially conceived as 'a DIY (Do It Yourself) piece on public property' (Williams, 2014, pers. comm., 21 February). Our observations of Town Park reveal an almost grassroots and makeshift feel, with wooden ramps built with graffiti and artistic elements. Then, taking up an entrepreneurial approach, Williams has signed an agreement with Levi's Jeans, a San Francisco–based corporation, to fund a more permanent skate space. Levi's has launched a skateboarding clothing collection and are subsequently promoting their brand by direct involvement with skateboarding culture.

Town Park and the associated Hood Games together demonstrate how private–public partnerships are inextricably linked with the logics of neoliberalism. These endeavours led by Williams reflect the contemporary ethos of market deregulation, predicated upon the belief that corporations and individuals pursuing their own economic interests can drive modern societies (Hursh & Henderson 2011). In this regard, Williams suggested to us during an interview that his relationship with the local parks and recreation department was ambivalent; he needed to make deals with corporate sponsors to develop a skatepark that would be accessible to all members of the local community. Williams's propensity for utilizing private interests rather than public agencies and resources to build urban space raises questions about the competing agendas of his private backers. Within his neoliberal vision of community building, we ask: what are the ramifications for creating a socially inclusive space? It has been argued by Jodi Melamed (2006) that the discourse of neoliberalism continues to structure unequal terms for citizens, despite the claims of openness and inclusion that underpin this discourse. In what follows, we examine how Williams's 'open' approach may in practice privilege certain individuals over others.

Despite the infusion of private support from local companies and multi-national corporations, Williams (2014, pers. comm., 21 February) claimed to us during an interview that 'I don't want the brand, I don't want a skateboard company, I want the platform and everybody's welcome'. He distinguishes himself from others who are 'really pushing the brands' and claims that his focus is on community building for youth development and their skill building. Williams (2014, pers. comm., 21 February) described the clientele of Town Park as 'multi-cultural and

The 'legitimate' skateboarder   115

local', including African-Americans, white youth from wealthy suburbs, and rock musicians who practice in warehouses nearby. Yet following Melamed (2006, p. 16), we argue that social inclusion assertions can be problematic when housed within neoliberalism, as structural inequalities are often subsumed under claims of 'open societies'. The clientele referenced indeed speaks specifically to male skate participants, and there is limited engagement with providing for women and girls to skate in Town Park. For example, when asked about being socially inclusive regarding gender, Williams (2014, pers. comm., 21 February), noted to us that 'Girls come through for a minute and don't stay with it'. He suggested that other sports such as soccer, surfing, and softball were capturing the interest of girls and young women. We contend that Williams is reproducing a DIY view that closely aligns with neoliberalism. The DIY philosophy, in which individuals 'find their own mode of production and distribution to match exactly what it is they just might have to say' (McCormick 2004, p. 78), arguably mirrors the individualistic rhetoric of neoliberalism. DIY similarly provides currency for those who embody the attitude of being 'self-made'. Williams's view thus suggests that females must also find their own means to access Town Park, like the men seemingly can.

Therefore, even as Williams welcomes both male and female skateboarders, females are much less visible in Oakland's Town Park. This suggests that his open approach does not directly focus on how to break down gendered barriers reinforcing male privilege. Williams enacts a 'hands-off' approach to controlling clientele who use this skatepark; this view elides with a neoliberal perspective of fairness and neutrality (Melamed 2006) despite structural and ideological barriers that currently exist for women in urban skateboarding culture. In this way, the emergence of Town Park as a locally driven urban skatepark does not account for women's lack of access or marginalization. Thus, an open approach to social inclusion only maintains the status quo, as women continue to be marginalized by male power. The operation of male power can only be disrupted when direct practices to include women are enacted, so that the 'symbolic capital that is integrally associated with masculinity' can be seen as feminine as well (Atencio, Beal, & Wilson 2009, p. 17).

The Bay Area Skatepark

In a grassroots fashion, the Bay Area Skatepark culture came into existence largely through the efforts of 'Jane'[1] and a local group of like-minded parents. Jane became involved because her son was a skateboarder, and she saw the need for a safe place for young people like him to skate. The local group of parents created a volunteer group with a Facebook site to keep the community informed about the plans and development of the skatepark. As noted on their Facebook webpage, this group 'was created to support the new skatepark from design and construction through opening day and beyond!' The skatepark was built with public funds and is under the auspices of the city parks and recreation department. Currently, the volunteer group plays a crucial role in developing the culture

116   *Matthew Atencio and Becky Beal*

and ethos of the skatepark as noted on their website: 'The Bay Area Skatepark Group is a group of skaters, parents and community members who work with the City . . . to ensure our free, public skatepark is safe, welcoming and inclusive for skaters and their families'.

Jane (2014, pers. comm., 14 March) commented during an interview with us that the relationship this volunteer group has with public agencies is constantly in negotiation: 'We agreed to an open, free, public, family skatepark. We're still working on that'. When asked if Jane was essentially the 'on-site manager', she replied to us, 'That's the other [thing] too, every time we want to do something here, we have to go through the city. It would be nice if we had some of our own money so that if we said, "okay, we want to do this"' (2014, pers. comm., 14 March). Her group is considering being incorporated as an official non-profit organization so they would have more autonomy from the city. Jane (2014, pers. comm., 14 March) described another situation in which the city placed responsibility for programming back on her volunteer group:

> They (Parks and Recreation Department) want us to do things . . . the city they sponsor Mike (an ex-professional skater who now gives lessons) and then when we approached them to also sponsor Girl Riders Organization, they basically said 'No, we're doing enough'. It's not that they don't want to; it's that they just don't have the capacity for all this programming. They can't manage it all, so they said 'Why don't you do it, why don't you do that?'

The views expressed here reflect a tension around gaining full city support that was highlighted by Williams, too. Williams makes recourse to private funding from sponsors through his non-profit status, and Jane's mission is similarly to leverage the skatepark's supporter groups into non-profit status in order to gain more private funding. Yet her key priority is to provide more access to families, including females. Thus, while gender issues remain unaddressed within the skate contexts led by Williams and Dyrdek, the Bay Area Skatepark has already made explicit links with female-focused skate groups such as Girl Riders Organization (GRO) and Skate Like A Girl (SLAG).

Observations at this skatepark reveal how female-only events provided structured opportunities for females to learn skills in an environment they felt comfortable in. The local leaders of GRO and SLAG were regularly present at these events, mentoring young skateboarders, gathering their feedback, and handing out token gifts from skate shops. Parents frequently commented during interviews that their daughters would 'light up' and gravitate toward other females during these events. Observations in the park on Saturday mornings reveal how females are regular participants, with parents observing from the side in a manner reminiscent of traditional youth sport.

Other community events aimed at creating a safe and welcoming place for newcomers are regularly hosted here, including a 'rider safety day'. These events aim to instil a particular type of youth culture, one that is focused on safety, social

The 'legitimate' skateboarder   117

inclusion, and being family friendly. This formal programming arguably translates into the intentional development of social relations at the park. Jane (2014, pers. comm., 14 March) even suggested that certain elements were not welcome in the park:

> Well, we don't want police coming by and giving people tickets and hassling the skaters. We need a community of parents and skaters that give the skatepark that sort of a vibe, so that you don't have people vandalizing and . . . people still smoke pot up on the hills and stuff like that, but the whole presence of parents, and more of a family atmosphere just keeps those kind of people out so we get serious skaters and people who just want to enjoy the park.

The Bay Area Skatepark supporters group, led by Jane, attempts to increase access for all by creating a family-friendly environment at a city-sanctioned skatepark. In a grassroots sense, they are attempting to create a safe environment in which females and people of all abilities, backgrounds, and ages are welcome. This view counters what it typically means to be the 'authentic' urban skater: a young, risk-taking, independent male (Atencio & Beal 2011). Within this public space they have created both formal mechanisms (e.g., Park Rangers) and informal mechanisms (e.g., a core volunteer group and Facebook web presence) to surveil and shape the culture of that space. These concerted efforts attempt to open up opportunities for otherwise excluded groups, such as women and young children. This approach challenges the more traditional hierarchies of skate culture. While Williams was focusing on developing Oakland youth through an open-door policy, this group was strategically focused on creating safe social spaces for males and females to develop their skateboarding skills. Crucially, this volunteer group is based in a more affluent urban community compared to Oakland. This community already had the infrastructure of a high-quality skatepark in place. Additionally, adult leaders such as Jane have access to parents, volunteers, ex-professional skateboarders, skateboarding coaches, and some city funding and support mechanisms to manage this space in a more formal sense. In contrast, in our visits to Town Park, we rarely saw parents unless it was during a skate contest or event.

Throughout this chapter, we have argued that both private and public stakeholders supporting urban skatepark development work to construct codes of legitimacy that directly implicate the construction of acceptable or devalued identities. Following on, we aver that these codes of legitimacy have severe consequences for urban skateboarders' identities and their practice within skateparks. Supported by a highly organized adult volunteer group, the Bay Area Skatepark utilized various mechanisms to instil a family-friendly discourse. This approach directly involved the inclusion of females representing acceptable identities, while positioning the teenaged young men's identities as potentially disruptive and in need of adult control.

Conclusion

Madden (2010) notes that within advanced capitalist cities, urban spaces operate in complex ways to create ideals of acceptable citizenship as well as the public good. Madden (p. 188) reminds us that these spaces are increasingly 'centered upon surveillance, order, and the bolstering of corporate capitalism'. In many cases, this means that public spaces such as city parks have been transformed into private contexts where the 'intended public' is no longer the general urban population; that is, the desired users of these spaces are not 'faceless and certainly not classless' (p. 198). We took up this view, suggesting that within many community skate spaces infused with private investment, certain individuals are considered more legitimate than others based on specific socio-cultural markers. We developed this analytical frame in order to examine various private–public sponsorships that structured skateboarding practices in the San Francisco Bay Area.

Howell (2008, p. 477) specifically illustrates how the recent 'skatepark revolution', created out of diverse and complex public and private investments, can serve to 'promote neoliberal ideals, particularly as they pertain to the desired personal qualities of young citizens'. This view of neoliberalism's preference for certain forms of subjectivity largely speaks to Rob Dyrdek's entrepreneurial skate plazas. We argued that these skateparks are set up to privilege 'authentic' street skateboarding typically coded as masculine. Thus, even as his foundation is constructing more legal skateparks, we do not see any concerted effort at changing the notions of who counts as a 'legitimate' user within these skateparks. To uphold his claim to authenticity (and to help sell his brands), Dyrdek does not challenge male ascendency in skateboarding but rather reifies it through his linkages with his all-male Street League Skateboarding. Thus, we largely see his community-building efforts as reinforcing traditional codes of inclusion and exclusion that have been structured to prioritize male access and power. We questioned the Rob Dyrdek Foundation's claims that he is universally creating community skateparks for the sake of general public consumption.

Dyrdek's entrepreneurial and non-activist skate plazas can be viewed as essentially rootless in relation to his 'homogenizing' branding influence (Silk, Andrews, & Cole 2004). In contrast, Town Park (aligned with Tha Hood Games) and the Bay Area Skatepark reflect a more activist stance towards skateboarding. That is, these spaces have been initially framed around practices of social inclusion, and their remit remains to benefit all members within their local communities. As such, these spaces are less oriented toward monetization and personal profit making.

Under the logics of multiculturalism and social inclusion, the adult leaders of Town Park and the Bay Area Skatepark target particular youth who they believe have been marginalized in skateboarding culture. They are in essence trying to expand and codify what groups of people may be considered 'legitimate' skateboarders within skateboarding spaces. Keith Williams views himself as a 'bridge' between public and private entities, using his entrepreneurial and creative abilities to benefit Oakland's multicultural youth, who are seemingly in need of role

The 'legitimate' skateboarder   119

models and increased life opportunities. However, Town Park still refracts the neoliberal value that those with 'strong character, determination' and appropriate 'lifestyle' will succeed (Giardina & Metz 2004, p. 111); gender exclusion is explained as lack of motivation on the part of women to skateboard.

The Bay Area Skatepark has a more limited entrepreneurial presence mostly pertaining to skate coaches that are hired to benefit both boys and girls on a limited basis. Mostly, this park draws upon the social and material capital found within its volunteer steering group; these adults program and monitor the social space to maintain a family-friendly environment. This skatepark thus provides an intentionally designed case of social inclusion maintained by adult surveillance of youth behaviour. Madden (2010) reminds us, however, that this increasing trend of surveillance within public parks works to divide users as either legitimate or not. In this case, adults are trying to promote family-friendly skateboarders while marginalizing traditionally 'core' members of this activity through surveillance and behaviour control.

The discourse of community development was invoked to build each skatepark and associated program highlighted. Accordingly, our findings suggest that each skatepark had different workings of private–public partnerships that influenced how these spaces operated in relation to specific codes of legitimacy. Following Madden (2010), we advocate that these codes of legitimacy must be examined as they exist in tension with claims of social inclusion that are now being used to frame and construct skateparks in the United States.

Note

1. 'Jane', the 'Bay Area Skatepark', and 'Mike' the skate coach are pseudonyms. Also, websites including Facebook that are associated with this skatepark have not been referenced to protect anonymity.

References

Atencio, M & Beal, B 2011, ' "Beautiful Losers": The symbolic exhibition and legitimization of outsider masculinity', *Sport in Society*, vol. 14, no. 1, pp. 1–16.

Atencio, M, Beal, B & Wilson, C 2009, 'Distinction of risk: urban skateboarding, street habitus, and the construction of hierarchical gender relations', *Qualitative Research in Sport and Exercise*, vol. 1, no. 1, pp. 3–20.

Atencio, M & Wright, J 2008, ' "We be killin' them": hierarchies of black masculinity in urban basketball spaces', *Sociology of Sport Journal*, vol. 25, no. 2, pp. 263–280.

Beal, B 1996, 'Alternative masculinity and its effects on gender relations in the subculture of skateboarding', *Journal of Sport Behavior*, vol. 19, no. 3, pp. 204–220.

Beal, B 2013, *Skateboarding: the ultimate guide*, ABC CLIO Extreme Sport Series, Santa Barbara, CA.

Cole, CL & King, S 1998, 'Representing black masculinity and urban possibilities: racism, realism, and hoop dreams', in G Rail (ed), *Sport and postmodern times*, State University of New York Press, Albany, pp. 49–86.

Dumas, A & Laforest, S 2009, 'Skateparks as health resource: are they as dangerous as they look?', *Leisure Studies*, vol. 28, no. 1, pp. 19–34.

Giardina, M & Metz, J 2004, 'All-American girls? Corporatizing national identity and cultural citizenship with/in the WUSA' in M Silk, DL Andrews & CL Cole (eds), *Sport and cultural nationalism*, Berg, Oxford, pp. 109–126.

Hartmann, D 2001, 'Notes on Midnight Basketball and the cultural politics of recreation, race, and at-risk urban youth', *Journal of Sport and Social Issues*, vol. 25, no. 4, pp. 331–371.

Howell, O 2005, 'The "creative class" and the gentrifying city: skateboarding in Philadelphia's Love Park', *Journal of Architectural Education*, vol. 59, no. 2, pp. 32–42.

Howell, O 2008, 'Skatepark as neoliberal playground: urban governance, recreation space, and cultivation of personal responsibility', *Space and Culture*, vol. 11, no. 4, pp. 475–496.

Hursh, D & Henderson, J 2011, 'Contesting global neoliberalism and creating alternative Futures', *Discourse*, vol. 32, no. 2, pp. 171–185.

Kelly, D, Pomerantz, S, & Currie, D 2005, 'Skater girlhood and emphasized femininity: "you can't land an Ollie properly in heels"', *Gender and Education*, vol. 17, no. 3, pp. 129–148.

Madden, D 2010, 'Revisiting the end of public space: assembling the public in an urban park', *City and Community*, vol. 9, no. 2, pp. 187–207.

McCormick, C 2004, 'The beaten path' in A Rose & C Strike (eds), *Beautiful losers: contemporary art and street culture*, Iconoclast and Distributed Art Publishers, Inc., New York, pp. 73–80.

Melamed, J. 2006 'The spirit of neoliberalism: from racial liberalism to neoliberal multiculturalism', *Social Text*, vol. 24, no. 4, pp. 1–24.

Németh, J 2006 'Conflict, exclusion, relocation: skateboarding and public space', *Journal of Urban Design*, vol. 11, no. 3, pp. 297–318.

Porter, N. 2003 'Female skateboarders and their negotiation of space and identity', *Journal for Arts, Sciences, and Technology*, vol. 1, no. 2, pp. 75–80.

Rob Dyrdek Foundation, The, 2014, Available from: http://robdyrdekfoundation.org. [28 March 2014].

Silk, M, Andrews, DL & Cole, CL 2004, 'Corporate nationalisms? The spatial dimensions of sporting capital' in M Silk, DL Andrews & CL Cole (eds), *Sport and cultural nationalism*, Berg, Oxford, pp. 1–12.

SLS Certified Skate Plazas, 2014, Available from: http://streetleague.com/foundation/sls-certified-plazas. [2 April 2014].

Taylor, M & Khan, U 2011 'Skate-Park builds, teenaphobia and the adolescent need for hang-out spaces: the social utility and functionality of urban skate parks', *Journal of Urban Design*, vol. 16, no. 4, pp. 489–510.

Tha Hood Games, 2014, Available from: www.facebook.com/pages/Tha-Hood-Games/400702643377. [21 March 2014].

Turner, D 2013, 'The civilized skateboarder and the sports funding hegemony: a case study of alternative sport', *Sport in Society*, vol. 16, no. 10, pp. 1248–1262.

Wheaton, B 2013, *The cultural politics of lifestyle sports*, Routledge, Abingdon, UK.

Zukin, S 1991, *Landscapes of power: from Detroit to Disney World*, University of California Press, Berkeley, CA.

9 Spreading the Skirtboarder stoke

Reflexively blogging fluid femininities and constructing new female skateboarding identities

Steph MacKay

Why explore the relationship among media, gender, and skateboarding? The media are a central element of modern life, gender remains an important aspect of our identities, and skateboarding challenges traditional ways of 'seeing' and 'doing' sport. For more than thirty years, scholars have alleged that the discursive marginalization, (hetero) sexualization, and trivialization of sportswomen (including skateboarders) in media representations diminish women's athletic accomplishments and discourage women from participating in sports. When women do participate, media messages insinuate that they are socially acceptable only if they adopt and perform in ways that legitimize the dominant discursive constructions of sportswomen circulated in and through media texts (Bernstein 2002).[1] Dominant discursive strategies that construct sportswomen in media texts focus on gender marking (Koivula 1999), establishing heterosexuality (Wright & Clarke 1999), emphasizing female stereotypes (Christopherson, Janning, & McConnell 2002), infantilizing women (Koivula 1999), non–sports-related aspects (Eastman & Billings 2000), comparisons to men's performance (Donnelly, MacNeill, & Knight 2008), and ambivalence (Wensing & Bruce 2003). Despite the documented emergence of reverse gender discourses in some sports media contexts and findings that suggest that not all women consider the dominant discursive constructions of such media as problematic, (some consider them empowering[2]), scholars suggest that for many women (including skateboarding women), media texts normalize, discipline, and classify their sporting bodies (Pirinen 1997; Thorpe 2008; Wright & Clarke 1999).

In the skateboarding world, male skaters represent the standard in media representations, while female skaters are marginalized, (hetero) sexualised, and trivialized (Beal & Wilson 2004). When skateboarding is featured in mainstream media,[3] skateboarding women are represented in the same way as sportswomen from the mainstream sports world[4] (i.e., [hetero] sexualized and trivialized). Such forms of marginalization are even worse in niche skateboarding media (Beal & Wilson 2004).[5] This reinforces rather than challenges ideologies of gender difference and perpetuates the positioning of women as outsiders in skateboarding culture (Donnelly 2008).

Fortunately, scholars are 'seeing' media spaces that challenge the confining, discursive constructions of gender conveyed in skateboarding contexts (MacKay &

122 Steph MacKay

Dallaire 2013a; Porter 2003). However, the continued underrepresentation and purported misrepresentation of skateboarding women in the mainstream and niche media, coupled with the contradictory and increasing prevalence of skateboarding as a viable activity for young women (Wheaton 2009), calls for a more extensive investigation of skateboarding media. Furthermore, as suggested earlier and as claimed by Laura Azzarito (2010), through their interactions with media texts, audiences may adopt subject positions that contradict or challenge dominant discursive constructions of sportswomen and sportsmen and the institution of sport in general. Numerous scholars have complained about the scarcity of studies exploring media text production processes and audience reception of them. Karen Ross (2010, p. 6) noted that 'much research has been done looking at how media frame us, as gendered subjects, but it is crucial to also examine how we use the media, thus how we act as architects of our mediated world'. Concerning lifestyle sport, Belinda Wheaton (2013, p. 6) argued, 'there are limitations with approaches to understanding the meaning and significance of lifestyle sport that do not also engage with individuals and groups of people's contradictory and shifting experiences of it'. What is needed and what is being called for (MacKay & Dallaire 2013b) are explorations of how girls and women 'produce' and 'read' skateboarding media texts, rather than simple analyses of what researchers 'see'.

Communications researchers, including cyberfeminists[6] and feminist sports media scholars,[7] have also called for research projects that explore how their use of digital media affects women's individual and collective experiences of identity and difference. Although the rise of the Internet has led to a proliferation of online sport sociological research exploring the everyday meanings and practices of sport and physical cultures, David J. Leonard (2009, p. 2) writes that 'sports studies continues to lag behind in terms of analysis and critical interrogation of new media'. Too few studies examine improvements in the material and political positions of sportswomen resulting from Internet practices, while sportswomen are using digital media technologies to construct and express their gender identities on community media platforms. In the context of skateboarding, Emily Chivers Yochim (2010, p. 183) defined 'community media' as media 'designed by skateboarders using equipment and materials developed for personal use'. These media are created to be not for profit, small in scale, and distributed to and shared among community members rather than a mass audience. The proliferation of digital media in contemporary society and the shortage of related studies are further reasons for studying how Web-based community media representations may be affecting young skateboarding women.

Lifestyle sports are an interesting phenomenon for feminist researchers because of their increasingly central role in the cultural identities of young women. In her recent book, *The Cultural Politics of Lifestyle Sports*, Wheaton (2013, p. 6) attempted to determine whether these activities offer 'alternative identities and spaces that challenge the dominant ideologies of sport and the broader politics of identity, in the twenty-first century'. Other scholars claim that these practices can and do, as argued by Lucy Spowart, Lisette Burrows, and Sally Shaw (2010), provide sites for challenging dominant discursive constructions of gender. While

Spreading the Skirtboarder stoke 123

some investigations have explored how discursive constructions of gender are deployed in media representations of lifestyle sports cultures (Beal & Wilson 2004; Donnelly 2008; Henderson 2001; Thorpe 2008), only a few scholars have examined representations specifically constructed with and circulated through digital media platforms.[8] Few works have studied gender, skateboarding, and digital media (MacKay & Dallaire 2013a, 2013b, 2014; Porter 2003). No written analyses have investigated numerous angles of a single skateboarding text produced and shared on the Web by and for women, including an analysis of the text itself, an analysis of the producers' intentions, and an analysis of users' interpretations of discursive constructions of gender.

The purpose of this chapter is to address scholarly calls for action and examine a skateboarding blog,[9] Skirtboarders.com, from three angles: (a) discursive constructions of gender circulated on the blog produced by the Skirtboarders, a group of women skateboarders based in Montréal, Canada; (b) the Skirtboarders' reflexive use of blogging to challenge discursive constructions of women deployed in skateboarding media and construct an alternative gender identity; and (c) the ways in which users make sense of Skirtboarders.com.[10] Two types of materials were analyzed: (a) Skirtboarders' blog posts[11] in their entirety, including English and French text, photos, videos, links to other sites, and comments from users and (b) transcripts from semi-structured interviews.[12] All materials were analyzed using a discursive approach. Michel Foucault's (1969, 1971) discourse theory and Chris Weedon's (1997) understanding of the fluidity, complexity, and multiplicity of gender identities constructed through discourse were drawn upon to analyze how the Skirtboarders represent their gendered skateboarding performances on their blog[13] and how blog users take up these representations.

The analysis of the blog involved identifying and categorizing how skateboarding women were constructed in each text, situating the discursive constructions within a wider discourse and closely examining the contexts in which the discursive constructions were deployed. For example, how did the Skirtboarders' constructions compare to Becky Beal and Charlene Wilson's (2004) descriptions of female skateboarding media texts? Did the Skirtboarders use the same strategies that reproduce the dominant discursive constructions of sportswomen identified by sport studies scholars, or did they use different strategies and offer alternatives? Were the Skirtboarders skating amongst other women and girls at the skatepark, partying at a nightclub, or eating lunch on one of their skateboarding trips?

Researchers have been critical of the Internet, particularly how governments, armed forces, and companies nefariously use it as a panoptic mechanism to classify and discipline populations (Batra 2008). Paul Gilchrist and Belinda Wheaton (2013, p. 184) caution sport scholars not to 'uncritically laud web-based media as instruments for self-expression, creativity and enhanced democratic communication' in lifestyle sport cultures. However, feminist scholars[14] and sport scholars[15] have suggested that although disciplinary and constraining mechanisms (e.g., economic, geographical) may come into play, the Internet can also serve as a tool for social change. This chapter furthers this argument by suggesting that although the Internet is problematic in many ways, it also has 'immense revolutionary potential

124 *Steph MacKay*

in sport-related contexts' (Wilson 2007, p. 457). The Internet is a place where women can access predominantly masculine sports, such as skateboarding, create more fluid definitions of skateboarding femininity, and control their own digital media representations, which may ultimately challenge the male-dominated skateboarding media organizations.

The Skirtboarders and their blog, Skirtboarders.com

The Skirtboarders crew became an official entity in 2002 when a group of female skateboarding friends registered the Internet domain name 'Skirtboarders.com'. The fifteen primarily white[16] women aged twenty-one to thirty-six, identified as the Skirtboarders and profiled on the blog, travel to skate, make videos (they produced the first Canadian all-female skateboarding film in 2007), meet other girls and women through skateboarding, and share stories, including photos and videos on the blog. They engage in different skateboarding practices in various locales: from exclusive crew member gatherings to larger events organized through their blog in Montréal, other cities in Canada, or international tours, where they invite all girls and women to join them. They sometimes compete but usually skateboard for pleasure. Although some of the women have official sponsorships (e.g., Sitka, Volcom, Spy Optics, and Hurley) that help fund their skateboarding trips and clothing and equipment purchases, most pay for their sporting activities and travel themselves. Featured in the Canadian mainstream and niche media several times since the blog started, they have also attracted international media attention from *Transworld Skateboarding* magazine and Mexican and Swedish magazines and newspapers, as well as numerous skateboarding websites, including other women's skateboarding websites.

The Skirtboarders produce the written and visual representations contained in the blog. Three members post most of the entries, elected by the group to perform this task on the group's behalf, and no administrator (gatekeeper) decides who can post or censors crew members' representations. Most postings are initiated by crew members, although a considerable number of respondents present themselves as young women who see the Skirtboarders as role models. The Skirtboarders also cross-post their stories and videos on numerous social networking sites (including Facebook and Twitter) and video sharing sites (including Vimeo and YouTube), where they have developed an extensive following (including almost 25,000 Facebook 'likes'). Young women who engage with the Skirtboarders through the Internet come from Quebec and elsewhere in Canada or from countries like Sweden, Mexico, the United States, England, and Vietnam.

What makes the Skirtboarders blog an interesting case for analysis? First of all, the Skirtboarders have managed to self-produce and distribute representations of female skateboarders on the site on their own terms, without bending to mainstream media conventions, for example modelling their coverage after other female skateboard media coverage primarily to sell a product (Beal & Wilson 2004). They have also deliberately constituted themselves as 'ethical subjects'

Spreading the Skirtboarder stoke 125

and, perhaps most importantly, have constructed and circulated a wider collective identity (Taylor & Whittier 1992) that could prompt young women who access and interact with their blog to become (more) engaged in the movement to promote skateboarding among women.

Using third-wave politics to create and spread fluid femininities

The Skirtboarders explicitly state in various places on the blog that they want to challenge certain aspects of skateboarding culture and representation. Mary Celeste Kearney (2006, p. 13) noted:

> recognizing that what is represented in commercial popular culture has little to do with their identities and experiences, many girl [and young women] media producers rely on the practices of appropriation and *détournement* [emphasis in original] to reconfigure commercial cultural artifacts into personalized creations that speak more directly to their concerns, needs, fantasies and pleasures, a practice bell hooks refers to as 'talking back' and relates to the politics of liberation.

However, they do not explicitly identify themselves as feminists or state any specific political goal that involves promoting certain forms of femininity on their blog. Although the Skirtboarders do not explicitly claim to have a political agenda for the blog, they nonetheless make a political statement through the discursive constructions they circulate. The fact that the Skirtboarders turned to the Web to self-represent and to fill a void says something about their position on gender relations within skateboarding culture.

Furthermore, the findings of the blog discourse analysis suggest that in photos, videos, and the way they write about themselves on their blog, the Skirtboarders embrace various femininities and, at the same time, reject binaries of male/female, exemplifying what Dayna Daniels (2009) describes as 'polygenderedness'. Daniels claimed that the concept of gender is created socially and culturally and calls for recognition and a celebration of the polygendered nature of individuals (especially girls and women). In other words, we all, to some extent, embody 'a mix of those characteristics, interests, behaviours and appearances that have been traditionally used to sort females and males into exclusive categories called feminine and masculine' (pp. 1–2). Given that polygendered subjectivity is a site of disunity and conflict produced through a whole range of embodied masculinities and femininities and is therefore never fixed or coherent, Daniels encouraged people to allow others (and ourselves) to self-express and self-identify in terms of masculinity and femininity as they (we) please.

On the Skirtboarders blog, numerous action photos (with no accompanying captions) depict skateboarders mid-trick wearing loose t-shirts (with no bra straps showing) and long hair not tied back or under baseball caps. The lack of signs of

126 *Steph MacKay*

overt femininity (and masculinity) may lead some users to conclude these skateboarders are men. Others would 'see' women. The complexity in reaching a conclusion about whether the skateboarders in the photos are male or female suggests that the Skirtboarders' photos are polysemic, in that they have a number of meanings, interpretations, or understandings. These representations of fluid gender performances depart significantly from representations of female skateboarders in mainstream and niche media (see Beal & Wilson 2004).

Furthermore, the women do not explicitly identify crew member gender in their blog and rarely establish heterosexuality by references to a crew member's romantic relationships. They also rarely emphasize female stereotypes, compare their performance to that of men, or post ambivalent materials. In fact, they often challenge female sporting stereotypes (such as giggling, hugging, and crying) in the blog. For example, the Skirtboarders spit and fart in videos of skateboarding sessions and gorge on nachos and other food in photos, behaviours that do not fit with representations of stereotypical femininity described by Neal Christopherson, Michelle Janning, and Eileen Diaz McConnell (2002) in their study of how the media constructs or promotes certain gender ideologies through the 1999 soccer World Cup. The Skirtboarders occasionally reproduce some of the normative discursive fragments commonly found in media representations, such as images of them with long hair, long painted nails, jewellery, and tight jeans, which could be read as an emphasis on femininity, or when they ambivalently post photos of themselves in bikinis. They also post links to mainstream and niche media coverage of their crew, which in most cases perpetuate the 'problems' of historical media coverage, such as marginalization, (hetero) sexualization, and trivialization. However, they rarely express approval or disapproval of how this coverage represents them.

Despite the occasional reproduction of some dominant discursive constructions of skateboarding women found in mainstream and niche media representations, most of the Skirtboarders' online productions portray them as polygendered skaters. This is a radical departure from other media representations. The circulation of paradoxical discursive constructions in which young women embrace various femininities (including sexualized versions) and at the same time reject binaries (male/female) reflects a third-wave (or at least a new kind of) feminist approach. Indeed, scholars (Harris 2008) have suggested that younger women have developed new feminisms that complicate the contradiction between persistent sexism and increased opportunities for women. Holly Thorpe (2008) notes that while second-wave feminist researchers argue that the sexualisation of female athletes reduces women to docile bodies for the consumption of the male gaze, young women today often applaud sports media representations of feminine physical attractiveness. They do not view 'feminine' and 'sporting' as mutually exclusive identities but rather as inextricably intertwined. The Skirtboarders' blog, though somewhat paradoxical, supports the notion that young women can transform their own experiences by creating and circulating representations that contain the 'potential beginnings of an altered subjectivity, an altered identity' (Holland et al. 1998, p. 18).

Blogging reflexively: the Skirtboarders as ethical subjects

The way that the Skirtboarders produce, circulate, and use feminist materials differs radically from other mainstream and niche media sources. In this way, they expand the space occupied by girls and women in the Internet skateboarding landscape. But do they accomplish this reflexively? Findings from the interviews with crew members suggest that, unlike a disciplined subject who spontaneously and unthinkingly takes up and reproduces discursive constructions of gender circulating in media, the Skirtboarders consciously and strategically create themselves as alternative skateboarding women (and thus as ethical subjects).[17]

For example, during interviews, the Skirtboarders confirmed that the creation and circulation of alternative discursive fragments about skateboarding and gender on their blog are not accidental. Prior to the crew's formation and the blog's creation, these women were aware of the socially constructed codes of gender conduct reinforced by power relations. They also knew that they had some flexibility within these codes to construct and ultimately represent themselves on their blog. As noted by Shauna Pomerantz, Dawn Currie, and Deirdre Kelly (2004) and Alana Young (2004), this critical awareness of gender norms is not uncommon among female skateboarders, known for challenging forms of femininity they disagree with. With respect to the Skirtboarders' crew and blog, co-founder of the blog and crew Mathilde Pigeon[18] (pers. comm., 19 February 2011) stressed that a central goal of the Skirtboarders (and their blog) is to represent skateboarding women as a diverse group of sportswomen who express a variety of femininities both on and off a skateboard. In fact, all eight of the Skirtboarders interviewed suggested that they are not coherent, stable, rational selves but rather an embodiment of what Rhiannon Bury (2005) calls 'interdiscursive collision'. Interdiscursive collision speaks to Judith Butler's (1990, p. 97) argument that 'gender ought not to be construed as a stable identity or a locus of agency from which various acts follow; rather gender is an identity tenuously constituted in time, instituted in an exterior space through a stylized repetition of acts'. Therefore, gender discourses (both dominant and alternative) offer subject positions, which may or may not be taken up or refused. According to Butler (p. 97–98),

> the possibilities of gender transformation are to be found precisely in the arbitrary relation between such acts, in the possibility of a failure to repeat, a de-formity or a parodic repetition that exposes the phantasmatic effect of abiding identity as a politically tenuous construction.[19]

The Skirtboarders recognized that they did not have to take up and perform the dominant discourse of gendered (hetero) sexuality. Instead, they transformed their skateboarding lifestyle into a site (for women, at least) where femininity, masculinity, and polygenderedness are acceptable on and off a skateboard. Over time, they also claimed that their feminine identities changed both on and off the skateboard, confirming that they understand the complex and fluid aspects of gender.

Interviews further suggest that the Skirtboarders aspire to become engaged female skateboarders (although crew members defined 'engaged' in different

128 *Steph MacKay*

ways) and to set an example for other young women. Their blog work, which challenges dominant discursive media constructions of skateboarding women, attempts to move them closer to this way of being. For some, this means using the blog (as well as complex and fluid representations of femininity) to actively promote involvement by girls and women in the skateboarding world. For others, it means *doing* (i.e., skateboarding), maintaining a public profile, and meeting other skateboarding women. Ultimately, the interviews suggest that the Skirtboarders' collective goal is to challenge the gender order in the skateboarding mediascape by circulating alternative discourses *and* by getting more girls and women on skateboards (i.e., participating). Thus, they are reflexively attempting to counter the effects that the (hetero) sexualization and trivialization of female skateboarders in media representations purportedly creates.

Building a collective female skateboarding identity through blogging

A thorough appraisal of the Skirtboarders' case thus far suggests that these women are reflexively offering alternatives to persistently sexist mainstream and niche media representations of female skateboarders by creating and posting stories that express a variety of femininities (both on and off a skateboard). In so doing, they are creating a polygendered Skirtboarder identity. Through comments on the blog and in interviews, users confirmed that they are also constructing a larger collective identity through this Web project. According to Verta Taylor and Nancy Whittier (1992), collective identities are negotiated and built through the symbolic and everyday actions used by subordinate groups to resist existing systems of domination. Blog comments from non–self-identified Skirtboarders suggest that the Skirtboarders are achieving their goals of representing skateboarding women differently than elsewhere in the skateboarding mediascape by challenging feminine codes that constrain the practice of skateboarding. Users felt that this endeavour ultimately establishes a community where skateboarding women (disenfranchised by sexist media representations) can virtually congregate and advocate for a collective female skateboarding identity that openly challenges gender constructions. Additionally, users felt that the blog highlights young women having fun and forming communities centred on their participation in physical activity. It motivates users to either start or continue to pursue skateboarding. In blog comments and interviews, the Skirtboarders were celebrated for reflexively advancing the female skateboarding 'movement' (term used by numerous blog users on the blog and in interviews).

The story of Skirtboarder Roux is a particularly interesting example of a user who intensified her skateboarding (practice) because of the gender identities circulated on the blog (representation). Roux claims that without the blog, she would not have taken up skateboarding as a lifestyle and would certainly not have become a Skirtboarder, a significant identity for her today. Prior to accessing the website, she skateboarded occasionally with boys in her neighbourhood and with one female friend but was afraid to go to skateparks and did not identify

Spreading the Skirtboarder stoke 129

as a skateboarder. She said her life changed after discovering the blog. She contacted crew members, began skateboarding with them at local parks, was invited to continue skateboarding with them, eventually joined the crew, and now proudly adopts and expresses the Skirtboarder identity. Roux suggested that the blog inspires young women not only to skateboard but also to gather together for other sporting and non-sporting activities that may challenge gender discourses.

Ultimately, the interviewees felt that the best way to embrace the collective female skateboarding identity and become actors in the female skateboarding 'movement' was not to spend time on representational sites like the Skirtboarders' blog or try to become a Skirtboarder. They preferred to actively challenge oppressive, male-dominated milieus like skateparks by getting on their boards and skateboarding. Indeed, some scholars claim that women have always been considered 'intruders' in masculine territories like skateparks, beaches, and cliff-jumping areas (Kelly, Pomerantz, & Currie 2008; Laurendeau 2004; Wheaton 2004). To encourage more girls and young women to participate and to counteract this territorialism, some users supported strategies such as opening up parks for women-only sessions, while others suggested running women-only clinics and contests and inviting role models like the Skirtboarders to skateparks to meet girls and women, a practice the Skirtboarders have followed since the crew's formation. However, they also felt that more positive media representations of female skateboarders were necessary in order to challenge the current gender skateboarding culture. Therefore, they viewed the blog (and the collective identity circulated on it) as one of many political strategies for changing the global female skateboarding landscape.

Spreading the Skirtboarder stoke – conclusions

The Skirtboarders' blog is a powerful community media innovation, facilitated by digital media technologies, that spreads the Skirtboarders stoke. This consists of a love of skateboarding that celebrates fluid sporting femininities and promotes the construction of new female skateboarding identities. This analysis shows that the blog is, indeed, a public space where skateboarding women can voice alternative, discursive constructions of gender identity by creating and posting personal stories that would otherwise be marginalized in the mainstream and niche media. Furthermore, through a process that Foucault (1986) referred to as ethical conduct, involving intentional work to subject oneself to a moral code of conduct, the Skirtboarders consciously constructed a 'Skirtboarder' identity as well as a collective female skateboarding identity. This suggests that women are using the Internet in ways that enable collaboration, social activity, critical thought, democratic action, and, ultimately, individual and collective identity building. The Skirtboarders and non-Skirtboarder blog users understand that the Internet is one of many political tools for constructing alternative gender identities while contending that the physical practice of skateboarding is equally if not more important for change to occur.

In their analysis of photos in female sports magazines, Marie Hardin, Susan Lynn, and Kristie Walsdorf (2005, p. 115) suggested that the emergence of

130   *Steph MacKay*

female-only sports media texts 'signals an emergent discourse about women and sport that has the potential to make "gender trouble" in ways that will chip away at male hegemony'. Other scholars claim the opposite (Shade 2002; Worthington 2005), that cyberspace has not been an empowering space for women. One reason is that endeavours such as the Skirtboarders' blog (i.e., when women create their own sports media) leave male-dominated structures unchallenged. For example, in her analysis of the relationship young women have to snowboarding media, Thorpe, (2005, p. 94), noted that

> while women only magazines, films and competitions see positive steps toward female equality, in reality, separatist endeavours actually let the big brother structures avoid social responsibility in terms of the moral requirement publishers, filmmakers and organizers have to accommodate and represent women . . . [and allowing them to] justify their male-exclusive approaches.

The Skirtboarders and Skirtboarder blog users are aware of the representational and practical struggles that female skateboarders face and are committed to joining the 'movement' to challenge the current system. Female skateboarders have not yet been able to convince those involved in producing 'real' niche sport media and events to represent them differently. However, if women continue to turn to the Internet to self-represent and actively choose to consume community media produced by other women rather than mainstream or niche media produced by corporations and other (usually male) community members, the skateboarding world will have to change. Representations of skateboarding women that deviate from the 'rules' of the current discursive landscape will have to be included alongside representations of skateboarding men. This will challenge male-dominated institutions, such as mainstream and niche skateboarding media organizations, and ultimately open up spaces for women to participate in predominantly masculine sports (like skateboarding) in new and exciting ways.

Notes

1. Foucault (1969) argued that dominant discourses are constructed within our societies by 'experts' such as government departments, scientific bodies, and so forth. The statements (also known as constructions, fragments, or strands) that make up these discourses underpin what is considered 'commonsense knowledge', and the circulation and repetition of these constructions is what produces us as subjects.
2. See Antunovic and Hardin (2013) and Thorpe (2008).
3. Skateboarding features in mainstream media are produced for a mass audience by non-skateboarding journalists and producers who often have little knowledge of skateboarding culture.
4. Reinhart (2005, p. 234) defined mainstream sports as those 'that have been embraced by spectators and participants alike . . . are taught in the schools, that run through a patriarchal culture to such an extent that both terminology and attire deriving from those sports remain unremarkable to casual observers'. By contrast, lifestyle sports (which have been referred to in both academic and popular discourse as extreme or

Spreading the Skirtboarder stoke 131

alternative) consist of a range of primarily individualized activities such as surfing, skateboarding, snowboarding, parkour, wakeboarding, rock climbing, B.A.S.E. jumping, and kite surfing. Researchers coined the term 'lifestyle sports' based on their findings that members of the cultures themselves defined what they do as 'a lifestyle' rather than as a sport practiced in a specific time and space. However, some scholars (e.g., Wheaton, 2013) question whether there is, in fact, a rigid dichotomy between mainstream and lifestyle sports.

5. Niche skateboarding media tend to be created by journalists, editors, photographers, and filmmakers who are or were active skateboarders. These media are not necessarily centered on profit making but reach a relatively wide audience compared to 'community media'. Niche media that communicate skateboarding discourses and cultural knowledge are the most instrumental in skateboarder identity building.

6. Cyberfeminists are feminists critically examining the relationship between gender and digital culture, such as Bury (2005), Consalvo and Paasonen (2002), Gajjalla (2009), and Passonen (2005).

7. Such as Antunovic and Hardin (2013), Hardin (2011), and MacKay and Dallaire (2013b).

8. Such as websites, blogs, Twitter, and Facebook. See Olive (2012) and Pavlidis and Fullagar (2013).

9. Blogs (or weblogs) allow bloggers (blog writers) to post regularly dated entries, often including opinions, journal entries, or commentary.

10. Each of these angles is written about in more depth in MacKay and Dallaire (2013a, 2013b, 2014).

11. A total of 262 blog posts (including photos, videos, and 1,128 user comments) from March 2007 to May 2010 were analyzed.

12. Digitally recorded interview material with twelve women (eight 'core' Skirtboarders and four users) was gathered between August 2010 and September 2011 and included in the analysis. Users ranged in age from eighteen to twenty-seven years, lived in different geographical locations (one in Hanoi, Vietnam, three in Ottawa, Canada), maintained different relationships with the blog (e.g., one woman visited the blog daily while three others visited monthly), and different skateboarding lifestyles (e.g., two women identified as skateboarders and two as former skateboarders). All interview participants self-identified as female. All of the Skirtboarders were white (as identified by the researcher), and two of the users were white. The other users were Vietnamese and Asian-Canadian (unverified). This reflects Brayton's (2005) assertion that while skateboarding may offer opportunities for challenging the normativity of whiteness, structural barriers still make entry more difficult for some than for others. Although the women were not explicitly asked about their class backgrounds, it would seem from their education levels and employment histories that they belong to the 'professional middle class' (Fletcher 2008). Ultimately, the perceived primarily white, middle-class classification of the women interviewed is consistent with Wheaton's (2004) demographic profile of lifestyle sport participants.

13. As advocated by Smith Maguire (2008), the discursive analysis extended beyond a simple categorization of a priori constructions that confirmed or challenged 'truths' about sportswomen circulating in mainstream and niche media; it also attended to the Skirtboarders' emergent discursive constructions of gender (e.g., gender play).

14. For example, Consalvo and Paasonen (2002).

15. Including Gilchrist and Wheaton (2013).

16. While thirteen of the fifteen women featured in the Skirtboarders.com blog photos appear to be white, visual representations of their tours to Mexico, for instance, do

132 *Steph MacKay*

trouble the predominant whiteness of their skateboarding media production and of larger skateboarding culture. Nevertheless, their Web project, which strategically reproduces a variety of feminine identities, opening up the potential for various gender skateboarding performances, does nothing to challenge the whiteness of skateboarding. In this sense, it resembles media portrayals of male skateboarders that reinforce the privileged position of white men (Yochim 2010).

17. The Skirtboarders do this through their engagement in the four aspects that Foucault (1986) suggested frame the task of ethics. For a detailed explanation of how Foucault's framework was adapted to understand how the Skirtboarders engage in ethical constitution, see MacKay and Dallaire (2013b).

18. Mathilde, who is thirty years old and a co-founder of both the blog and the crew, wrote most of the blog posts, filmed and edited most of the videos, and took many of the photographs between May 2007 and September 2011. She directed *Skirtboarders, Le Film*, released in 2007, the Skirtboarders all-female skateboarding video and the first of its kind in Canada and among the first worldwide. She also managed all of the Skirtboarders' media requests and emails and acted as the Skirtboarders' 'gatekeeper' (media outlets and others who wanted to connect with the Skirtboarders outside the blog had to contact Mathilde). She dedicated herself to promoting female skateboarders and the Skirtboarders in particular, often focusing more on producing blog material than on her own skateboarding. The Skirtboarders have used their names and/or posted photos or other identifying personal information on the Internet and were advised at the outset of this research project that their anonymity could not be guaranteed, since the readers of texts arising from this research might be able to identify individuals from their interview responses. The Skirtboarders interviewed agreed to be named in the research.

19. It should be noted that social groups and individuals do not all have equivalent opportunities to challenge gender discourses. The act of challenging dominant discourses is contingent of the historical moment and location as well as a person's other identities such as class, race, ethnicity, ability, and so on. The Skirtboarders' social positions in the 'professional middle class' may make it more possible for them to challenge gender discourses than other girls and women.

References

Antunovic, D & Hardin, M 2013, 'Women and the blogosphere: exploring feminist approaches to sport', *International Review for the Sociology of Sport*, vol. 34, no. 1, pp. 1–17.

Azzarito, L 2010, 'Future girls, transcendent femininities and new pedagogies: toward girls' hybrid bodies?', *Sport, Education and Society*, vol. 15, no. 3, pp. 261–275.

Batra, ND 2008, *Digital freedom*, Rowman & Littlefield, Plymouth, UK.

Beal, B & Wilson, C 2004, "Chicks dig scars': commercialisation and the transformation of skateboarders' identities', in B Wheaton (ed), *Understanding lifestyle sports: consumption, identity and difference*, Routledge, Thousand, New York, pp. 31–54.

Bernstein, A 2002, 'Is it time for a victory lap? Changes in the media coverage of women in sport', *International Review for the Sociology of Sport*, vol. 37, no. 3/4, pp. 415–428.

Brayton, S 2005, "Black-lash': revisiting the 'White Negro' through skateboarding', *Sociology of Sport*, vol. 22, no. 2, pp. 356–372.

Bury, R 2005, *Cyberspaces of their own: female fandoms online*, Peter Lang, New York.

Butler, J 1990, *Gender trouble: feminism and the subversion of identity*, Routledge, New York.

Spreading the Skirtboarder stoke 133

Christopherson, N, Janning, M & Diaz McConnell, E 2002, 'Two kicks forward, one kick back: a content analysis of media discourses on the 1999 women's World Cup soccer championship', *Sociology of Sport Journal*, vol. 19, no. 2, pp. 170–188.

Consalvo, M & Paasonen, S (eds) 2002, *Women and everyday uses of the Internet: agency and identity*, Peter Lang, New York.

Daniels, D 2009, *Polygendered and ponytailed: the dilemma of femininity and the female athlete*, Women's Press, Toronto, Canada.

Donnelly, P, MacNeill, M & Knight, G 2008, *Enough, already! A comment on gender representation research*. Unpublished manuscript.

Donnelly, M 2008, '"Take the slam and get back up": hardcore candy and the politics of representation in girls and women's skateboarding and snowboarding on television', in MD Giardina & MK Donnelly (eds), *Youth culture and sport*, Routledge, New York, pp. 127–146.

Eastman, ST & Billings, AC 2000, 'Sportscasting and sports reporting: the power of gender bias', *Journal of Sport and Social Issues*, vol. 24, no. 2, pp. 192–213.

Fletcher, R 2008, 'Living on the edge: the appeal of risk sports for the professional middle class', *Sociology of Sport Journal*, vol. 25, no. 3, pp. 310–330.

Foucault, M 1969, *L'archéologie du savoir [The archaeology of knowledge]*, Éditions Gallimard, Paris.

Foucault, M 1971, *L'ordre du discours [The order of discourse]*, Éditions Gallimard, Paris.

Foucault, M 1986, *The history of sexuality. Volume 2: the use of pleasure*, First Vintage Books, New York.

Gajjala, R 2009, 'Response to Shani Orgad', in AM Markham & NK Baym (eds), *Internet inquiry*, Sage, Thousand Oaks, CA, pp. 61–68.

Gilchrist, P & Wheaton, B 2013, 'New media technologies in lifestyle sport', in B Hutchins & D Rower (eds), *Digital media sport: technology and power in the network society*, Routledge, New York and Abingdon, UK, pp. 169–185.

Hardin, M 2011, 'The power of a fragmented collective: radical pluralist feminism and technologies of the self in the sports blogosphere', in A Billings (ed), *Sports media: transformation, integration, consumption*, Routledge, New York, NY, and UK, pp. 40–60.

Hardin, M, Lynn, S & Walsdorf, K 2005, 'Challenge and conformity on "contested terrain": images of women in four women's sport/fitness magazines', *Sex Roles*, vol. 5, no. 1/2, pp. 105–117.

Harris, A 2008, 'Introduction', In A Harris (eds), *Next wave cultures: feminism, subcultures, activism*, Routledge, New York, pp. 1–16.

Henderson, M 2001, 'A shifting line up: men, women, and *Tracks* surfing magazine', *Continuum: Journal of Media and Cultural Studies*, vol. 15, no. 3, pp. 319–332.

Holland, D, Lachicotte, W, Skinner, D & Cain, C 1998, *Agency and identity in cultural worlds*, Harvard University Press, Cambridge, MA.

Kearney, MC, 2006, *Girls make media*, Routledge, London.

Kelly, DM, Pomerantz, S & Currie, DH 2008, '"You can break so many more rules": the identity work and play of becoming a Skater Girl', in MD Giardina & MK Donnelly (eds), *Youth culture and sport*, Routledge, New York, pp. 113–125.

Koivula, N 1999, 'Gender stereotyping in televised media sport coverage', *Sex Roles*, vol. 41, no. 7, pp. 589–604.

Laurendeau, J 2004, 'The "Crack Choir" and the "Cock Chorus": the intersection of gender and sexuality in skydiving texts', *Sociology of Sport Journal*, vol. 21, no. 4, pp. 397–417.

Leonard, DJ 2009, 'New media and global sporting cultures: moving beyond the clichés and binaries', *Sociology of Sport Journal*, vol. 26, no. 1, pp. 1–16.

134 *Steph MacKay*

MacKay, S & Dallaire, C 2013a, 'Skirtboarder net-a-narratives: young women creating their own skateboarding (re)presentations', *International Review for the Sociology of Sport*, vol. 48, no. 2, pp. 171–195.

MacKay, S & Dallaire, C 2013b, 'Skirtboarders.com: skateboarding women and self formation as ethical subjects', *Sociology of Sport Journal*, vol. 30, no. 2, pp. 173–196.

MacKay, S & Dallaire, C 2014, 'Skateboarding women: building collective identity in cyberspace', *Journal of Sport and Social Issues*, vol. 38, no. 6, pp. 548–566.

Olive, R 2012, '"Making friends with the neighbours": blogging as research method', *International Journal of Cultural Studies*, vol. 16, no. 1, pp. 78–84.

Paasonen, S 2005, *Figures of fantasy: Internet, women and cyberdiscourse*, Peter Lang, New York.

Pavlidis, A & Fullagar, S 2013, 'Becoming roller derby grrrls: exploring the gendered play of affect in mediated sport cultures', *International Review for the Sociology of Sport*, vol. 48, no. 6, pp. 673–688.

Pirinen, R 1997, 'Catching up with men? Finnish newspaper coverage of women's entry into traditionally male sports', *International Review of the Sociology of Sport*, vol. 32, no. 3, pp. 239–249.

Pomerantz, S, Currie, DH & Kelly, DM 2004, 'Sk8er girls: skateboarders, girlhood, and feminism in motion', *Women's Studies International Forum*, vol. 27, no. 5/6, pp. 547–557.

Porter, NL 2003, *Female skateboarders and their negotiation of space and identity*, Masters thesis, Concordia University.

Reinhart, R 2005, '"Babes" and boards: opportunities in new millennium sport?', *Journal of Sport and Social Issues*, vol, 29, no. 3, pp. 232–255.

Ross, K 2010, *Gendered media*, Rowman & Littlefield Publishers, Plymouth, UK.

Shade, LR 2002, *Gender and community in the social construction of the Internet*, Peter Lang, New York.

Smith Maguire, J 2008, 'Leisure and the obligation of self-work: an examination of the fitness field', *Leisure Studies*, vol. 27, no. 1, pp. 59–75.

Spowart, L, Burrows, L & Shaw, S 2010, '"I just eat, sleep and dream of surfing": when surfing meets motherhood', *Sport in Society*, vol. 1, no. 7–8, pp. 1186–1203.

Taylor, V & Whittier, NE 1992, 'Collective identity in social communities: lesbian feminist mobilization', in AD Morris & C McClurg Mueller (eds), *Frontiers in social movement theory*, Yale University Press, New Haven, CT, pp. 104–129.

Thorpe, H 2005, 'Jibbing the gender order: females in the snowboarding culture,' *Sport in Society*, vol. 8, no. 1, pp. 76–100.

Thorpe, H 2008, 'Foucault, technologies of the self and the media: discourses of femininity in snowboarding culture', *Journal of Sport and Social Issues*, vol. 32, no. 2, pp. 199–229.

Weedon, C 1997, *Feminist practice and poststructuralist theory*, Blackwell Publishing, Malden, MA.

Wensing, EH & Bruce, T 2003, 'Bending the rules: media representations of gender during an international sporting event', *International Review for the Sociology of Sport*, vol. 38, no. 4, pp. 387–396.

Wheaton, B 2004, 'Introduction: mapping the lifestyle sport-scape', in B Wheaton (ed), *Understanding lifestyle sports: consumption, identity and difference*, Routledge, New York, pp. 1–28.

Wheaton, B 2009, 'The cultural politics of lifestyle sport (re)visited: beyond white male lifestyles', in J Ormond & B Wheaton (eds), *On the edge: leisure, consumption and the representation of adventure sport*, vol. 104, Leisure Studies Association, Eastbourne, pp. 131–160.

Wheaton, B 2013, *The cultural politics of lifestyle sports*, Routledge, Abingdon, UK.

Wilson, B 2007, 'New media, social movements, and global sport studies: a revolutionary moment and the sociology of sport', *Sociology of Sport Journal*, vol. 24 no. 4, pp. 457–477.

Worthington, N 2005, 'Women's work on the World Wide Web: how a new medium represents a old problem', *Popular Communication*, vol. 3, no. 1, pp. 43–60.

Wright J & Clarke, G 1999, 'Sport, the media and the construction of compulsory heterosexuality: a case study of women's rugby union', *International Review for the Sociology of Sport*, vol. 34, no. 3, pp. 227–243.

Yochim, EC 2010, *Skate life: re-imagining white masculinity*, University of Michigan, Ann Arbor, Michigan, USA.

Young, A 2004, 'Being the "alternative" in an alternative subculture: gender differences in the experiences of young women and men in skateboarding and snowboarding', *Avante*, vol. 10, no. 3, pp. 69–81.

Part 3
Skate shifts

10 Skateboarding as a technology of the collective

Kona Skatepark, Jacksonville, Florida, USA

Michael J. Lorr

> Kona Skatepark is the oldest outdoor, privately owned, skatepark in the United States, and possibly the world. Kona is a legendary skatepark, and should be on every skater's list of parks to skate.
>
> *(Park info* n.d.)

This is the claim on the promotional website of the historic Kona Skatepark in Jacksonville, Florida. My first time at Kona Skatepark was in virtual reality when playing Tony Hawk's *Pro Skater 4* video game, released in 2002. My first actual visit took place on a temperate December day in 2013. At this first 'real' visit to Kona, my main purpose was to get trucks, wheels, and bearings so I could ride the new deck I had just purchased from a brewery called Revolution in my hometown, Chicago, Illinois. Also, I could finally cross Kona off my list of parks to skate.

I began skateboarding around 1989, when I was in fifth and sixth grades in a middle class suburb of Chicago. I was embedded in the skate and punk subcultures as a skatepark employee at a YMCA and as a punk rocker. At the time, skateboarding was considered a form of youthful resistance by skaters, who were doing something unsanctioned and seemingly disorganized in the built environment. The popular adolescents in junior high and high school, who played sports like football, considered skateboarding a subcultural outsider activity for their unpopular peers. Parents, police, and other agents of adult society considered skateboarding at best a nuisance and at worst a crime, punishable by arrest, fines, and hours of mandatory community service or worse. Shortly after I started skating, skateboarding began riding a wave of popularity that turned the subcultural outsider activity from an act of deviance, where to skateboard meant to risk harassment on a spectrum from teenage bullying to punishment by the criminal justice system, to a sporting activity, where to skateboard meant to practice, to be coached, and ultimately to have a shot at making big money as a professional athlete (Lorr 2005). One explanatory factor in this shift or co-optation of skateboarding from subcultural outsider activity to sport was the appearance of extreme sports in mainstream culture on cable networks like ESPN and MTV and then on broadcast television networks. Large-scale televised skate contests like the X Games, which started in 1995, tended to legitimate skating, incorporating the practice into commercial,

140   *Michael J. Lorr*

mainstream, and everyday life (Lombard 2010). Now, in 2015, skateboarding has become so normal that a diverse group of many of my students ride longboards, trick boards, and penny boards to class. Skateboarding is no longer for subcultural outsiders – everyone does it.

This chapter utilizes the recent normalization of skateboarding as a way to compare how different generations of skateboarders at Kona Skatepark conceptualize and embody their individual and collective identities. By drawing on Tia DeNora's (1999, 2000, 2011) concept of the 'technology of the self' as a resource for identity work and on William Roy and Timothy Dowd's (2010) concept of the 'technology of the collective', this chapter focuses on how skaters use skateboarding to create their individual and collective identities with emphasis on how skateboarders use the skateboard, the act of skating, and the place Kona Skatepark to construct a collective intergenerational identity. Employing two dominant modes of skateboarding practice for exploration, street skating and park skating, illustrates the similarities and differences between generations. This approach helps us understand how the practices of skateboarding operate and consider how social interactions constitute emerging individual and collective identities. This chapter pinpoints how skateboarding works as an iterative intergenerational 'technology of the collective' by focusing on skateboarding practices, thereby contributing to the ongoing dialogue about how practice and identity matter to individuals and communities.

Shifting subcultural/normal individual/collective identities and practices

Michael Brooke's (1999) brief history of skateboarding gives context to the subculture's connections to surfing subculture, skateboarding's normalization, and the formation of individual and collective identities by identifying skateboarding history as a succession of waves. According to Brooke, the first wave of skateboarding grew in 1959 to 1965. In this era, skateboards were fad items like the hula-hoop and were usually created in a do-it-yourself fashion by youth themselves. The second wave took place from 1973 to 1980. During the second wave, skateboarding became more common, but this wave broke when many private skateparks had to close due to the high insurance rates needed to keep them open and lack of youth interest in the activity. Skateboarding receded further from the mainstream during its third wave in 1983 to 1991. 'Skate and destroy' became the mantra and identity of this wave of skating, and street skating became the preferred form of skate practice. With no place of their own, skaters went into the streets, solidifying their individual and collective identities as subcultural outsiders due to skaters' multiple run-ins with authorities for disrupting and inconveniencing pedestrians and automobile drivers anywhere there was pavement. The fourth wave of skateboarding started in 1993 and crested in the early 2000s, leaving in its wake a new mainstream and commercial identity for individuals and the collective group. The individual and collective identity shift that took place during this era was manufactured in part by the greater prevalence of extreme

Skateboarding as a technology of the collective 141

sports on televised cable stations like ESPN and on broadcast stations like PBS, FOX, CBS, NBC, and ABC. This shift in individual and collective identity was also encouraged by an influx of many new skaters. The previous generation of third-wave skaters called many of these new skaters 'groms'.[1] The influx of new skaters into the subculture and the desire of commercial interests to make money from these 'newbies' began to turn skateboarding away from its subcultural outsider status and identity to becoming a pastime similar to football, baseball, or any other mainstream sport. In many ways, when this fourth wave receded, it left in its wake a much higher tidal level of interest in skateboarding across mainstream Western culture.

Many people draw on physical activities, like skateboarding, as resources to construct their individual and collective identities. Prior to 1991, individuals and collectives involved in the practice of skateboarding constructed and embodied a subcultural outsider identity. However, starting in the early 1990s and continuing with greater intensity well into the 2000s, individuals and collectives started to shift the practice of skateboarding to construct and embody a 'normal' mainstream commercialized identity. Studying this phenomenon within skateboarding helps us understand how individual and collective physical practices interactively mediate between subcultural, oppositional identities and more normalized and mainstream identities. Skateboarding practices can be understood as both a technology of the self and of the collective, as a resource and socializing medium through which to learn socially constructed modes of intergenerational identity and conduct comportment, and the cultural configuration of people's social worlds (DeNora 1999, 2000, 2011; Hancock & Lorr 2013).

To skateboard is to construct an individual and collective identity. The technology of this identity-construction process is the skateboard itself and the application of this technology to the body in the form of falling and skinning knees and elbows, learning new tricks, being chased out of parking garages, or encouraged by parents in a skatepark and sharing this practice with others who skate. To address these matters, I discuss two central skateboarding practices based on twenty-five years of participant observation of skateboarding subculture and one year of intensive participant observation and interviews at Kona Skatepark. First, I describe and analyze the third-wave skaters' predominant interest in and practice of street skating. Secondly, I similarly describe and analyze the fourth-wave skaters' predominant interest in and practice of park skating, while at the same time problematizing the interactions between these waves of skaters and identifying the ways they construct a new intergenerational collective identity.

The third wave: 1990s old-school street skaters

When I bought my skate supplies and was having my deck set up, the current owners of Kona, Marty Ramos[2] and his wife, were the ones behind the counter. Kona has been in Ramos's family since it opened in 1977. Marty and his wife have been taking care of Kona for about sixteen years or so. In their role as proprietors of Kona, the Ramoses have also become stewards of the Jacksonville

142 *Michael J. Lorr*

skate community. Marty grew up skating – doing the family business. He became a professional skateboarder as a part of that process. After that, he moved away from Jacksonville for school and then moved back from Colorado. During our interview, Marty (2013, pers. comm., 26 December) said,

> I fell into . . . well I really grew up into the family business. It's really cool because I have such a history with this place that I see parents skate with their kids and sometimes I even see grandparents skate with their kids and their grandkids. Skating here has become important over the past couple of generations. It is really meaningful beyond us being in the Tony Hawk Pro-Skater video game.

Clearly, Marty understands the opportunity he has as the proprietor of Kona Skatepark to witness the culture and practice of skateboarding. He also understands the importance of the role he holds in the skateboarding and wider communities as a role model to new skaters and as an ambassador of skateboarding.

Marty, confirming his role as an ambassador of skateboarding, told me,

> There were some pretty lean years as a skatepark in the late 1980s and early 1990s before skateboarding really hit it big in the mid 1990s and on. We only survived then because of a small group of rollerbladers. Most of the skateboarders were really into street skating at that time. And as you can see now even with the promotion provided by the inclusion of our park in the Tony Hawk video game, we are at the whim of what kids see as popular, cool, and edgy.
>
> (Marty Ramos, 2013, pers. comm., 26 December)

Marty acknowledges that when he began skating, street skating was the most prominent skating practice, but since his family owned Kona, Marty was able to park skate more than the average third-wave skater. Marty is elucidating the cyclical conditions of co-optation that Thomas Frank outlines in *The Conquest of Cool* (1997, p. 9): 'If American capitalism can be said to have spent the 1950s dealing in conformity and consumer fakery, during the decade that followed, it would offer the public authenticity, individuality, difference, and rebellion'. The processes Ramos and Frank highlight illustrate how people in a consumer society make skateboarding their own, incorporating and perpetuating that practice as a technology of self and collective. A part of the process of making a technology of the self your own is to make it normal, to turn it into a technology of the larger set of collective everyday practices. Failing to do that, the practice dissipates or may disappear completely until it is rediscovered by a new generation.

Nineties-style street skating looks abnormal, like a pack of wild youth 'ollying' and falling all over public streets, sidewalks, parking lots, stairwells, and alleyways. Many of the skaters growing up during this generation embraced the outsider activity's anarchist stylistic tendency both physically and in their fashion. Many street skaters see themselves and the way they practice skating as a form of oppositional identity. Chris (2014, pers. comm., 28 February), a thirty-seven-year-old male Asian third-wave skateboarder, suggested in our interview that

> Yes, it is resistance and rebellion. You're not doing what everyone else is doing and you do it for the love, not for the corporate career – to go against 'corporateness' is very threatening to certain mainstream segments of the public.

Similarly, another 'old-school' nineties skateboarder, Jessie (2014, pers. comm., 7 May), a thirty-five-year-old white female, said, 'by street skating you are destroying the corporate structures – literally the concrete planters, benches, stairs, and other forms of corporate art – of society'. Many street skaters see their practice as a form of resistance and rebellion to some extent, even if it is just because it rubs certain people the wrong way. But as these nineties skaters had more frequent interactions with an angry public, business owners, and law enforcement, they became more interested in park spaces and other less illicit places to practice their activity. Marty and others argue that this is what makes Kona special. It is a place that embraces the original oppositional impulse of street skateboarders by offering a substantial variable street section, providing a relatively safe place, and space to cultivate a simulacrum of street skating practice away from the multiple hassles faced by third wavers attempting to skate in the streets.

Dick Hebdige's seminal work *Subculture: The Meaning of style* (1979), finds that subcultures are resistant to mainstream culture as a kind of experiential bricolage meant to subvert boredom, the sad reality of the marketing and high cost of fun in a capitalist society. He explains that bricolage 'is the way in which commodities are used in a subculture which mark the subculture off from more orthodox cultural formations' (p. 103). The skateboard reveals the skateboarder's 'secret' identity while at the same time communicating its and the owner's forbidden meanings. This interpretation meshes well with the way many nineties third-wave skaters talk about why they began skating. As illustrated in our interview, John (2014, pers. comm., 9 April), a now thirty-eight-year-old white male skateboarder from the third-wave 'skate and destroy' era, says,

> I got into skateboarding because it was a way for me to express my angst at normal school oriented activities like football and all that 'jock', 'preppie' garbage. Skateboarding is fun, healthy exercise, anti-authority and after paying for the board was mostly free. What more could you want?

Adding to the contradictions and double meaning of the practice and identity formation involved in skateboarding, Hebdige (1979, p. 77), like Stan Cohen (1972), contends that subcultures provide 'magical solutions' to social problems. In such an analysis, skateboarding can provide an activity for bored youth, a safety valve for disgruntled teens to blow off steam instead of doing anything more politically threatening, which might partially explain the resistant yet accommodating apolitical stance skateboarders take.

144 *Michael J. Lorr*

Still, many street skaters feel that they embody a type of oppositional identity both individually and collectively. At least while they are actively street skating, skateboarders effectively do not participate in the normal operations of space, and they challenge normal conceptions of what a space should be used for and who ultimately has control over a space. Skaters yearn for stairs, ledges, planters, railings, loading docks, and untended concrete ramps of all types in the built environment. They transform this ubiquitous mundane urban concrete space into architectural 'heterotopias' – a place meant for one often mundane purpose and group, which is then repurposed in a surprising, sometimes utopian way by another group for a short period of time (Foucault 1999). Skaters create heterotopias by using the pervasive urban concrete in ways that are in direct contradiction to the original planned use of a space. Heterotopias are to architecture what bricolage is to consumer commodities for skateboarders. Office stairs for safe transportation of office workers turn into a playground for 'ollying' and otherwise tumbling through the air for a short time. The skaters' heterotopic alternate use of space creates ephemeral liberatory *frission*, the excitement and empowerment of individually and collectively changing the meaning of structures by hurtling through space on revolving wheels with friends creates a fleeting feeling of possibility and progress, of going somewhere, of creating new individual and collective identities. Third-wave skaters used the skateboard as a technology to create and embody new, subcultural, outsider identities, which were normalized later on.

One of the reasons for the staying power of Kona and other skateparks in contemporary skating is that they became safe places where skaters could organize and defend their practice of skateboarding and their individual and collective identities. In the process of nineties street skaters fighting for places of their own, they were subsumed and co-opted by governmental and corporate consumer cultures, which began to shift the individual and collective identities of skateboarding. Frank (1997, p. 27) writes that 'In its hostility to established tastes, the counterculture seemed to be preparing young people to rebel against whatever they had patronized before and to view the cycles of the new without the suspicion of earlier eras'. The same perspective can be applied to skateboarding. As a result, skateboarding found itself morphing into a 'normal' youth sport such as football, baseball, basketball, and the like. The new 'playing field' of this outsider activity turned 'sport' was the skatepark, not the street. Many of the younger skaters exposed to the sport on television via the X Games, which occurs in a skatepark setting, now see the skatepark as the 'normal' place to skate. Park skating became the embodied practice, shifting subcultural, oppositional identities towards 'normal', mainstream individual and collective identities.

Beyond the fourth wave: 2000s groms and Kona Park skaters

The third wave of skateboarding and the individual and collective identities those skaters embodied were a response to a particular time, place, and context prior to 1991, which forced skateboarders out of skateparks and into the streets. From the mid-1990s onwards, the conditions of skateboarding changed when many cities

Skateboarding as a technology of the collective 145

and local authorities moved to criminalize street skating, thereby pushing skaters into skateparks. This was the fourth wave of skateboarding. Hebdige's (1979, p. 89) notion that a subculture has 'specificity and conjuncture' or place, time, and context explains why skateboarders' individual and collective identities changed from the third wavers' street-skating generation to the fourth wavers' park-skating generation. But as we saw in the previous section, skaters' identities were more fluid than discretely subcultural or normal. Steve Redhead (1990), Andy Bennett (1999), David Muggleton (2000), and Muggleton and Rupert Weinzierl (2003) offer a postmodern and post-subculture critique of Hebdige's (1979) idea that each subculture is bound by geography or elements of style. The postmodern perspective sought to collapse subcultural oppositions, such as subculture and conventional norms, essence and appearance, style-as-resistance and style-as-fashion.

But context and social interactions are still important when it comes to skateboarding as a form of identity formation, especially because of the ways in which generational identities can meld together through the act of skating. Third-wave nineties skaters got into skating when it was at its most underground, confrontational phase and there were relatively no skateparks. Skateboarding and street skating were embodied practices used to construct and reinforce oppositional identities. In contrast, the fourth wavers got into the sport during the time when skateparks and ramp skating became the preferred 'normal' places to skate. These parks came into existence because the older skaters fought to create the parks after being accosted by police and other agents of social control. Third-wave skaters did not take this public censorship, banishment, and 'topographical evisceration' lightly (Ferrell 2001). Third-wave skaters were consistently banned from their heterotopia of the concrete world, which partially explains why so many skaters, especially the older street skaters who have already gotten in trouble with the arbiters of space and younger skaters whose parents do not want them to get in trouble, skate in parks like Kona. Iain Borden (1996) argues that street skating threatens dominant society in a conventional physical way. Skateboarders also threaten the dominant society because they use space in a similar way to the homeless, questioning the social, spatial, and economic arrangements of society. Skateboarders use architecture in a way that does not engage the economic activity of the built environment. As a result, street skaters continually face harassment by business owners and law enforcement. Borden calls the street skater experience of fines, bans, and imprisonment 'spatial censorship' (1996, 2001). Starting in the early to mid-1990s, many cities moved to criminalize skateboarding, and in response, there were many battles fought by youth and parents in Jacksonville and across the United States to build skateparks or to keep ones like Kona open. One of the more iconic and successful battles was the do-it-yourself building and maintenance of Burnside Skatepark in Portland in the 1990s, during which the builders were essentially building and maintaining the park illegally (Hamm 2010).

In Jacksonville, Marty Ramos, supporting the needs of the skateboard community, created 'old-school night' to reinvigorate the hard-core contingent of skater grandparents and parents and 'grom night' to introduce the next generations to skateboarding at Kona. These generationally specific skate nights and the

146   *Michael J. Lorr*

multigenerational skaters that skate at Kona are part of a core group of skateboarders who keep skateboarding going, both as a practice and as a kind of individual and collective identity formation. What used to be at the heart of skateboarding for the older generations of skaters at Kona was its subcultural edge, based on its performance in public street spaces. Skateboarding, to them, is a practice of resistance to the mainstream generally or specifically to the corporate manner in which society is run. In contrast, many of the fourth-wave park skaters see skating as a mainstream, commercial sport like baseball. During an interview with Tony (2014, pers. comm., 28 February), an eleven-year-old grom, he said, 'parents and teachers encourage us to skate'. Sue (2014, pers. comm., 7 May), a twelve-year-old skater, said she does it because 'people think it's cool'. Mark (2014, pers. comm., 12 March), a fourteen-year-old fourth waver, said, 'skateboarding is an all-encompassing lifestyle, just not one of rebellion or resistance. It's just fun'. Skateboarding may be a practice-based identity, but that identity viewed through the perspective and skatepark practice of fourth-wave skaters is more normal, mainstream, and commercial than compared to how past generations of street skaters embody their identity, but this identity is fluid and influenced by the old-school skaters skating at Kona.

The descriptive statements offered by the nineties third-wave street skaters mirror some of the analyses offered by Theodor Adorno and Max Horkheimer (1999) about the culture industry and Thomas Frank's (1997) critique of sixties counterculture. These arguments revolve around the notion that the culture industry places its stamp on everything. The cultural power of capitalism seeps into and commodifies practices and identities like that of skateboarding and the skater, which were once perceived by the older generation as forms of subcultural resistance. The culture industry is said to create pseudo-individuality, which creates a cycle of perpetual disappointment or a perpetual-motion machine, which ultimately creates an eternal consumer. For instance, Tim (2014, pers. comm., 9 April), a forty-five-year-old skater, said, 'groms are a manifestation of skateboarding's shift towards being mainstream and a manifestation of how society is a corporately run marketing scheme'. Skateboarding and skateboarders were once subcultural and oppositional practices and identities, and they have shifted into hollow consumer costumes anyone can buy at the online mall. The practice of skateboarding can similarly be purchased, coached, officially controlled in the confines of a skatepark, closing off the spontaneity and creativity of street skating. During another interview Steve (2014, pers. comm., 9 April), a forty-year-old skateboarder, reported,

> You will find Vans stores and other skateboard oriented shops in and around Jacksonville, Florida, reinforcing the reality of a commercial skate culture that is much more divorced from the edgier anti-authority roots of skateboarding. That's not a bad thing. It brings people in to the sport and in to Kona Skatepark and then us old skaters can teach the groms some of the other things at the heart of skateboarding culture, like underground punk and hip hop music and the general anti-authority style and perspective.

Skateboarding as a technology of the collective   147

These old-school skaters highlight that in order for there to continue to be a skateboarding culture, there needs to be some level of commercialization and yet also an infusion of some of their subcultural ideas into the younger generation of skaters. The communication that occurs between these generations of skaters at the skatepark occurs through the act and focal point of skating together.

The shift from subcultural, oppositional identities towards mainstream, commercial ones is still in process at Kona, although it was apparent that the balance has heavily shifted towards the commercial end of the spectrum. During an interview with Ken (2014, pers. comm., 8 January), a thirty-five-year-old third-wave street skater, he relayed his ambivalence towards this new generation of groms:

> [A]fter school on Fridays, maybe 4:30 or 5:00 p.m. is the worst time to be here because this is when you see what skating is becoming – the 15 year old kid, preppy-looking, dressed by his or her parents, dropped off by his or her middle to upper class parents, decked out in all the helmets and pads to practice skating as if it were a sport like any jock would play in high school. I guess somebody has to keep skating going.

Ken is identifying how the past subcultural dress of skaters has now turned into more of a 'preppy' look complete with khakis and buttoned-down cotton plaid long-sleeve shirt. While the skateboard and skating are the primary technologies of the self and collective, in this case, fashion and music are secondary technologies. In this example, the clothing and music have either been co-opted or the skaters themselves have shifted their tastes to more normalized looks.

Jane (2014, pers. comm., 12 March), another third-wave street skater, speaks to the instant rapport and camaraderie that develops across generations based on the embodied demonstration of common skating practices,

> Walking into the park and strapping on my helmet, I see the large contingent of groms. They always look at me now like I'm a ghost . . . like "really you are going to skate"? After they see me do my limited mini ramp riding abilities – 'drop in', '50–50' or sometimes '5–0 grind', 'rock 'n' roll' – they are actually mildly impressed, probably because of how old they think I am. Anyway they talk to me a little and they want to know how long I've skated and we begin to share tricks we've learned, informally coaching each other.

Jane illustrates how embodied social practice reduces the barriers between intergenerational skateboarding identities. The act of skateboarding is more critical to the creation of intergenerational identity formation than secondary technologies of the self like dress or music. The intergenerational bridge is the bodily knowledge and competence to skate.

Many of the groms I talked to at Kona have been skating from as little as two weeks to one year and three months. Johnny (2013, pers. comm., 26 December), a ten-year-old grom, told me, 'A salesman told me that skateboarding was the cool thing to do so I bought a board'. But the older groms also said that they got

148   *Michael J. Lorr*

into skating because their older brothers and uncles introduced them to the sport. This older group of skaters has been skating for at least six years, but one of the five had been skating for ten years and another has been skating for sixteen years. During an interview, Dex (2014, pers. comm., 7 May), a thirteen-year-old grom, underscored the important function that Kona plays in constructing and reconstructing his individual skater identity and his connections to skateboarding as an intergenerational collective identity:

> I began skating because there was nothing better to do. It was very fulfilling mainly because as I learned my older cousin showed me more tricks and then I showed other kids my own age how to do those tricks. I also learned what music to listen to and how to look like a skater.

These park skaters' responses reinforce the ambivalent shift between subcultural and commercial skateboarding identities. These responses further illustrate how the technology of the self and collective, the skateboard and the act of skating, are the tools by which individuals relate to one another, within and across generations. During an interview with Sean (2014, pers. comm., 28 February), a thirty-four-year-old third-wave street skater, he said,

> Yes, Kona is run like a business. But it's still better than school football, baseball, or basketball teams. How could anyone have fun being told what to do like that? Kona and park skating offer us a space to create something we have control of that's all our own – a new anti-'sporto' sport.

While many of the older skaters reported they were not happy with playing mainstream sports because that was what 'jocks' and 'preppies' did and their dislike of team sport organization, in many ways, Kona and park skating practice offer a space for an alternate type of skater organization, socialization, and individual and collective identity.

Compared to my research in the late nineties and early 2000s, the contemporary skaters at Kona Skatepark are much more intergenerational and less antagonistic towards each other (Lorr 2005). They see skateboarding as simultaneously forms of sport, the mainstream, commerce, as well as forms of subculture, oppositional identity, and anti-commercial activity. During an interview, Sue (2014, pers. comm., 9 April), a now twenty-five-year-old Hispanic female from the fourth-wave era of skateboarding, claimed,

> I got into skating because it was in all of the cartoons, movies, and television shows I watched and it was also a bad boy thing to do too. Skateboarding is just something you do when you are a kid and you have family and friends who skate and it's cooler than golf or other sporty activities. It's normal and edgy at the same time.

Hebdige's more recent work *Hiding in the Light* (1988) offers insight on how and why this ambivalence exists. Hebdige argues that youth actually resist by doing

Skateboarding as a technology of the collective 149

so in an approved activity where everyone can see. So in some sense the more popular skating becomes, the more oppositional it becomes as well. Skateboarding as a technology of the self and the collective helps explain how, when skating in a park together, multi-generational skaters begin to construct identities that blend the third wave's subcultural tendencies and the fourth wave's commercial mainstream tendencies.

On one of my last visits to Kona, Marty Ramos told me to keep an eye out for a father-and-son duo in the park because they illustrate so many of the subcultural, mainstream, intergenerational topics we discussed before. The father wore a 1980s-styled jean jacket with a flaming skull patch on the back in vintage punk fashion and was riding an old-school board with a definite nose and tail. His young six- or seven-year-old son dressed in loose T-shirt and jeans, picked an eight-foot-tall quarter pipe to drop in on first with his 'new school' double kick tail trick board. He 'dropped in' on his trucks to 'tailstall' on the ramp. The father skated while coaching and suggesting tricks. The kid was 'shredding'. The father helped contribute to the velocity his son generated while skating by 'slingshotting' the kid down ramps to give him more speed. After a short time of shredding, this duo left, only to be replaced by other intergenerational skaters.

Kona Skatepark creates the critical space in which the seemingly contradictory oppositional and normal individual and collective identities of skateboarding coalesce. This tension is addressed in the practice of park skating and street skating. While park skating has become more popular, street skating has fallen out of favor not because there are fewer practitioners of street style than park style but because now many parks offer a street course and because skating on the public streets is just too much of a hassle. This transformation of practice has occurred for a variety of reasons; skaters want a safe place to skate, parents like their children in safe spaces, the public does not like the way street skaters act, skating can be big business, and skating in the streets results in more frequent contact with law enforcement. These changes have led to a fusion or hybridization of oppositional and normal skateboarding identities. While the commercialization of skateboarding works in tandem with the shifting of subcultural practices and identities into what mainstream commentators would call a sport, many of the nineties generation of skaters in the context of Kona Skatepark have retained parts of skateboarding's subcultural practices in a controlled environment where they do not have to risk arrest or other inconveniences. In the context of Kona Skatepark, the groms begin to see skating as both another mainstream activity like soccer or baseball and also as a subcultural practice, identity, and community. In the context of Kona Skatepark, skateboarders form an individual, collective, and intergenerational identity that embraces both subcultural opposition and normal, mainstream commercialism.

Conclusion

Street skating and park skating reflect how skateboarders construct individual, collective, and intergenerational identities. Skateboarding's role in relation to

150 *Michael J. Lorr*

physical self and collective expression and the way that street and park practices differentiate the intensity of the social bonds with and to the collective validate the solidarity individuals feel towards the community. Similar to the analyses Black Hawk Hancock and Michael J. Lorr (2013) outline in their essay on the musical practices of hard-core punk, this chapter examines how skaters use skateboarding as a technology of the self for individual identity construction. Skaters also use skating as a technology of the collective, which binds groups together through collective corporeal, symbolic, and intergenerational interactions. By focusing on the practices of street skating and park skating, the nuances involved in how individuals and collectives construct and reconstruct their identities as skateboarders become clear. For Kona skateboarders, skating is more than just a subculture or mainstream sport; it is a lifestyle paramount to one's social activity. This case study of skateboarding at Kona opens a window to the ways that sport is not reflective of social life but rather constitutive of it. The value of skateboarding resides neither in the abstract nor in the singular personal experience but in the localized social interactions between individuals and groups, whether that happens in a skatepark or while street skating. Skateboarding draws on and is embodied in skaters' actions. Skateboarding practices become social practices. Skateboarders enact these practices and experiences individually and collectively in order to construct meaningful membership within the wider skateboarding community. Skateboarders use the skateboard and skateboarding practice as technologies of self and collective to shift between oppositional identities and normal identities, providing the foundational resources for a sense of collective investment and collective intergenerational identity.

This chapter moves beyond the technology of the self, by which individuals are constituted through their use of skateboarding as cognitive and corporeal resource, and adds to the technology of the collective concept by illustrating the intergenerational aspects of individual and collective identity formation. By exploring skateboarding at Kona Skatepark, the two skateboarding practices discussed here highlight how skateboarders embody practices that frame their individual and collective identities, as well as how they use skateboarding as a generational resource to draw on and into the constitution of social life. Skateboarding channels interaction and expression into practice and identity for individual skateboarders whose shared activities construct the skateboarding community. The experiential character of the collective multigenerational skateboarding community cultivates their identities and investments in each other as skateboarders. Advancing past the specificities of particular subcultures, this study also explores more generally the ways people utilize and embody social practices as mediums and mechanisms of collective intergenerational expression. This approach affords new possibilities by which we can begin to understand skateboarding as a visceral and meaningful artistic expression that is not in addition to or on top of social life but emanates outward from the inside of cultural practices to structure social interaction and collective understanding. By focusing on skateboarding practices, this chapter contributes to the ongoing dialogue about how practice and identity matter to individuals and community.

Notes

1. 'Groms' or 'grommets', also spelled 'grommits', are board sports participants (skateboarding, surfing, snowboarding, etc.) usually younger than fifteen who are either novice and particularly good or particularly annoying.
2. I use Marty's real name because he is a public figure as the owner of Kona. For other interview subjects, I use pseudonyms as required by research ethics, IRB approval, and the conventions of ethnographic research.

References

Adorno, T & Horkheimer, M 1999, 'The culture industry: enlightenment as mass deception', in S During (ed), *The cultural studies reader*, Routledge, London and New York, pp. 31–41.
Bennett, A 1999, 'Subcultures or neo-tribes? Rethinking the relationship between youth, style and musical taste', *Sociology*, vol. 33, no. 3, pp. 599–617.
Borden, I 1996, *Beneath the pavement, the beach! Skateboarding, architecture, and the urban realm*. Available from: www.interlog.com/~mbrooke/borden.htm. [20 April 2015].
Borden, I 2001, *Skateboarding, space and the city: architecture and the body*, Berg, Oxford.
Brooke, M 1999, *The concrete wave: the history of skateboarding*, Warwick, Toronto.
Cohen, S 1972, *Subcultural conflict and working class community*, University of Birmingham, Birmingham.
DeNora, T 1999, 'Music as a technology of the self', *Poetics*, vol. 27, pp. 31–35.
DeNora, T 2000, *Music in everyday life*, Cambridge University Press, Cambridge.
DeNora, T 2011, *Music-in-action: selected essays in sonic ecology*, Ashgate, London.
Ferrell, J 2001, *Tearing down the streets: adventures in urban anarchy*, Palgrave, New York.
Foucault, M 1999, 'Space, power, and knowledge', in S During (ed), *The cultural studies reader*, Routledge, London and New York, pp. 134–141.
Frank, T 1997, *The conquest of cool*, The University of Chicago Press, Chicago.
Hamm, K 2010, *Burnside turns 20*, ESPN. Available from: http://espn.go.com/action/skateboarding/news/story?id=5741014. [23 April 2015].
Hancock, BH & Lorr, M 2013, 'More than just a soundtrack: toward a technology of the collective in hardcore punk', *Journal of Contemporary Ethnography*, vol. 42, no. 3, pp. 320–346.
Hebdige, D 1979, *Subculture: the meaning of style*, Routledge, London.
Hebdige, D 1988, *Hiding in the light*, Routledge, London.
Lombard, K-J 2010, 'Skate and create/skate and destroy: the commercial and governmental incorporation of skateboarding', *Continuum: Journal of Media and Cultural Studies*, vol. 24, no. 4, pp. 475–488.
Lorr, M 2005, 'Skateboarding and the X-gamer phenomenon: a case of subcultural cooptation', *Humanity and Society*, vol. 29, no. 2, pp. 140–147.
Muggleton, D 2000, *Inside subculture: the postmodern meaning of style*, Berg, Oxford.
Muggleton, D & Weinzierl, R 2003, *The post-subcultures reader*, Berg, Oxford.
Park info n.d., Available from: www.konaskatepark.com/PARKINFO/tabid/56/Default. aspx. [31 January 2015].
Redhead, S 1990, *The end of the century party: youth and pop towards 2000*, Manchester University Press, Manchester.
Roy, W & Dowd, T 2010, 'What is sociological about music?' *Annual Review of Sociology*, vol. 36, pp. 183–203.

11 Steep Transitions

Spatial-temporal incorporation, Beasley Skate Park, and subcultural politics in the gentrifying city

Simon Orpana

Hamilton is a city of more than half a million people located on the western tip of Lake Ontario, about an hour south of Toronto. Historically a site of heavy industry that earned the city its 'Steeltown' nickname, Hamilton's fortunes have suffered under the neoliberal restructuring of the past several decades. Skateboarders have been practicing their moves at Beasley Park in downtown Hamilton for more than thirty years, a period that overlaps with the city's faltering industrial economy. What began as a 'found' street spot that made use of the curved contours of a children's wading pool then became one of the first municipal skateparks in central Canada and most recently has gained new life as a rehabilitated do-it-yourself (DIY) spot. Throughout these transformations, the site has served as a focal point of the local skate culture, registering more than three decades of skateboard history in its chipped, cracked, and painted surfaces.

Located in the heart of what has historically been a working-class and immigrant neighbourhood, both the skateboard site and larger park have recently received increased attention due to plans to renovate a flanking abandoned knitting mill into a possible hub for 'creative industries' based on arts, culture, information, and technology. Attempts to gentrify the downtown core according to Richard Florida's 'creative cities' model of redevelopment have placed Beasley and the skaters who use it in a new position. Whereas skateboarders have historically been cast (and have cast themselves) as marginalized and even criminalized 'outsiders', the cultural capital of the Beasley skateboard scene is now being recognized as part of what makes downtown unique and desirable to the professionals and artists the city would like to attract in its redevelopment projects. In this context, skateboarding has been celebrated as useful for turning 'blighted areas and neglected space into useful and safe destinations' (Heywood 2011, p. 30). At the same time, the skatepark's location directly beside the knitting mill makes Beasley's rough and gritty character a possible hurdle to attracting investors and clients.

This ambiguous positioning of the skaters as both celebrated and problematic points to the contradictions inherent in a model of urban development that increasingly turns to commonly produced and historically unique culture in the service of schemes that primarily generate privatized wealth.[1] It also illustrates how, at a time when the cultural sphere plays an important pedagogical role in socializing subjects, a subculture like skateboarding serves to ease the transition between an emergent 'post-industrial' neoliberal service-and-information economy and the older Fordist society of industrialized mass production. Highlighting this changing historical context can help us retain some of the potential for challenging the status quo that theorists like Dick Hebdige identified in subcultures while still acknowledging the ways in which subcultures often reproduce dominant values under the guise of rebelling against them.[2]

Key to realizing the political potential of subcultures in a contemporary context is recognizing and countering what I call 'spatial-temporal incorporation', or the way in which contemporary accumulation strategies excel at appropriating relatively autonomous common cultures, re-privatizing and ultimately undermining them in the process.[3] Spatial-temporal incorporation is one of the means by which capitalism has managed the shift in Western economies from an industrial, Fordist social order (of hierarchical corporate structures and social norms externally imposed) to a post-Fordist, neoliberal regime (of more fluid, 'permissive', and internalized control structures).[4] It is this process that has allowed a subculture like skateboarding to transition from being a criminalized, 'oppositional' practice to a tolerated and even valued component of the socio-economic machinery. However, though subcultures like skaters and artists might enjoy increased political and cultural capital in this new context, the gentrification processes they inadvertently enable threaten to instrumentalize and undermine the progressive, common character of these cultures. Furthermore, the public championing of subcultures can obscure the exploitation and displacement of less visible and celebrated subjects like the homeless, immigrants, the working poor, sex workers, and street-involved youth. Unless material, legislative, institutional, and cultural measures are taken to counteract the inherent tendency of 'organic' gentrification strategies to displacement and exploitation, it is the common and inclusive, shared nature of our societies and cities that will be further damaged and lost.

The vision of subcultural politics sketched here emerges from my personal history as a skateboarder, researcher, and activist. When I was growing up in northern Ontario in the eighties, there were no skateboard parks, amateur events or organizations, just a ragged band of misfits combing small town streets for new places to skate. Arriving in Hamilton in 2002 as an adult, I found an opportunity to get involved with a skateboard community that had its own organization in the Hamilton Skateboard Assembly (HSA), amateur events, and an informal, spatial epicentre at Beasley Skateboard Park. Between 2009 and 2011, I served as the secretary for the HSA, a role that provided the opportunity to meet with City of Hamilton workers and councillors, to get involved with the local Beasley Neighbourhood Association (BNA), and that has recently led to my serving as a member of the Beasley Park Redevelopment Public Stakeholder's Group. My engagement with skateboarding developed into a research project in 2008 when I began pursuing a Master's and then a PhD project in English and cultural studies at McMaster University. During this time, I was also conducting interviews and collecting footage for a documentary film, *Beaz Steez: Skateboarding at Beasley Park* (Orpana 2013), available online.

154 Simon Orpana

Blood, sweat, and concrete: a visual map of the history of skateboarding

The history of skateboard culture at Beasley offers a good example of the process of spatial-temporal incorporation that has helped facilitate the shift from a Fordist to a neoliberal regime of accumulation. It also illustrates several distinct shifts in the history of street skateboarding from the late 1970s to the present. These histories are inscribed into the very topography of the current skateboard park, revealing a dialectical process by which subcultural innovation has both elicited and constructively informed responses by the city and surrounding neighbourhood. I divide this history into three phases, each of which is represented by a physical feature of the existing park.

Creative appropriation: the Beasley Bowl and the emergence of street skating

Beasley Park's current footprint was first developed in 1978 as a site of much-needed parkland in the city's core. Located in downtown Hamilton, both the skatepark and larger green space are embedded in the fabric and flow of the city in ways that many other skateparks, often relegated to out-of-the-way locations in the suburbs, are not. Beasley Park is close to the downtown police headquarters, a prison, several homeless shelters, soup kitchens, a hospital, and (until 2013) a mosque. The skatepark is thus embedded amongst a number of institutions that speak to the working-class and immigrant histories that have shaped the life of downtown Hamilton during its heyday as an industrial center and its more recent

Figure 11.1 Skaters using Beasley Bowl in the eighties. Courtesy of Derek Lapierre ©.

history of deskilling and unemployment. When heavy industry began to suffer in the 1980s, the downtown core entered a period of what has been perceived as decline. But during this same period, Beasley began to entice skateboarders, who were attracted by a children's wading pool with a nicely sloped transition that is perfect for carving across and launching out of on a skateboard.

What is now known as 'the Beasley Bowl' was retained in the modern skatepark installed by the city in 1992. Similar children's pools from the same era exist in other downtown parks, but local skaters verify that none of them have the particular transition and contour that makes Beasley enticing to skateboarders. The curb that surrounded the shallow end of the pool and the hat-shaped concrete form that contained the fountainhead (called 'the sombrero' by skaters) were used as skateboarding obstacles. Skaters would also add parking blocks, garbage cans, and other elements to the bowl to do tricks upon and over. They further modified the area by removing a metal railing that was installed at the top of the bowl and that prevented them from using the incline as a launching pad. The inclusion of a repurposed, pre-existing element into a municipal skatepark is rare, as most such facilities start by clearing the ground and erecting all new structures. This quirk of Beasley Park is one of the features that makes it a site of living history, as the repurposed bowl supplies a physical trace of the emergence of street skateboarding in the late seventies and early eighties when, with the closing of many privately run skateboard parks, skaters took to the streets in search of new terrain.[5]

Spatial-temporal incorporation: the Widow Maker and municipal skate parks

In the early 1990s, Jesse-Lee Wolter, an artistic and enterprising local skater, procured the architect's plans for Beasley Park from the public library. He approached city officials with the argument that having a wading pool so close to an electrical transformer station (which flanks the east side of the park) was unsafe and that the area would be better suited for the dry use of a skateboard park.[6] In 1992, the city agreed, incorporating the bowl into a larger paved delta and adding a quarter pipe, hump, railing, and some other contoured areas. Rumour has it that the quarter pipe, called 'the Widow Maker' due to its steeply inclined transition, was accidentally installed upside down.[7] However, the skaters have turned this difficulty into a virtue: mastering tricks on the Widow Maker is one of the markers of authenticity and skill amongst Beasley skaters, proof that one has spent enough time at the park to learn to navigate the steep transition.

In 1992, Derek Lapierre, another local skater, started what would become the annual Beasley Skate Jam, a popular amateur event that has been running for more than two decades, which attracts skateboarders from all over Ontario and further afield. In 1994, Lapierre spearheaded *Nomads* magazine, a publication chronicling the skateboarding, music, and rave culture in Hamilton and surrounding areas. What started as a photocopied zine quickly developed into a printed, glossy-covered magazine with advertising and one paid staff member. The Hamilton Skateboard Assembly (HSA), a volunteer organization that runs the Skate Jam

156 *Simon Orpana*

Figure 11.2 Beasley Skateboard Park in the mid-nineties, with the Widow Maker in the background. Source: Courtesy of Derek Lapierre ©.

and other events, was formed in 2002 by Lapierre and other local skaters. With the installation of Beasley Skateboard Park as a site where skaters could practice their sport, the development of events like the Skate Jam, publications like *Nomads*, local skate shops like DMBC, and organizations like the HSA, Hamilton skateboard culture began to solidify its own unique identity.

In downtown Hamilton, the growing number of riders in the mid-1990s allowed for the development of a common culture based on the social and physical act of skateboarding. I use the term 'common culture' to designate forms of culture that emerge from the actions of ordinary people and that are held in common rather than being 'owned' by either state or private agents.[8] A common culture may have key innovators, such as Wolter and Lapierre, but these figures focus the energies of a much larger group. Common culture is also different from the commoditized, mass-produced cultures of consumer capitalism, though in the case of skateboarding, there is considerable overlap between the two categories. However, despite the widespread contemporary popularity of skateboarding and the commodity culture that supports it, the physical act itself remains a commons in its adaptation of a shared set of continually evolving 'tricknowlogies' (Willard 1998). Though particular individuals are often credited with the invention of certain tricks, these rapidly become common property as a set of moves that are applied to new environments in endless variations. Furthermore, given the increasing privatization, surveillance, and control of social space, the appropriation of space by skateboarders, if not constituting an act of what David Harvey calls 'commoning' (2012, pp. 73–75), at least creates symptomatic friction that reminds us of the absence of truly common space in our cities (Howell 2001, p. 21).

Steep Transitions 157

As one of the first municipal skateparks in Eastern Canada, Beasley became a space of subcultural innovation where riders could practice on specially designed terrains that were previously not widely accessible. The development of grass-roots institutions like the Skate Jam, the HSA, and *Nomads* magazine also served as focal points for the common skateboard culture that started to flourish in Hamilton and the surrounding area in the 1990s. These initiatives were created and pursued by volunteers aided by the city (who issued permits and supplied staff for events), the state (Lapierre first learned the skills to run the Jam while enrolled in the Canadian Special Event Development Program), and private enterprise (such as local skate shops and businesses that provide prizes for the Jam). But city, state, and private interests did not dominate the common culture at Beasley, which issued from the skaters themselves and their particular use of the space of the park.

It is important to note that the common skateboard culture at Beasley, though it began as a spontaneous appropriation of the wading pool by skaters, was furthered by an enclosure strategy on the part of the city. By giving skateboarders their own designated place, cities like Hamilton were responding to the growing number of skateboarders who were posing a potential hazard to pedestrians, motorists, and property owners by skating the sidewalks and streets. The city's installation of Beasley Skateboard Park thus constituted an attempted form of spatial-temporal incorporation. Hebdige (1979, pp. 92–99) articulated two ways in which subcultural innovations are domesticated and incorporated: the *commodity form* by which subcultural styles are mass marketed and the *ideological form* by which subcultures are made less threatening through strategies of mediation and legislation. *Spatial-temporal incorporation* provides a third form cantered upon the spatial sites and embodied practices of subcultural production. Given the intensified interest since the 1980s in the redevelopment of urban spaces according to neoliberal models of aggressive marketization (Harvey 2012, p. 29) and globalization (Sassen 2006), the spatial incorporation of subcultures has become increasingly important for property managers, developers, and governments (Howell 2001).

Furthermore, in light of the shift from a society based on 'repressive' disciplinary enclosures (such as the factory, prison, school, hospital, etc.) to a post-Fordist, consumer-oriented capitalism based on more permissive and 'libidinal' control structures, subcultures have become important for their production of *pleasures* and *temporalities* that can be appropriated and used by dominant agents as a means of maintaining hegemony.[9] In the post-disciplinary, fluid, and permissive *societies of control* (Deleuze 1992), it is not just the commodity form that incorporates and profits from subcultural innovations but structures of socialization, management, and governmentality as well (think here of the utopian vision of Google's corporate offices as a space that blurs the lines between work and play or of the DIY ethic that city governments have begun to promote as a means to compensate for the privatization of formerly socialized services such as park and roadway maintenance).

Spatial-temporal incorporation is further illustrated by considering the differences between Beasley and the newer Turner Skateboard Park located in Hamilton's suburban outskirts. Turner is a modern skatepark built between 2008 and

2009 for half a million dollars generated when Hamilton privatized its hydroelectric utility. The park is thus a physical token of the kinds of liquidation of previously socialized resources that characterizes the shift from Fordism to neoliberalism. Like many skateparks, Turner works to contain and reconfigure the common, resistant practice of skateboarding in the streets, individualizing, regulating, and rationalizing the subculture (Chiu 2009; Howell 2008). Being in opposition to vehicles, pedestrians, property owners, and security guards fosters a sense of solidarity amongst street skaters. In contrast, the crowded confines of skateboard parks force riders to compete with *each other* for space and attention, turning the activity into more of an individualized performance. At Turner and other suburban parks, the presence of small children on scooters and bikes, often accompanied by parents, also tends to further regulate the space. These disciplinary and policing functions at Turner are dramatically highlighted by its particular location: to quell local residents' concerns that a skatepark would increase crime and vandalism in the area, the park was installed directly beside a police headquarters.[10] Nestled between the police station, a library, and a YMCA, Turner Park provides a contradictory space of controlled rebellion, a fitting emblem of the 'biopolitical societies of control' (Hardt & Negri 2000, pp. 22–27) where '[e]verywhere surfing has already replaced the older sports' (Deleuze 1992, p. 6).

One important difference between Beasley and Turner involves the range in age of the skaters at the respective parks. Because more than three generations of skaters have grown up skating Beasley, there are many older skaters who regularly use the park. Several Beasley regulars are in their thirties or forties. The older skaters keep alive skating styles that have fallen out of contemporary skate

Figure 11.3 Skaters at Turner Park in suburban Hamilton. Illustration by Simon Orpana ©.
Source: author

culture but which at Beasley are being adopted by younger skaters. This pedagogical relationship, with several generations of skaters learning from each other, is reinforced by the circumscribed topography of the park. Though the skatepark is much smaller than Turner, skaters at Beasley develop a sense of 'flow' that allows for many skaters to efficiently use the space. When they are not navigating a line, skaters watch each other and shout encouragement, creating an atmosphere of support and camaraderie. These factors combine at Beasley to counteract many of the alienating and regulating tendencies of newer skateboard parks.

Though Turner and Beasley host two very different skateboard scenes, they both offer examples of spatial-temporal incorporation. In the suburban context, Turner Park is contiguous with the flanking police station and recreation center, a location that transforms skateboarding into another middle-class recreational activity, akin to the swimming or yoga classes that take place just next door. Here, the proximity of the skatepark to other options for recreation and leisure serves to domesticate skateboarding's more unruly aspects. As an example of this, the annual Cop-Shop Skate Jam organized by the neighbouring police station has been running for several years and helps build a positive community presence for the police. Such an event would be difficult to stage at Beasley, where park users are more likely to have been subjected to police discipline or to have friends or family members who have been. And yet, incorporation takes a different form at Beasley, where a sense of gritty 'authenticity' can generate the frisson of transgression needed to make the space enticing to the cultured artists and professionals that the city and investors hope to attract to downtown. In this context, it is the anarchic tendencies of skateboarding that need to be encouraged and celebrated, but only insofar as they do not become a disincentive to economic development. By celebrating and attempting to capitalize upon the alternative spatialities and temporalities of skateboard culture, the incorporation at work at Beasley is perhaps less explicit than at Turner Park, but it also has potentially damaging repercussions that extend beyond the community of skaters themselves.

In this regard, Hamilton's bid to re-brand itself has given birth to a troubling discourse (Antwi & Dean 2010) casting downtown as in need of 'fixing', with prominent figures, such as Hamilton's former mayor, arguing that downtown has been 'abandoned to the poor' (Bratina cited in Hume 2013). This discourse casts Hamilton's precarious subjects – people whose situation is the direct result of deskilling and de-industrialization – as an impediment to urban renewal. Instead of addressing poverty as an issue of the redistribution of social wealth (providing funds for services, re-training, housing, transportation, etc.), this discourse seeks a *spatial fix*, encouraging development that will disperse the concentration of poor people rather than alleviating hardship. One deployment of this strategy is through the increased surveillance and policing of downtown, where the concentration of the poor, disabled, and homeless is characterized as a detriment to the preservation of the city's 'heritage' buildings.[11] This, in turn, is part of a larger strategy of gentrification whereby a more affluent class is encouraged to colonize previously affordable neighbourhoods, thus raising property values and rents, which further force the original inhabitants to move elsewhere. The skaters

160   *Simon Orpana*

of Beasley inadvertently encourage this strategy of displacement in two ways. First, as already mentioned, the skaters' subcultural capital makes the neighbourhood attractive to the artists and professionals who often comprise the first wave of the gentrification of neighbourhoods. Second, the skateboarders' spectacular presence at Beasley provides a policing function, increasing the number of eyes that monitor the park and providing socially legitimated bodies that give the space a 'lived in' feel.[12]

Alongside their willingness to frequent areas in which other people might feel uncomfortable, we must examine why skateboarders in particular are useful as the 'shock troops of gentrification' (Howell 2005, p. 40). Many times while skateboarding at Beasley, I have seen police stop to search, question, and detain men (and sometimes women) who, attracted by the nearby food bank and shelters, have been quietly sitting on the steps of the abandoned knitting mill that flanks the park. Had these people been holding or riding skateboards, they would not likely have been subjected to the same treatment. Michael Nevin Willard (1998, p. 330) points out the 'similarities of spatial exclusion' faced by street skateboarders and homeless people. He argues that 'skaters create relationships of affinity with the homeless to intentionally dramatize their own kind (but not degree) of spatial poverty' (p. 330). Despite this strategically deployed rhetoric on the part of skaters, in the context of the gentrifying city, skateboarding also helps authorities distinguish between acceptable and unacceptable kinds of bodies. Like some 'undesirables', skateboarders also sometimes drink alcohol, do drugs, or act in an unruly manner, and yet they are tolerated and even celebrated in gentrifying cities. Why? I suggest it is skateboarders' physical discipline, their public performance of a spectacular activity, and their willingness to expose themselves to individually assumed risk in the pursuit of sport that makes their presence acceptable to the ruling order.

Matthew Atencio, Becky Beal, and Charlene Wilson (2009) identify the assumption of risk as an indicator of authenticity in skateboard culture, one that reproduces masculinist hierarchies that subjugate and devalue women, who are perceived as being averse to such risk taking (Beal 1996). Here, the alignment of neoliberal capitalism with patriarchal value structures is reinforced by skateboarding subculture. The skateboarding body is a hyper-performing, predominantly masculine, individualized and active body. Though the skaters of downtown Hamilton share an environment with the poor and the homeless, skaters are granted a larger right to public space because they perform a socially accepted version of risk-taking masculinity. This spectacular form of activity distinguishes skateboarding men from the unwanted kinds of downtown bodies whose presence is only slimly tolerated, even in the allegedly 'public' spaces of parks and streets.

Beasley is a neighbourhood that has wrestled for several decades with social stigmas associated with poverty. Examples of Fordist institutions of social care are still visible in downtown Hamilton in the form of food banks, addiction-management clinics, homeless shelters, youth drop-in centers, used-goods stores, and the like. Forty years of neoliberal restructuring have cast a disparaging shadow over these institutions, dismantling them wherever possible and replacing them with market-driven 'solutions' to poverty and unemployment. As Hamilton struggles to re-brand itself as 'post-industrial', the skateboarders offer a cultural presence that downtown can celebrate. But this endorsement carries with it a hidden control structure: skateboarding makes the bodies of young, precarious, and often working-class men socially acceptable, allowing them their own space within the city, but only insofar as their bodies *perform* the values of individualized risk management demanded by patriarchal neoliberalism.

This highlights the role subcultures play in easing the transition between a Fordist and neoliberal social order. In the context of an industrial downtown designed to keep the working class fixed in place, skateboarding in the streets provided an accessible vehicle for freedom and agency, creatively appropriating infrastructures designed to limit rather than enable the kinds of social pleasures enjoyed by skateboarders. The emergent post-Fordist capitalism, by relocating industrial production to other parts of the globe, has largely succeeded in undermining the hard-won gains made by the Western working classes. In place of the job security, benefits, protections, and standard of living fought for by workers throughout the nineteenth and twentieth centuries, the neoliberal decades have effected generalized precariousness, debt, and underemployment as central levers of social control. In this context, rather than repressing subcultural pleasures, neoliberal governance works *permissively*, selectively encouraging these practices in ways that reinforce competitive market values and forming alliances with subaltern subjects in a manner that consolidates hegemonic rule.[13]

Returning to the steep, possibly upside-down quarter pipe that Beasley skaters call the Widow Maker, though it exemplifies the paternalistic structures that Fordism imposed on subjects – structures that only imperfectly reflected their needs or desires – this quirky feature has become part of Beasley's unique character, serving as a mark of distinction and subcultural capital for skaters who are able to master its challenging slope. The quarter pipe thus illustrates the defiant posture of skateboarders to the repressive aspects of the older, Fordist control structures while simultaneously signalling a willingness to face the steep and uneven contours of an aggressive and individualistic neoliberalism. The losers in this new configuration are those who cannot navigate the transition between the more predictive disciplinary structures of Fordism and the new, precarious order: the unemployed or underemployed, the disabled, aging, and often racialized bodies of a Western industrial workforce no longer useful to global capitalism. These people are left to fend for themselves, and their presence in the city is an embarrassment to the governments who are no longer willing or able to care for them.[14] They haunt the streets and parks of downtown like living ghosts, subjected to police harassment and negative media attention, while the skateboarders performing their agile, daring moves garner new admiration.

Haunted by Fordism: the Beasley DIY project and gentrification

While skateboarders' ability to be self-governing, risk-taking neoliberal subjects makes them fitting figures of the transition to neoliberal modes of social control,

162 *Simon Orpana*

the Beasley example provides another, more progressive aspect that involves the reconstitution through play of the sense of solidarity and community struggled for by workers and activists in the context of Western industrial society. Something of this collaborative spirit is found in the recent wave of DIY renovations. Since around 2010, skaters have been working with the city and local Beasley Neighbourhood Association (BNA) to repair and add new skateboard elements to the existing park. Skaters show up on designated weekends with bags of cement, tools, paint, and a portable radio and work alongside neighbours and friends through hot summer afternoons to fill in cracks, create new inclines, and decorate the park with mural art. This activity is part of a larger trend in which skaters, inspired by user-built spaces like the now famous Burnside Park in Portland, Oregon, fashion custom skateboarding environments using their own materials, energy, and ideas.[15] Though DIY skateparks are often done without the prior permission of governments or property owners, the Hamilton skaters have formed alliances with the local BNA and city councillors, gaining support and funds from these quarters and ensuring that the DIY changes made to the park are officially endorsed. Members of the HSA have also participated in a stakeholders' group charged with helping plan a 2016 overhaul of the entire park. By raising public awareness regarding the history of skate culture at Beasley, the skaters have thus far been able to safeguard the space they have helped create, and plans are under way for the city to actually expand the skatepark while preserving historic elements of the existing terrain. This process highlights Kara-Jane Lombard's (2010) insight that the governmental incorporation of skateboarding gives skaters the opportunity to shape political and cultural processes from within, an opportunity missed by the vision of skaters as merely defiant outsiders.

Alongside downtown locals who have long skated at Beasley, the DIY improvements have attracted talented skaters from other parts of town such as the suburban 'mountain' area and neighbouring municipalities. Many of these skaters have taken an active role in the weekend repair sessions as well. I suggest that the appeal held by Beasley for the diverse (but still largely male) skaters who use it lies in the way the DIY park combines elements of neoliberal subjecthood (the focus on individual risk management) with vanishing elements of industrial society such as a sense of group solidarity grounded in shared physical space and work. Skate cultures like Beasley's offer a combination of physical, embodied, and repetitive labor (largely industrial in character) with the promise of creativity, excitement, and personal satisfaction that the post-Fordist economy tries to leverage. Beasley Park thus provides a compensatory experience of un-alienated, collective, but also individualized and creative labor and sociality. With concerted political pressure being placed on workers' institutions such as unions, the Beasley skate scene offers an alternative sense of solidarity through embodied, spatial stewardship. With perhaps unintended irony, local skate shops reference this heritage in such promotional slogans as 'Support Your Local' ('local' here referring to the skate shop), translating the heritage of workers' struggles for empowerment and solidarity into often factious and divisive loyalty to individual shops and brands.[16] And yet the persistent traces in skateboard culture of legacies of political activism,

Figure 11.4 Skaters working on a Jersey barrier at Beasley Park. The photo shows skaters working on one of the two concrete Jersey barriers, dropped off in the park by the city in 2011 and regularly modified by the skaters. The collaborative, volunteer labour invested in these elements illustrates the grassroots, community-oriented, DIY ethic that informs the skaters' response to the degeneration of the skatepark. Photo by Simon Orpana ©.

even in such diluted and distorted form, retain symptomatic echoes of the desire for equity and autonomy that informed the original movements being referenced.

Conclusion

If building public skateparks constitutes a spatial-temporal incorporation strategy on the part of cities, the skaters' ongoing shaping and caring for Beasley Park is part of a longer history of enacting subcultural agency and forming subcultural community. We can identify the progressive elements of the DIY process as offering skateboarders a form of solidarity, pride, and embodied sociality that might be lacking in post-Fordist societies in which spaces of both labor and leisure have been dramatically fragmented and restructured. Building, maintaining, and using the skatepark gives skaters a concrete, immediate experience of accomplishment, making the space their own in ways that a park like Turner does not allow. At the same time, the model of risk-taking masculinity that informs skateboard culture is continuous with rather than in opposition to neoliberal values. This partially explains why skate culture can be useful for gentrification projects, since

164   *Simon Orpana*

its self-reliant ethos can work against cultivating solidarity and alliances with a growing number of subjects who are simply not needed by post-industrial, Western capitalism.

We can challenge subcultures being used in this way by remembering the histories of the often contingent and fragile spaces in which subcultural difference flourishes. Part of the reason for Beasley's unique character is that the institutions that support and surround it (the school, prison, community center, hospital, soup kitchens, homeless shelters, workers' unions) hearken from a Fordist period when significant state and private funds were directed toward the production of shared and socialized resources that helped reproduce the industrial labor force. In Hamilton, these institutions and values have been buffered from neoliberal restructuring due to the city's strong working-class character and industrial heritage. The recent attempt to re-brand the city as a creative hub celebrates the city's cultural capital in the form of art, history, and subcultural investments.[17] But key measures of progress and equity, such as living wages, steady employment, accessible education, and the material securities that allowed these cultural innovations to flourish in the first place are increasingly undermined by a post-Fordism that encourages flexible, precarious contract work, low-paying service-sector jobs, higher housing and transportation costs, and increased educational debt.[18]

The steady erosion of free time, security, and resources in the new, entrepreneurial 'creative economies' makes it increasingly difficult for people to make and enjoy the kinds of common culture that were possible under Fordism. To give one example, for almost twenty years, the Beasley Skate Jam operated under the City of Hamilton's insurance. In 2012, the City changed its stance and required the HSA to secure its own insurance coverage, a development that is in keeping with the predominant neoliberal climate of privatized risk. In order to run events, the HSA now must buy expensive private insurance. Registration fees from the events no longer generate the revenue needed to keep them going, and the organizers have had to host annual fund-raising drives. In the future, they might have to rely more heavily on the private sector, commercial advertising, and sponsorships, a tendency that could undermine the amateur, grassroots character of the Skate Jam and other events.

In the face of these challenges, it is important to remember that spatial-temporal incorporation always *reacts to* subcultural challenges and innovations: it is likely that the same impetus to thwart systems of control that informed the skaters' spontaneous appropriation of the Beasley Bowl and that inspired the ongoing project of repairing, improving, and using the park for a common skateboard culture will continue to manifest in unexpected developments on the part of the skateboard community and larger neighbourhood. At the same time, it is likely that the cultural capital and policing practices associated with skateboarding at Beasley will further encourage the gentrification projects that are already transforming the character of the neighbourhood and that threaten to reduce its diversity and displace existing residents. The degree to which this comes to pass will largely depend on the actions of residents and user groups, like the skateboarders, and the pressure they can put on governments, investors, and themselves to enlarge the culture of solidarity, engagement, and care of place and inclusive community that they have thus far managed to keep alive.

Notes

1. For more on how urban culture and history is used to generate profit, see Harvey (2012, esp. ch.4).
2. Critics who accuse Hebdige of perpetuating a 'heroic version' (Marchart 2003 p. 83) of subcultural alterity, resistance, and incorporation overlook that the Birmingham researchers themselves saw subcultures as compromised and largely 'symbolic' solutions to the social contradictions of their day (Clark 1993, p. 159; Cohen 1999, p. 57). Contemporary critics of skateboarding's rebellious stance range from Heath and Potter's (2004, pp. 131–132) polemic dismissal to Dinces's (2011) more nuanced and convincing analysis, yet both accounts, in focusing upon representations of skate culture, miss the key element of how skateboarders themselves relate to their physical surroundings, embodied practice, and wider relations with communities. In contrast to these dismissals, Lombard (2010) offers analysis and examples of the ways in which skateboarders, while never 'outside' dominant culture, can yet pose significant challenges that might transform society from within.
3. The idea of spatial-temporal incorporation is informed by Cohen's (1999) insights into the ways in which subcultural subjects work out the contradictions of their familial and social situations via territorial solutions and Howell's (2001, p. 3) insights into how contemporary urban design incorporates elements of subcultures through a process of 'surveillance and simulation'.
4. The term 'Fordism' was coined in the 1930s by Antonio Gramsci (2010) to describe an American society based on mass production in which industry and the developmental state collaborated to reproduce the labor force and to provide the level of wages and security necessary to leverage consumption of the commodities thus produced. Neoliberalism signals the dissolution of this arrangement when, starting in the 1970s, Western governments began to relax corporate regulations, privatize social infrastructure, and aggressively impose market capitalism on developing parts of the world (Brown 2003; Gilbert 2013; Harvey 2005).
5. For accounts of the emergence of street skating out of the demise of the private skateparks in the seventies, see Borden (2010, ch. 7) and Howell (2001).
6. This is one version of the skatepark's origins.
7. Thanks to Scott McDonald for this piece of Beasley lore.
8. For further development of this idea, see Hardt and Negri (2005, pp. 196–208, 2009, p. viii).
9. For the shift from a repressive, disciplinary society to contemporary, 'permissive' biopolitical capitalism see Žižek (2009, pp. 295–317), Deleuze (1992), and Marcuse (1968, pp. 74–81).
10. A report from the City of Hamilton 'recommends the construction of a new skateboard facility at Turner Park with the understanding that the Hamilton Police Service will provide video surveillance of the park 24 hours a day, seven days a week' (Makins 2005, p. 1). The park is described as enhancing 'Community Well-Being' by providing a 'much needed designated space for the skateboarders, moving them out of the streets and parking lots of businesses' (ibid., p. 4).

166 *Simon Orpana*

11. See, for instance, the recent, contested proposal to change Hamilton city bylaws involving loitering, spitting, and other 'nuisance behaviour' (Craggs 2014).
12. Howell (2008, pp. 484–485) critiques the policing function performed by skateboarders. This tendency was also recognized (and celebrated) at several neighborhood meetings that I attended from 2011 to 2014.
13. This strategy is at work in Florida's (2002) articulation of the 'creative class' that attempts to group artists and professionals under the banner of 'creativity' in service of urban revitalization. Howell's (2005, p. 39) sharp insight that these subjects are actually united by 'their participation in the process of gentrification' challenges this rhetoric. For more critiques of creative class ideology, see Cazdyn and Szeman (2011), Krätke (2010), Malanga (2004), Maliszewski (2003), Mann (2014), and Peck (2005).
14. Cazdyn (2012) calls those subjects whom society has effectively 'killed' but who have yet to die the 'already dead' and sees a revolutionary potential in the mounting prevalence of this condition. One of the current Canadian government's strategies for dealing with this ongoing crisis is to remove poverty and inequality from official records by dismantling the mandatory long-form national census (Carter 2013).
15. For more on these DIY projects, see Howell (2005, pp. 485–488).
16. The 'Support Your Local' slogan was initially incorporated into the logo of Flatspot, an independently owned skateboard shop in downtown Hamilton. In 2013, a second independent shop opened, referencing the rival shop's slogan in its own name, the Local.
17. For instance, a video on the investinhamilon.ca website interviews artists and architects to highlight Hamilton as a hub for 'creative industries' (Creative Industries, n.d.).
18. For critique of how the new 'creative economy' colonizes free time, replacing collectivized struggle and protections with a neoliberal emphasis on entrepreneurialism, individualization, and commercial sponsorship, all under the guise of a model of 'freedom' appropriated from artistic and academic subcultures, see McRobbie (2002) and Ross (2000).

References

Antwi, P, & Dean, A 2010, 'Unfixing imaginings of the city: art, gentrification, and cultures of surveillance', *Affinities: A Journal of Radical Theory, Culture and Action*, vol. 4, no. 2, pp. 17–27.

Atencio, M, Beal, B & Wilson, C 2009, 'The distinction of risk: urban skateboarding, street habitus, and the construction of hierarchical gender relations', *Qualitative Research in Sport and Exercise*, vol. 1, no. 1, pp. 3–20.

Beal, B 1996, 'Alternative masculinity and its effects on gender relations in the subculture of skateboarding', *Journal of Sport Behaviour*, vol. 19, no. 3, pp. 204–20.

Borden, I 2010, *Skateboarding, space and the city: architecture and the body*, Berg, New York.

Brown, W 2003, 'Neoliberalism and the end of liberal democracy', *Theory & Event*, vol. 7, no. 1, n.p.

Carter, A 2013, 'Poorest Hamilton neighbourhoods vanish from new census', *cbc.ca*. 16 September. Available from: www.cbc.ca/news/canada/hamilton/news/poorest-hamilton-neighbourhoods-vanish-from-new-census-1.1856549. [27 January 2015].

Cazdyn, E 2012, *The already dead: the new time of politics, culture, and illness*, Duke University Press, London.

Cazdyn, E & Szeman, I 2011, *After globalization*, Blackwell Publishing, Malden, MA.

Chiu, C 2009, 'Contestation and conformity: street and park skateboarding in New York City public space', *Space and Culture*, vol. 12, no. 1, pp. 25–42.

Clark, J 1993, 'Style' in S Hall & T Jefferson (eds), *Resistance through rituals: youth subcultures in post-war Britain*, Routledge, New York, pp. 147–161.

Cohen, P 1999, *Rethinking the youth question: education, labor and cultural studies*, Duke University Press, Durham, pp. 48–63.

Craggs, S 2014, 'City wants to stop downtown loitering, spitting and other "nuisance behaviour"', *cbc.ca*, 4 July. Available from: www.cbc.ca/news/canada/hamilton/news/city-wants-to-stop-downtown-loitering-spitting-and-other-nuisance-behaviour-1.2695805. [24 January 2015].

Creative Industries n.d., *Hamilton Economic Development*. Available from: www.investinhamilton.ca/key-industries/creative-industries/. [27 January 2015].

Deleuze, G 1992, 'Postscript on the societies of control', *October*, no. 59, Winter, pp. 3–7.

Dinces, S 2011, '"Flexible opposition": skateboarding subcultures under the rubric of late capitalism', *International Journal of the History of Sport*, vol. 28, no. 11, pp. 1512–535.

Florida, R 2002, *The rise of the creative class: and how it's transforming work, leisure, community and everyday life*, Basic Books, New York.

Gilbert, J 2013, 'What kind of thing is "neoliberalism"?' *New Formations*, no. 80/81, pp. 7–22.

Gramsci, A 2010, *Selections from the prison notebooks*, International Publishers, New York.

Hardt, M & Negri, A 2000, *Empire*, Harvard University Press, Cambridge, MA.

Hardt, M & Negri, A 2009, *Commonwealth*, The Belknap Press of Harvard University, Cambridge, MA.

Harvey, D 2005, *A brief history of neoliberalism*, Oxford University Press, Oxford.

Harvey, D 2012, *Rebel cities: from the right to the city to the urban revolution*, Verso, New York.

Heath, J & Potter, A 2004, *Nation of rebels: why counterculture became consumer culture*, HarperBusiness, New York.

Hebdige, D 1979, *Subculture: the meaning of style*, Routledge, New York.

Heywood, W 2011, 'Navigating the new fortress: skateboarding's constant answers to an exclusionary urban environment', *Urban Action 2011*, pp. 19–32.

Howell, O 2001, *The poetics of security: skateboarding, urban design, and the new public space*. Available from: http://urbanpolicy.net/wp-content/uploads/2013/02/Howell_2001_Poetics-of-Security_NoPix.pdf. [27 January 2015].

Howell, O 2005, 'The "creative class" and the gentrifying city: skateboarding in Philadelphia's Love Park', *Journal of Architectural Education*, vol. 59, no. 2, pp. 32–42.

Howell, O 2008, 'Urban governance, recreation space, and the cultivation of personal responsibility', *Space and Culture*, vol. 11, no. 4, pp. 475–496.

Hume, C 2013, 'Hamilton is no longer Toronto's poor cousin', *The Hamilton Spectator*, 15 October.

Krätke, S 2010, '"Creative cities" and the rise of the dealer class: a critique of Richard Florida's approach to urban theory', *International Journal of Urban and Regional Research*, vol. 34, no. 4, pp. 835–853.

Lombard, K 2010, 'Skate and create/skate and destroy: the commercial and governmental incorporation of skateboarding', *Continuum: Journal of Media & Cultural Studies*, vol. 24, no. 4, pp. 475–488.

Makins, G 2005, *Skateboard park construction at Turner Park (HCS04031b) (City Wide)*, City of Hamilton, Public Health and Community Services Department, Culture and Recreation Division.

Malanga, S 2004, 'The curse of the creative class', *City Journal*, Winter. Available from: www.city-journal.org/html/14_1_the_curse.html. [27 January 2015].

168 *Simon Orpana*

Maliszewski, P 2003, 'Flexibility and its discontents', *The Baffler*, vol. 16, pp. 69–79.

Mann, S 2014, 'Creative class struggle: gentrification and sex work in Hamilton's downtown core', *Briarpatch Magazine*, July/August. Available from: http://briarpatchmagazine.com/articles/view/creative-class-struggle. [27 January 2015].

Marchart, O 2003, 'Bridging the micro-macro gap: is there such a thing as a post- subcultural politics?', in D Muggleton & R Weinzierl (eds), *The post-subcultures reader*, Berg, New York, pp. 83–97.

Marcuse, H 1968, *One-dimensional man: studies in the ideology of advanced industrial society*, Beacon Press, Boston, MA.

McRobbie, A 2002, 'Clubs to companies: notes on the decline of political culture in speeded up creative worlds', *Cultural Studies*, vol. 16, no. 4, pp. 516–531.

Orpana, S 2013, *Beaz Steez* (Short Version). Available from: www.youtube.com/watch?v=pRzI4KOtjo4. [27 January 2015].

Peck, J 2005, 'Struggling with the creative class', *International Journal of Urban and Regional Research*, vol. 29, no. 4, pp. 740–770.

Ross, A 2000, 'The mental labor problem', *Social Text*, no. 63, Summer, pp. 1–32.

Sassen, S 2006, *Cities in a world economy*, Pine Forge Press, London.

Willard, MN 1998, 'Seance, tricknowlogy, skateboarding, and the space of youth', in J Austin & MN Willard (eds), *Generations of youth*, New York University Press, New York, pp. 326–346.

Žižek, S 2009, *The parallax view*, The MIT Press, Cambridge, MA.

12 Trucks, tricks, and technologies of government

Analyzing the productive encounter between governance and resistance in skateboarding

Kara-Jane Lombard

The governance of skateboarding has taken varying forms, from legislation to building skateparks to the attention paid to the 'criminogenic situation' (Lombard 2010). These forms have exhibited various responses, as Iain Borden (2001, p. 251) explains:

> [W]hile some parts of the world, notably Tasmania, Brisbane and Melbourne have recently begun to actively encourage skateboarding in certain parts of the city, the more general pattern of anti-skate legislation has been repeated worldwide, whether in Australia, Sweden, the Netherlands, Brazil, Canada and so on.

There are a number of actors involved in governing skateboarding, from public forms such as police, local governments, and state authorities to those employed in a private capacity to enforce the rules of property owners, such as security guards. Skateboarders encounter a politics of space whereby they occupy space without engaging in economic activity, and consequently urban authorities often brand skaters as trespassers or as the cause of criminal damage (Borden 1998). Complicating the governance of skateboarding is its legitimate aspect – it is a form of transport as well as a recreational activity. As Nicholas Nolan (2003, p. 320) puts it, 'the recognition that skateboarding is a legitimate mode of transport and source of recreation for young people complicates the transgression label because it creates a distinction between "good" skateboarding and "bad" skateboarding that cannot be accommodated by total bans'. Furthermore, measures against individual skateboarders are generally ineffective, and skaters transgress the boundaries between public and private spaces, making them difficult to govern.

In this chapter, I examine a particular aspect of resistance in the governance of skateboarding by considering the appropriation of 'indigenous governance', which is based in the everyday lives of subjects and not imposed from the outside. Examples such as skater-built skateparks and other skateboarding projects are analyzed. I argue that it is important to theorize the productive encounter between governance and resistance and that resistance plays a constitutive role in the formation of rule. Indigenous forms of governance are increasingly appropriated to achieve the ends sought by political programmers. In the process, however, it is

170   *Kara-Jane Lombard*

also apparent that resistance can alter the programmed vision of rule, and the subjects of rule are able to bring the governors into alignment with their wills and their governances.

Governmentality and indigenous governance

According to Nikolas Rose and Peter Miller (1992, p. 183), government is a domain of

> strategies, techniques and procedures through which different forces seek to render programmes operable, and by means of which a multitude of connections are established between the aspirations of authorities and the activities of individuals and groups. These heterogeneous mechanisms we term *technologies of government*.

In analyzing the technologies of government responding to skateboarding, Foucault's rubric of 'governmentality' is a useful starting point. Governmentality is described as an analytics: a type of study 'concerned with an analysis of the specific conditions under which particular entities emerge, exist and change' (Dean 1999 pp. 20–21). As Mitchell Dean (p. 3), points out, studies of governmentality are problem centered and present oriented. According to such a perspective, it is the field of power that is in question, because as Michel Foucault (1980, p. 98) puts it, power

> is never localised here or there, never in anybody's hands, never appropriated as a commodity or piece of wealth. Power is employed and exercised through a net-like organisation. And not only do individuals circulate between its threads; they are always in the position of simultaneously undergoing and exercising this power. In other words, individuals are the vehicles of power, not its points of application.

In examining the field of power, governmentality theory is also useful for its engagement with the concept of resistance. Pat O'Malley, Lorna Weir, and Clifford Shearing's article 'Governmentality, Criticism, Politics' (1997) is an important reference in this regard. First, they note that there is a tendency in governmentality literature 'to separate out programmes from the processes of their "messy" implementation, and the related silencing of the constitutive role of contestation' (p. 512). Furthermore, governmentality literature often discusses the formation of programs from the programmers' perspective, which results in resistance being viewed in terms of obstruction and failure. However, as O'Malley, Weir, and Shearing articulate in the quote, contestations and resistances actually shape rule. They state that separating contestation from rule 'leaves little space for theorizing the *productive engagement* between them' (p. 511).

One of the ways in which the productive engagement between resistance and rule can be theorized is through an analysis of what Pat O'Malley terms 'indigenous governance'. Although exploring aspects of Australian policies of self-determination for Aboriginal people, O'Malley's concept can be more widely deployed. He argues that resistance can take the form of indigenous governances, that is, 'the forms of government that arise in, and are endemic to, the everyday lives of subjects' (1998, p. 158) which render governmental rule unworkable. Identifying the focus on mentalities of rule and the lack of sociological analysis in governmentality literature, O'Malley (1996b, p. 310) argues that this trend tends to produce a programmatic vision of governance which renders resistance as a negative: 'a source of programmatic failure'. Instead, he argues that 'Government and resistance articulate, mingle and hybridize, so that resistance cannot readily be thought of as external to rule. In this way, liberalism's governmental relations with resistance are characterized by incorporation of resistant, "indigenous" governance' (p. 310).

Furthermore, as O'Malley indicates, the appropriation of indigenous governance can be seen as an effect of the neoliberal (or advanced liberal) form of political-economic governance: 'Among the many forms of such "government at a distance", one of the most attractive to advanced liberalism is the appropriation of "indigenous' governances"' (p. 313). In his 1979 course, 'The Birth of Bio-Politics', Foucault moved away from tracing the genealogy of governmentality to a study of liberal and neoliberal forms of government. Liberalism superseded the earliest form of governmentality in Europe – the science of police (*Polizeiwissenschaft*). This refers to a program of detailed regulation concerned with taking care of living such as public tranquillity and order, security, health, and prosperity. As Foucault (1991, p. 91) explained,

> whereas the doctrine of the prince and the juridical theory of sovereignty are constantly attempting to draw the line between the power of the prince and any other form of power, because its task is to explain and justify this essential discontinuity between them, in the art of government the task is to establish a continuity, in both an upwards and a downwards direction.

He added, 'this downwards line, which transmits to individual behaviour and the running of the family the same principles as the good government of the state, is just at this time beginning to be called *police*' (p. 92). Police evolved to become a police of general morality and respectability (Dean, 1999, p. 91), and as David Garland (1997, p. 177) explains, 'was, from the first, criticized as unworkable, and liable to produce all manner of counter-productive consequences'.

In contrast, liberalism is thought to mark the instance when 'the dystopian dream of a totally administered society was abandoned' (Rose & Miller, 1992, p. 179). The art of liberal government 'abandons this megalomaniacal and obsessive fantasy of a totally administered society. Government now confronts itself with realities – market, civil society, citizens – that have their own internal logics and densities, their own intrinsic mechanisms of self-regulation' (Rose, 1993, p. 289). Wendy Larner (2000, p. 6) provides an interesting discussion which differentiates between 'analyses that understand neo-liberalism as a policy

172 *Kara-Jane Lombard*

framework, those that portray neo-liberalism as an ideology and those who conceptualize neoliberalism through the lens of neo-liberalism'. She points out that the most common conceptualization of neoliberalism is as a policy framework (p. 6), which is marked by a shift from Keynesian economics towards neoliberal principles such as the rule of the market, deregulation, and privatization. Larner goes on to describe the notion of neoliberalism as ideology as a more 'sociological' approach to neoliberalism which considers a wider range of institutions, organizations, and processes, such as Stuart Hall's analyses of Thatcherism (p. 9). Finally, Larner considers neoliberalism as a form of governmentality, which, as she points out, requires a move to Foucault and post-structuralism (p. 12). She adds, 'neo-liberalism is both a political discourse about the nature of rule and a set of practices that facilitate the governing of individuals from a distance' (p. 6).

Neoliberal forms of government have affected the ways authorities deal with skateboarding, such as 'governing at a distance', and the call to citizens to give their lives a specific entrepreneurial form. Thomas Lemke (2001, p. 203) works through two studies dealing with 'technologies of the self' to show that neoliberalism links a reduction in welfare state services and security systems to the increasing call for 'personal responsibility' and 'self-care'; thus individual bodies, collective bodies, and institutions must be 'lean', 'fit', 'flexible' and 'autonomous'. Responses to skateboarding increasingly appear to encourage skateboarding in many urban spaces, with the removal of skate stopper devices in cities, as well as a repeal on bans. However, neoliberal governance utilizes new kinds of governmental programs, strategies, and technologies to rule skateboarding, including appropriating indigenous governance.

Skater-built skateparks: Portland and San Diego

To explore the role of resistance and the incorporation of indigenous governance in the regulation and governmental rule of skateboarding, it is useful to examine some of the American skateparks which have been built by skateboarders without permission and later sanctioned by government authorities. Portland's Burnside Skatepark was the first instance of a DIY skater-built skatepark. Journalist Phillip Dawdy (n.d.) explains that in late 1990, the public right-of-way under Burnside Bridge was 'a flea market for junkies, alcoholics, prostitutes and drifters . . . Homeless men slept in abandoned cars; the pavement was littered with rigs for shooting heroin'. As a proposed skatepark in Gabriel Park had been rejected, on a Halloween night in 1990, 'five skaters – whose identities remain sketchy, even to this day – troweled a cement ramp into place against a disused loading dock and retaining wall'.

While business owners and authorities were initially suspicious, local businesses began to see the skaters as cleaning up the area, while police officers reported that the park had reduced auto thefts in the adjacent area significantly and that vandalism and break-ins of surrounding businesses had ceased (n.d.). One of the original skaters involved with the park, Mark Scott, recalls that the skaters made friends with business owners and police in the area, who 'thought it was cool that we were driving out the prostitutes and pushers' (Hamm 2010). In

Trucks, tricks, and technologies of government   173

June 1992, the City Council passed an ordinance legitimizing the park. Burnside Skatepark has now existed for more than 20 years, and it continues to evolve as elements are modified or updated.

A more recent example has occurred in San Diego. Like Portland, San Diego had banned street skating while building poorly designed skateparks. In April 1999, 'without asking for permission from the city or anyone else, skaters built obstacles – a funbox, flat rails, ledges, and pillar transitions – under the Washington Street Bridge to fulfil their desire for a skatepark' (Wagner 1999, p. 206). A month and a half later, the city stepped in and closed the park. It was then that skate shop owner Ken Lewis became involved and began 'sitting in at town-council meetings and doing the legwork, rallying skaters together' (Sullivan 2003). Once the city agreed to give the park a chance under certain conditions, it was 'just the first step in what turned out to be a long road of political obstacles' (2003). These obstacles included creating 'a non-profit organization to administer the park, land use permits, encroachment and removal permits, construction insurance, and most importantly the one and only Engineering Permit (a $2400 piece of documentation)' (WSVT n.d.). This process took until 2001, after which the park was completed (Balcom 2011). The park continued due to the 'generosity of skate companies, local businesses, and concerned citizens . . . [who contributed] anonymous cash to piles of dirt and truckloads of concrete' (Sullivan 2003). Fifteen years later, Washington Street Skatepark still operates as a public, free skatepark in San Diego and is a top-rated skateboard park in Southern California and winner of *Thrasher Magazine*'s T-Eddy awards (WSVT n.d.).

Examples such as Burnside and Washington Street have proliferated across the United States and led to what is widely considered a successful strategy for dealing with skateboarding. As O'Malley (1996a, p. 157) has stated, 'resistance may be an integral part of and contributor to programs regarded as successful, and be incorporated into programs rather than merely acting as an external source of program failure'. Skater-built skateparks are not only successful from the point of view of authorities, they also prove that resistance can alter the programmed vision of rule significantly and that it is possible for resistant subjects to inscribe their mark on rule.

Skater-built skateparks have emerged in sites where the increased presence of regulation of the use of public spaces renders street skating criminal, and skate facilities are lacking or are limited due to admission fees or other factors. Thus these forms of resistance, incorporated as indigenous governance, assert themselves not through overt opposition but by rendering practices of rule unworkable (O'Malley 1996b, p. 316). While skaters do enact more overt forms of resistance at times (for instance, the rallies that occurred to protest the Southbank Skate Park relocation in the UK), more subtle forms of resistance are often at work in skateboarding. Becky Beal (1992, p. 146) hints at the role of this form of opposition, which renders the practices of rule unworkable:

> [S]katers opposed dominant norms less intentionally by re-defining them. Skaters' use of public structures for their own needs is one example. Skaters

174 *Kara-Jane Lombard*

also re-defined the CSA sponsored competitions as a means to exclusive positions by demanding and creating them as inclusive, as a place for everyone to skate.

For Borden (1998), skateboarding may not create the explicit political critique of some groups, nor is it involved in very much social disruption. However, he argues that its resistive potential lies in its ambiguity, 'because it is neither explicit protest nor quiet conformism, game nor sport, public nor private activity, adult nor childish and, above all, precisely because it is a spatially and temporally diffused and dispersed activity'. Such conceptualizations of skateboarding demonstrate that it is able to disrupt 'good government' while not engaging in 'hostile conflict' (O'Malley 1996b, p. 315).

O'Malley (p. 313) points out that liberal government maximizes the freedom of the subject and involves 'governing at a distance'. This can clearly be seen at Burnside, where

> to this day no public funds have ever went [sic] into the facility. A majority of the materials were literally donated one bag of concrete at a time. The parks department doesn't include it as a sanctioned city park, but it does provide a trash dumpster and portable restroom.
>
> (Balcom 2011)

This governing at a distance through the incorporation of indigenous governance means that both the governed and the governing must compromise and accept forms of the other (O'Malley 1996b, pp. 316, 321–322).

The appropriation of indigenous governance in the instance of skater-built skateparks clearly involves a new way of governing skateboarding that differs from older strategies such as bans or fines, but it has also changed skateboarding culture. As photographer Bryce Kanights (cited in Hamm 2010) points out:

> The modern skatepark revolution began with the DIY construction of Burnside . . . Before Burnside, there were only a handful of skateparks, and it was painfully obvious that they weren't built by skateboarders. [Now there are] progressively constructed parks all over the world.

A further example of the way the increasing incorporation of indigenous governance has affected the culture of skateboarding can be seen on the Skaters for Public Skateparks website. Advocating DIY skateboarding projects, the organization states, 'The standard cost for a 10,000 square foot skatepark often lies in the $350,000 range – which is simply unattainable for most communities currently' (Balcom 2011). The website acknowledges the difficult decisions faced by community leaders, the increased budget shortfalls with no relief in sight, and so encourages skaters to provide skate opportunities for themselves 'to create facilities that everyone benefits from' (2011). As O'Malley (1998, p. 158) points out,

Trucks, tricks, and technologies of government 175

one of the reasons advanced liberalism favours the appropriation of indigenous governance is that it is more likely to appear to both the rulers and the ruled as the expression of those within the culture rather than as 'impositions from without'. This is evident on the Skaters for Public Skateparks website, which indicates that the responsibility for skatepark development lies with skaters. Furthermore, these skaters have clearly adopted the stance and language of neoliberal governance – which would not only require skaters to give their lives an entrepreneurial form but be active participants in their own governance.

On The Edge

To consider the role of resistance in governance in more detail, I want to turn to the Australian skateboarding project On The Edge: Skateboarding Is Not a Crime. While On The Edge does not exhibit the kind of 'visible' opposition seen in the skater-built parks of Burnside or San Diego, it illustrates another form in which indigenous governance has been incorporated into rule. On The Edge began in early 2003 and was described as 'a spectacular, dynamic, participatory live installation that contemplates intersections of skateboarding and art' (*On The Edge: Skateboarding Is Not a Crime*, 2004, p. 1). The initial concept was proposed by the Artistic Director of Area Theatre Company Melbourne, Rose Myers, to Awesome Arts in Perth, Western Australia. I first found out about On The Edge in May 2003 when Awesome Arts employee and Perth Youth Advisory Council (PYAC) member Bonnie Davies brought it to the attention of the PYAC, asking for support. Members were in support of this project, which would work to counter negative perceptions of skateboarding and challenge the divide between high and low culture.

On 19 June, I attended a meeting in which the organizations involved could discuss desired outcomes for the event. Representatives came from a variety of organizations for youth, including the West Australia Music Industry, Awesome Arts, Headquarters Skate Park, Skateboarding Association of Western Australia, and Perth Youth Advisory Council. Neoliberal forms of government often act through various organizations and institutions, as can be observed with On The Edge. It is interesting that one of the benefits of the project was seen to be the development of a productive, working relationship among all the youth organizations, which would 'help facilitate other collaborations or a sharing of resources between organisations in future years' (Davies 2004, p. 4). This inter-agency cooperation is particularly evident in neoliberal crime control (Garland 1997). The reason that neoliberal strategies of rule involve enlisting other organizations and individuals in governance is because

> "advanced liberal" government entails the adoption of a range of devices that seek to recreate the distance between the decisions of formal political institutions and other social actors, and to act upon these actors in new ways, through shaping and utilizing their freedom.
>
> (Rose 1993, p. 295)

176   *Kara-Jane Lombard*

At this initial meeting, there was some discussion of the negative stereotypes of skateboarding. As the minutes for the meeting stated, 'one of the important aspects of On The Edge was to encourage discussion and give balanced open views on skating and its culture' (Bonnie Davies, 2003, pers. comm., 19 July). This would become a central aim of the project – when Davies made a submission for PYAC sponsorship, the application stated that On The Edge would 'address the negative stereotypes that often surround young people and their interests (particularly skateboarding)' (Davies 2004, p. 3). It is interesting that even though skateboarding is so commercialized and mainstream, skaters report that it still has a negative reputation. The title for this project is particularly curious in that respect. 'On The Edge' seems to connect skateboarding to resistance and being 'extreme' while there is a tension with the subtitle: 'Skateboarding Is Not a Crime.' Although there was some early discussion of the title by representatives of some of the organizations involved in organizing the project, no alternatives were raised. It must be noted that none of the skate organizations were involved in this discussion.

By January 2004, a grant for a two-week workshop by Headquarters Skate Park was already approved, as well as a second grant applied for by Davies on behalf of PYAC, which allowed the artists in the two-week workshop to utilize skills and information developed from the workshop. In April, funding from ArtsWA, Community Arts Network Western Australia, and PYAC had also been approved for the first stages of the project. The first stage of the project – the workshop – ran in early May 2004. Eight young people participated in the workshop, which was facilitated by music and video artist Roly Skender and skater Raoul Willison. One of the participants of the workshop, skater and filmmaker Mathew de Koning (2004, pers. comm., 17 May), explained,

> [T]here was the eight of us and then two facilitators, Raoul and Roly, and we all just kind of discussed where we want to take this project and what we want to do with it. And got into HQ on the Saturday and looked at the equipment that we've got and just kind of went out and experimented really for the first 2 or 3 days with sights and sounds. We used some audio equipment and we filmed a bit – mainly at HQ and then on location, we went around to Claisebrook and stuff like that. And really just capturing whatever looked appealing to the eye or the ear. I mean, for example, one of the days there were a bunch of senior citizens waiting to go for a dance and I went up to them and they were all quite intrigued by what we were doing and I'd asked them if they wanted to participate by kinda standing among the stairs that we were skating down. And we sent four guys to jump down this flight of stairs and all the senior citizens were clapping and cheering for us, and they loved it, it was great. . . . and then from there we just kind of looked at what we'd done and collaborated the ideas of everybody and then just kind of thought alright well let's go for another 2 or 3 days of shooting to finish it off and then produced about a 7 and a half minute little clip with about four different local music tracks.

Trucks, tricks, and technologies of government   177

The final weekend of the workshop was a public event held at Headquarters at which the film clip made during the workshop was shown. The second stage of On The Edge involved the production of an original artwork, while the third stage would see a performance installation at the Awesome Festival in November 2005, which could possibly then be toured nationally.

While the aim of On The Edge appeared to be to educate and re-program the general public about skateboarding, the project attempted to bind individuals into games as players of certain types. As Garland (1997, p. 190) explains in relation to the new rationalities for the governance of crime in advanced liberal governance: 'The new economic rationality attempts to make up new kinds of individuals, or rather, to create and impart new forms of subjectivity, which individuals and organizations will adopt for themselves'. While skateboarding is not always construed as a crime, Garland's point is useful in identifying the new forms of subjectivity skaters are being encouraged to adopt under advanced liberal rule. In neoliberal government, 'the active citizen is obligated to act as an entrepreneur of his or her own capacities, skills, talents and so on' (Dean 1998, p. 102). In enrolling young people and skateboarders as active participants in their own governance, On The Edge certainly encouraged participants to give their lives a specific entrepreneurial form. The project was concerned with the professional development of the artists and aimed to give them skills and mentorship at a crucial, early stage of their lives (Davies 2004, pp. 2–3).

On The Edge is clearly an attempt to incorporate indigenous governance – not only was the project run by young people and skaters, but its promotional material repeatedly stressed its flexibility and that it is driven by those participating in the project. For O'Malley (1998, p. 158), government at a distance is central in neoliberalism and can be seen where indigenous governance is appropriated: 'this alignment permits the apparent retreat of formal, exogenous imposed government, as rule is carried out by the community "itself"' Of course there is no obvious indigenous governance in skate culture, (the point of skateboarding being that it is not organized like other sports). Unlike various hierarchies found in other forms of youth culture, (such as tags and pieces in hip hop graffiti, which constitute a form of governance of graffiti), there is no indigenous organization of skateboarding that liberal rule can appropriate (except for skill level perhaps). Since governmental programs cannot appropriate any obvious indigenous governance in skateboarding, On The Edge is much more open to the rule of indigenous governance (whereas similar strategies such as legal graffiti walls tend to be more controlled by the authorities administering them).

The incorporation of indigenous governance has many advantages for the governor. As the City of Perth *Skateboarding in the City – Strategy* document recognizes, real outcomes have been achieved in building skateparks for which the local skate community is consulted (City of Perth 2002, p. 2). Headquarters is an example of this. The skatepark, which opened in 2002 after six years of lobbying and planning, was not only developed in consultation with skaters and youth; it is

178   *Kara-Jane Lombard*

also run by young people. Also, rather than simply seeking to address unwanted street skating,

> Headquarters [sic] goal is to address the range of issues confronting young people today by providing an area which facilitates a broad range of activities – creative, cultural, access to multimedia, physical and educational . . . [and includes] youth development and youth service links.
>
> (Stoll 2002, p. 5)

In a background paper for the State Sustainability Strategy, Kerry Stoll (2002) argued that this is clearly significant, as it establishes more liveable communities, builds on social capital principles, and underscores the 'need for youth, community and government working together in partnership' (p. 2).

In terms of On The Edge, at the preliminary meeting to discuss the project, there was talk about creativity – how On The Edge could promote creativity as a development tool and that creativity takes a variety of forms. The project also intended to provide a 'legal platform for young people to express their ideas' (Davies 2004, p. 3) – in other words, to encourage young people to adopt legal forms of expression. In this way, rendering skateboarding creative and artistic was an attempt to incorporate (certain aspects of) skateboarding. As O'Malley argues, appropriations of indigenous governance valorize certain aspects of that which it seeks to rule (1996b, p. 318), generating a particular view of what constitutes that culture (p. 321). In this case, the aspects of skate culture being promoted and valorized were its creative and legal ones. On The Edge was thus able to capture the tendency by skaters to define skateboarding as creative and artistic, which accompanied the backlash against notions of 'extreme' and resistance in skateboarding. It is these aspects which are seen to function better in achieving the goals of liberal government (p. 317). Consequently, those aspects of skateboarding seen as counterproductive or incompatible with the project of rule, such as its resistive potential or 'rebellious roots' (Staple 2015), were neutralized or suppressed.

Despite the advantages it offers authorities, as the incorporation of indigenous governance requires a kind of governing at a distance, it is often problematic. As O'Malley (1998, p. 169) notes, the incorporation of actual or potentially disruptive elements may be unavoidable, and all manner of concessions may be necessary to achieve the desired result, compromising the project from the outset. This has occurred to an extent with On The Edge. Because young people and skaters directed On The Edge in a kind of government from below (p. 157), there was a possibility that there will be disruptive elements and concessions. For instance, this project clearly disrupted the City of Perth's skateboarding program (Lombard 2010).

Furthermore,

> [Y]outh policy in Australia has taken shape in response to a range of conceptions of the young and ambitions for their reconstruction. One response as

White (1991) points out in his study has been to define the young person as a social *problem*, the other has been to define young people as a *victim*.

(Bessant, Sercombe, & Watts 1998, p. 77)

On the other hand 'youth policy can also evoke images of youth as *the future*' (p. 78). On The Edge disrupts this view of youth by accepting 'young people as a relevant and important part of the community now, not just as society's "future"' (Davies 2004, p. 4). Although this has not compromised the governance of skateboarding, it does reflect the problem of incorporating indigenous governance.

Conclusion

From the quoted examples, it is possible to observe that governmental programs, strategies, and technologies arise out of a complex field of contestation (Rose 1999, p. 275) and are inscribed by many voices – including the subjects of governance. As Miller and Rose (1990, p. 14) explain, the

> "real" always insists on the form of resistance to programming; and the programmer's world is one of constant experiment, invention, failure, critique and adjustment . . . Whilst a particular political program sets out specific objectives for government . . . the operationalization of a programme is achieved through a complex and difficult process.

While governmentality literature tends to separate governance from resistance, ignore it, or theorize it out of the picture, it is important to consider, since resistance is so implicated in governance. This chapter has attempted to address the way in which resistance and rule relate to one another in productive ways by exploring the appropriation of indigenous governance in skateboarding. While it is possible to read the appropriation of indigenous governance as resistance being constitutive of rule, but only in ways allowed by governing mentalities (O'Malley 1996b, p. 322) or as the engulfing and neutralizing of resistance (p. 323), I concur with O'Malley (1998, p. 169) that 'the existence of indigenous forms within the subjugating regime provides sites within rule for the operation of counter-discourses and subordinated knowledges'. Furthermore, as political programmers increasingly appropriate indigenous forms of governance, it is apparent that resistance can alter the programmed vision of rule, and the subjects of rule have brought the governors into alignment with their wills and their governances. Reconsidering the role of resistance in any youth culture is important, particularly in light of post-subcultural forms and the various (competing and subordinate) discourses and knowledges that are revealed by such an analysis. Such investigations could also reveal the degree to which potential or actual progressive social change exists.

With the increase in civically engaged skateboarders and skaters who are taking an active role in their governance coupled with the new urban social control regimes of advanced liberal governments, there is the recognition that skateboarding is part of urban life, that it has a place in society and on the streets. Borden

180   *Kara-Jane Lombard*

(1998) locates skateboarding in a long struggle by the unempowered and disenfranchised for a distinctive social space in the history of cities. Exploring the changing roles of public space, Borden (1998) claims that 'cities are always places of contestation and contradiction, conflict and counter-cultural engagements'. The kinds of urban practices discussed in this chapter, like other forms of DIY or participatory urbanism, are reshaping urban spaces, potentially building a new city with new functions, meanings, and a new urban politics.

References

Balcom, C 2011, *Ten DIY skateparks*, Skaters for Public Skateparks. Available from: www.skatepark.org/park-development/2011/05/ten-diy-skateparks/. [28 April 2015].

Beal, B 1992, *The subculture of skateboarding: beyond social resistance*. PhD thesis. University of Northern Colorado.

Bessant, J, Sercombe, H & Watts, R 1998, *Youth studies: an Australian perspective*, Longman, South Melbourne.

Borden, I 1998, 'An affirmation of urban life: socio-spatial censorship in the late twentieth century', *Archis*, vol. 5. Available from: www.archis.org. [10 November 2003].

Borden, I 2001, *Skateboarding, space and the city: architecture and the body*, Berg, Oxford.

City of Perth 2002, *Skateboarding in the city – strategy*.

Davies, B 2004, *Submission for PYAC sponsorship*.

Dawdy, P n.d., 'Pariahs on the pavement', *W Week*. Available from: www.wweek.com/html2/leada122700.html. [1 February 2005].

Dean, M 1998, 'Administering asceticism: reworking the ethical life of the unemployed citizen', in. M Dean & B Hindess (eds), *Governing Australia: studies in contemporary rationalities of government*, Cambridge University Press, Cambridge, pp. 87–107.

Dean, M 1999, *Governmentality: power and rule in modern society*, Sage Publications, London.

Foucault, M 1980, *Power/knowledge*, Harvester, Brighton.

Foucault, M 1991, 'Governmentality', in G Burchell, C Gordon & P Miller (eds), *The Foucault effect: studies in governmentality*, University of Chicago Press, Chicago, pp. 87–104.

Garland, D 1997, '"Governmentality" and the problem of crime: Foucault, criminology, sociology', *Theoretical Criminology*, vol. 1, no. 2, pp. 173–214.

Hamm, K 2010, 'Burnside turns 20', *ESPN*, 30 October. Available from: http://espn.go.com/action/skateboarding/news/story?id=5741014. [28 April 2015].

Larner, W 2000, 'Neo-liberalism: policy, ideology, governmentality', *Studies in Political Economy*, vol. 63, pp. 5–25.

Lemke, T 2001, '"The birth of bio-politics": Michel Foucault's lecture at the College de France on neo-liberal governmentality', *Economy & Society*, vol. 30, no. 2, pp. 190–207.

Lombard, K-J 2010, 'Skate and create/skate and destroy: the commercial and governmental incorporation of skateboarding', *Continuum: Journal of Media and Cultural Studies*, vol. 24, no. 4, pp. 475–488.

Miller, P & Rose, N 1990, 'Governing economic life', *Economy & Society*, vol. 19, no. 1, pp. 1–31.

Nolan, N 2003, 'The ins and outs of skateboarding and transgression in public space in Newcastle, Australia', *Australian Geographer*, vol. 34, no. 3, p. 311.

O'Malley, P 1996a, 'Risk and responsibility' in A Barry, T Osborne & N Rose (eds), *Foucault and political reason: liberalism, neo-liberalism and rationalities of government*, University of Chicago Press, Chicago, pp. 189–208.

O'Malley, P 1996b, 'Indigenous governance', *Economy and Society*, vol. 25, no. 3, pp. 310–326.

O'Malley, P 1998, 'Indigenous governance', in M Dean & B Hindess (eds), *Governing Australia: studies in contemporary rationalities of government*, Cambridge University Press, Cambridge, pp. 156–172.

O'Malley, P, Weir, L & Shearing, C 1997, 'Governmentality, criticism, politics', *Economy and Society*, vol. 26, no. 4, pp. 501–517.

On the Edge: skateboarding is not a crime 2004. Awesome Arts, Perth, Western Australia.

Rose, N 1993, 'Government, authority and expertise in advanced liberalism', *Economy & Society*, vol. 22, no. 3, pp. 283–299.

Rose, N 1999, *Powers of freedom: reframing political thought*, Cambridge University Press, Cambridge.

Rose, N & Miller, P 1992, 'Political power beyond the State: problematics of government', *The British Journal of Sociology*, vol. 43, no. 2, pp. 173–205.

Staple 2015, *Hey guy, cool job: Morgan Campbell of Skateboarding Australia*. Available from: www.acclaimmag.com/lifestyle/hey-guy-cool-job-morgan-campbell-of-skateboarding-australia/. [28 April 2015].

Stoll, K 2002, *Youth and sustainability: social capital social entrepreneurship and youth civic engagement as building blocks for sustainable communities – a case study of the Headquarters youth facility*. Available from: www.sustainability.dpc.wa.gov.au/docs/BGPapers/KerryStoll.pdf. [3 March 2004].

Sullivan, A 2003, 'Skatepark a go-go', *Transworld Skateboarding*, July. Available from: www.skateboarding.com/skate/skate_biz/. [10 September 2004].

Wagner, G 1999, 'Build it and they will come', *Transworld Skateboarding*, October, pp. 204–209.

WSVT n.d., *History of the Washington Street Skatepark*. Available from: http://washingtonstreetskatepark.org/history/. [28 April 2015].

13 Transformative improvisation

The creation of the commercial skateboard shoe, 1960–1979

Thomas Turner

Improvisation is at the heart of skateboarding. The skateboarder creates a new ride each time, responding to the external and inner worlds, combining individual moves into a coherent whole. New tricks and styles are the result of playful experimentation, as skaters explore and push the boundaries of what is possible, reacting against the hard reality of the built environment. The architect Iain Borden (2001, p. 33) has argued that by appropriating and exploiting physical terrain, the earliest skateboarders offered a new way of using and thinking about architecture: '[t]he modernist space of suburbia was found, adapted and reconceived as another kind of space, as a concrete wave'. As Tony Alva (cited in Brooke 1999, p. 79), one of skateboarding's great pioneers, put it, the urban and suburban landscape was 'built by man to serve one purpose, but when you have the mentality of a skateboarder and you see this terrain, you can see moves that these people who built it never saw'.

The mentality to which Alva referred, the skateboarder's ability to perceive greater possibilities in objects created by others, has a long tradition. The skateboard itself began as a children's plaything improvised from broken roller skates and scavenged timber. Skateboarding – and the skateboard – developed when surfers reimagined this childish toy as a land-based surfboard. The polyurethane wheels that revolutionised skateboarding in the 1970s were a creative reinterpretation of something intended for roller skates hired to novices at roller rinks. Materially, the development of skateboarding has been characterised by the way in which manufactured objects have been appropriated and put to new uses, a process that has reconfigured perceptions of common goods and commodities.

The story of polyurethane wheels illustrates another theme in this history: the rapid commodification of skateboarders' creative reimaginings. Polyurethane roller skate wheels, repackaged and advertised as 'Cadillac Wheels' for skateboards, hit the Californian market after Frank Nasworthy, a young surfer-skater, visited Creative Urethane, a factory owned by his friend's father. He realised the soft plastic wheels produced for roller skates offered an improved ride over the steel or clay wheels fitted to skateboards, and before long, the polyurethane skateboard wheel was established as a commodity in its own right (Brooke 1999, pp. 46–7; Davidson 1985; Hiss & Bart 1976; Weiss 2004). In the same fashion, toy manufacturers began selling roller skate wheels attached to short wooden planks as stand-alone entities in the late 1950s, transforming an improvised plaything into a manufactured object. Californian surf companies introduced 'sidewalk surfers' in the early 1960s, rebranding a toy as sporting equipment. Through the 1970s, skateparks that replicated the pools, pipes, and ditches ridden by Californian innovators were built by entrepreneurs keen to cash in on skateboarding. As Borden (2001, pp. 57–88) points out, physical echoes of southern California reverberate in skateparks around the world.

This process of creative improvisation and commercial exploitation was crucial to the development of skateboarding, which needed constant collaboration between practitioners – those who skateboarded – and producers to reproduce itself as a practice. The two groups together created the products and attitudes necessary for it to flourish. This notion, that producers and consumers are vital for the reproduction of practice, has been highlighted by Elizabeth Shove and Mika Pantzar (2005). In their work on the invention and reinvention of Nordic walking, they argue that 'new practices consist of new configurations of existing elements or of new elements in conjunction with those that already exist' (p. 61). These elements include material products, but also ways of thinking. Their spread is dependent on the actions of consumers and producers. In Shove and Pantzar's example, new conceptions of walking with sticks were a necessary corollary to the spread of Nordic walking. These attitudinal shifts prompted both the reassessment of existing products (in their case, the ski pole) and the manufacture of new specialist equipment, which then further encouraged the growth of Nordic walking as a practice.

This chapter builds on their approach but foregrounds objects. It looks at how new ways of understanding goods develop and how shifts in perception contribute to the creation of new types of product. Focusing on the footwear associated with skateboarding in the United States in the 1960s and 1970s, it considers how improvisation within skateboarding was reproduced and commercialized and reveals the processes by which the skateboard shoe was created as a specific category of footwear. More generally, it shows how the originators and early adopters of practices and the entrepreneurial producers who seize upon their actions affect the way commodities are marketed and more widely understood.

Shoes for skateboarding – 1960s

It is possible, just about, to skate in any type of footwear, but it is easiest in shoes with flat soles that grip the surface of the board and which are sufficiently flexible to enable tricks to be performed. It helps if they are lightweight and hardwearing, as they need to facilitate movement, protect riders' feet, and cope with the knocks and scrapes needed to manoeuver the board. Skating exacts a heavy toll on footwear, so shoes need to be affordable and easily replaced. Perhaps most importantly, the shoes best suited to skateboarding offer very little intermediary between the soles of the feet and the board. As two British skaters suggested in 1989, '[t]he best footwear for skating is grippy . . . tough and flexible'. The rider needs to 'be able to "feel" the board through the sole', so '[f]lat bottomed shoes

184 *Thomas Turner*

hold a considerable advantage' (Adams & Hills 1989, p. 12). These are hardly the most exacting or precise requirements, and so almost anything with a flat sole can become an improvised skateboard shoe.

The idea that special footwear may have been a necessity probably did not trouble the kids who rode homemade or toy boards in the 1950s and early 1960s. Photographs show them wearing common shoes, usually mass-produced canvas-and-rubber sneakers made by Converse, United States Rubber, and other American manufacturers. These originated in the early twentieth century as basketball or tennis shoes but were later marketed as multi-purpose sports and leisure footwear. By the 1930s, manufacturers sold them as inexpensive children's footwear, and by the 1950s, they were staple footwear for American boys and, to a lesser extent, girls. In 1962, the *New York Times* declared them 'a symbol of admission to full-fledged boyhood' (Bender 1962, p. 48) and in 1966 published the results of a survey that showed sneakers remained popular among boys in New York's public schools (Cook 1966). It is hardly surprising that when in spring 1965 *Life* published an extended photo essay on skateboarding, their photographer, Bill Eppridge, captured skaters in Manhattan in a mixture of canvas sneakers, suede desert boots, and leather shoes. The boys he shot skating the city streets all wore high-topped basketball shoes (*Skateboard Mania* 1965, pp. 126–128). Similarly, when students from Wesleyan, Amherst, and Williams universities took part in a light-hearted skateboard competition that involved a beer can slalom for the 'coveted award – a hot dog mounted on an aluminum foil plate', they 'donned their oldest sneakers' (Weintraub 1965, p. 35).

In California, where in the early 1960s surfers developed skateboarding into 'sidewalk surfing', there was disagreement over whether shoes were even necessary. For surfers, being able to feel and control the board were paramount. Many surf-inspired skateboarders therefore skated barefoot. The teenagers filmed skating around southern California in Noel Black's 1965 short film *Skaterdater* do so without shoes. It is only when one of them abandons his skateboard to be with a girl that he puts on a pair of sneakers. Many of those who appeared in Surfer Publications' *The Quarterly Skateboarder* (later known as *Skateboarder Magazine*) in 1964 to 1965 were similarly barefoot, as were the Californian skateboarders photographed by *Life* (*Skateboard Mania* 1965, pp. 126, 132). The preference for barefoot skating was not universal, however, and many opted to protect against the '[b]ashed legs and scraped toes common among skateboard enthusiasts' by donning lightweight shoes (p. 132). California's warm weather and sporting culture meant shoes intended for boating, tennis, basketball, or leisurewear were widely available, and it was these that were commonly worn for skateboarding. Photographs of the Anaheim International Skateboard Championships in 1965 show some competitors in canvas shoes and others barefoot (McNulty & Stoner 1965, pp. 21, 23, 30). The team assembled by the Vita-Pakt Juice Company to promote its Hobie skateboards that appeared in *The Quarterly Skateboarder* (vol. 1, no. 1, winter 1964, pp. 19–27) skated both barefoot and in dark oxford-style deck shoes, a classic design with canvas uppers and flat rubber soles. Shoes like this were introduced for tennis and boating in the 1920s and 1930s but, like the similarly

Transformative improvisation 185

aged basketball shoes, had since passed into more general use. Their popularity among skateboarders reflected the comparable needs of participants in different activities; skateboarders, tennis players, and sailors needed lightweight shoes that provided good grip. Indeed, the use of boating and basketball shoes for skateboarding reflected the similarities between varnished wooden yacht decks, basketball courts, and early skateboards.

Skaters in the 1950s and 1960s could select from a variety of shoes, but in most instances, all but the wealthiest, dedicated, or professional would have worn the same shoes as they did for everyday or 'play' purposes. This generally meant rubber-soled canvas sneakers, which with their flat soles, wide availability, and low price were well suited to skateboarders' needs. More serious skaters, like those sponsored by equipment manufacturers, could determine which shoes best suited their needs and situation through experience and experimentation, but in the absence of anything designed explicitly for skateboarding, they improvised with footwear produced for other sports and leisure activities. The absence of fixed ideas about what should be worn was captured by an advertisement for Vita-Pakt's Hobie 27-inch Fibreglass Competition Model. It showed seven pairs of feet around a board: five wore battered canvas oxfords, one a pair of beat-up basketball sneakers, and one was barefoot (Vita-Pakt Juice Company 1965).

It was not until the mid 1960s that shoes were marketed directly at skateboarders. The Randolph Rubber Company, a shoe manufacturer with factories in Massachusetts and California, introduced the Randy '720', a flat rubber-soled oxford, with blue or green suede uppers, white rubber foxing, and a distinctive red-and-blue rubber sole in 1964 to 1965. It sold for around $15 in surfing and marine stores (Blümlein et al. 2008, p. 27).[1] Advertisements in *Skateboarder Magazine* and *Surfer* showed it being worn by Californian skateboarders and suggested it was designed explicitly for skateboarding (advertisements reproduced in Blümlein et al. 2008, pp. 24, 26). Copy highlighted that it was the 'Official Shoe of the National Skateboard Championship Association', a newly formed organisation that worked to promote skateboarding as a sport, and emphasised the hardwearing nature of the outsole: 'The Randy "720" SKATE BOARDER is designed with the new TUFF TOE 'N HEEL, guaranteed to withstand tuff treatment given by the skateboarder' (advertisement reproduced in Blümlein et al. 2008, p. 24).

This was the first time a shoe was advertised as being especially for skateboarding, yet from a material or production perspective, the '720' required nothing out of the ordinary. To most observers it would have been indistinguishable from a generic casual deck shoe. Technically and stylistically, it differed little from shoes sold for other purposes. The upper used tougher suede in place of canvas, but the pattern was the same as any other oxford-style leisure shoe. The sole was attached in the standard fashion, with a vulcanization process used across the industry for decades. Even the special 'Randyprene' compound used for the sole could, quite probably, have been the same as that used for other models. The patterns, moulds, and 'Randy knowhow' it required could easily be put to other uses. It was, in essence, simply a standard leisure shoe repackaged to appeal to a new market. Yet by marketing their shoe in this way, Randolph built upon the actions

186 *Thomas Turner*

of skateboarders, who had begun to wear generic leisure footwear as skateboard shoes, and so reinforced an imaginative transformation that had already started.

The '720s' popularity among skateboarders is difficult to assess, mainly because it looked so similar to other models. Many skateboarders wore oxford-style deck shoes, but from photographs, it is hard to tell if they are Randy's '720'. In a photograph of the South East Bay skateboard team taken around 1965, only one of four members has the distinctive red-and-blue soles of the '720'. The rest wear deck shoes or low-top basketball sneakers (South East Bay Skateboard Club c.1965). Some photographs of the Anaheim Championships in 1965, including one used on the cover of *Skateboarder Magazine*, show the '720', but more often on the feet of officials than competitors (McNulty & Stoner 1965, pp. 1, 39).

Why Randolph jumped on skateboarding is even less clear. The company lagged behind Converse and United States Rubber as the third-largest casual shoe manufacturer in the United States. Perhaps by entering the skateboard market before its bigger rivals and establishing links to the bodies that looked set to shape its future, it hoped to become as closely associated with skateboarding as Converse was with basketball. Certainly, with a production base in southern California, company executives would have been aware of the growing popularity of skateboards through the early 1960s. More tellingly, perhaps, Randolph was happy to exploit novelties and cater to short-term popular tastes; during the 1960s, similar rubber-soled deck shoes were produced to tie in with the *Batman* and *Mighty Mouse* television shows (Randolph Rubber Company c.1960, c.1966). The '720' may well have been another attempt to capitalise on youthful tastes. Whatever the reasons behind the shoe, the company's link with skateboarding was short lived. Skateboarding faded from public view during 1966, the victim of ordinances that banned skateboarders from city streets, concerns over safety, and unreliable boards that put off many novices. The market collapsed, and manufacturers bailed out. The small groups of skaters who continued to skate through the late 1960s and early 1970s did so largely without manufactured equipment and certainly without specialist shoes.

Shoes for skateboarding – 1970s

By the mid-1970s, when skateboarding enjoyed a second wave of popularity, the footwear market had changed. The canvas-and-rubber sneakers popular in the 1960s were joined by a variety of technically complex, increasingly specialised sports training shoes, designed to meet the needs of participants in different sports and leisure activities. These were developed during the 1950s and 1960s, primarily in Germany, where adidas and Puma pioneered new soling and plastics technologies and innovative production techniques as they fought to dominate international sports markets. Rival manufacturers around the world followed the German firms' technical lead and quickly introduced specialist shoes of their own, often based on copied designs. For American consumers, the reduction of trade tariffs that protected domestic rubber manufacturers and the arrival in the early

Transformative improvisation 187

1970s of dedicated sports shoe retailers meant shoes like this were an easily accessible, affordable alternative to more traditional leisure styles.

Shifts in the casual shoe market were apparent in the advice provided by the rash of skateboarding books published in the late 1970s. Although hastily assembled and often produced by writers with little connection to skateboarding, they nevertheless provide a picture of the shoes thought suitable for skating. Howard Reiser (1978, p. 16) told would-be skaters 'to wear rubber-soled shoes or athletic shoes that do not have any heels'. LaVada Weir (1978, p. 23) recommended 'shoes with non-slip soles. You can't beat sneakers. If your ankle needs more strength, wear high sneakers'. Adrian Ball (1977, p. 30) told novices to avoid 'everyday shoes or boots' and wear 'plimsolls – provided they offer a good grip – or the now popular "training" shoes with high lace-ups which give some ankle protection'. He also suggested '[l]eisure footwear intended to be worn when sailing' (p. 30). Glenn and Eve Bunting (1977, p. 28) recommended tennis shoes, so long as the laces were tied.

As they had in the 1960s, skateboarders found shoes designed for other activities were perfectly serviceable. *SkateBoarder* admitted specialist footwear was not necessary and acknowledged that '[m]ost of the well known shoe companies, such as adidas, Converse, Nike, Puma, have several styles which are ideal for skateboarders' (Schneider 1979, p. 21). Photographs in books, magazines, and the press show skaters in a variety of sports and leisure footwear, most often shoes associated with tennis or basketball. Branded models from the likes of adidas, Puma, Onitsuka, Converse, Pro-Keds, and Nike and a huge range of unbranded court, deck, and running shoes all appear to have been popular.

With rising interest in skateboarding, Californian skateboard and surf manufacturers seized the trend for footwear specialisation. In 1976, Hang Ten, a surfwear company, launched the Skateboarder, which it claimed was 'the first shoe designed exclusively for the sport' (Hang Ten 1976). Advertising said it was 'designed for skateboarders by skateboarders', but it was made of heavy leather, with a stiffened sole, and looked more like a bowling shoe than something that would provide flexibility and feel on a skateboard (1976). In all likelihood, despite the advertising claims, it was probably a style borrowed from elsewhere, hastily adapted to capture a new market. More suitable Makaha- and Hobie-branded shoes were launched soon after. The Makaha 'Radial' had green nylon and suede uppers that were almost identical to Nike running shoes and a rounded, moulded sole intended to allow movement on a board. Advertising claimed it was tailored to skateboarders' needs:

> Now, you don't have to wear a remade sneaker or deck shoe . . . because we've built Radials for skating instead of walking. Radials unique sole configuration (Patent Pending) is designed to achieve the ultimate responsiveness with maximum body flow. You get a faster new feel for your board. Try the REAL skateboard shoe. You never had to do so little to be so radical.
>
> (Makaha Sportswear 1978)

188 *Thomas Turner*

The Hobie shoe arrived in 1978 (Hobie Athletic Footwear 1978). A rubber-soled canvas high-top with bright blue uppers, it was made in Taiwan to a generic design. Similar models were available for other sports from adidas, Puma, and Nike; relatively minor cosmetic differences aside, the Nike All Court, a shoe intended for basketball and racket sports, was virtually identical. Nevertheless, the legend 'FOR SKATEBOARDING USE ONLY NOT DESIGNED FOR OTHER ACTIVITIES' was stitched into the tongue label (Blümlein et al. 2008 pp. 46–47).

The new generation of specialist skateboard shoes drew upon growing expertise in the manufacture of modern sports shoes, particularly in Asia. Factories in Japan, Taiwan, and Korea had become proficient in the production of shoes like those made in Europe and regularly made shoes to order for export. Imitation and copying were rife, and it was common for essentially identical models to be produced for a number of different brands. Blue Ribbon Sports, the company that created the Nike brand, began as an importer of Japanese-made sports shoes for the American market. The first Nike basketball shoes were off-the-shelf designs produced by Nippon Rubber and branded with the company's swoosh logo (Strasser & Becklund 1993, p. 119). In the late 1970s, skateboard companies like Makaha and Hobie followed a similar approach, improvising and making do with available designs but tweaking them to appeal to their customers. Generic shoes that were sold by some companies as tennis, basketball, or training shoes were rebranded and remarketed as skateboard footwear with only minor material alterations.

Skateboard shoes – the Van Doren Rubber Company

Films and photographs from the 1970s suggest the Hang Ten, Makaha, and Hobie shoes enjoyed limited success. The Makaha and Hobie models were worn by some elite Californian skaters, most likely recipients of free shoes, but were absent from images taken elsewhere. Either they were hard to find outside California or ordinary skaters preferred shoes made by other companies. By contrast, many skaters wore shoes produced by Van Doren Rubber, a company that had not set out to make a skateboard shoe. Celebrity skaters like Stacy Peralta, Tony Alva, Shogo Kubo, and Jay Adams wore them, and they routinely appeared in magazine photographs and advertisements for other companies. Because of this, they were the shoes to which many young skaters aspired and, by the early 1980s, were so closely associated with skateboarding that in Britain they became a way by which skaters identified each other (Whitter 2005). Yet Van Doren was not a skateboard or surf manufacturer, and its shoes were not made initially with skateboarders in mind. Its experience in the late 1970s demonstrates the power of skateboarding to transform ideas about goods and the importance of collaboration between producers and consumer-practitioners.

The company was established in 1965 by Paul Van Doren in Anaheim, California (see interviews with Steve Van Doren in Le 2005; Palladini 2009, pp. 6,

Transformative improvisation 189

11–17). Born in 1930, Van Doren was raised in Massachusetts, the heartland of the American shoe industry, and began his working life on the floor of Randolph's Boston factory. He worked through the ranks to become an executive vice president and in the early 1960s was given responsibility for the company's Californian factory. He quit soon after and moved west permanently to establish his own business. He aimed to make shoes and sell them directly to the public, integrating manufacturing and retail, and by so doing hoped to lower prices and increase profits. A factory equipped with second-hand machinery and a connected store opened in March 1966. The business expanded fast. Ten more stores opened in southern California in the first ten weeks of business, and within eighteen months, there were fifty Van Doren stores across the region. By 1974, there were almost seventy (Brooke 1999, p. 124). For the next decade, Van Doren (or Vans) shoes were available only through Californian House of Van stores or by mail order. The company advertised that customers could 'save up to 50% at Van's factory-direct prices' (Van Doren c.1972).

The warm weather of southern California created a year-round market for casual footwear that Van Doren hoped to exploit. The range offered was simple: generic canvas and leather leisure shoes with chunky vulcanized rubber soles. The core men's shoe, the #44, was a simple, lightweight canvas oxford, similar to the Randolph '720' and countless other shoes produced since the 1920s. In his study of innovation and the forces that surround everyday objects, Harvey Molotch (2003, p. 1) argues that

> to understand any one thing you have to learn how it fits into larger arrays of physical objects, social sentiments, and ways of being. In the world of goods, as in worlds of any other sort, each element is just one interdependent fragment of a larger whole.

The Van Doren range was shaped by the climate and social habits of Southern California, but also by the aged plant installed in the company's factory. As Molotch has shown, creativity is frequently affected by the hard reality of machine tooling (p. 107). Van Doren was equipped only to produce shoes with vulcanized rubber soles. Footwear manufacturers can vary upper styles relatively easily by changing the shape and size of the pieces that are sewn together to make them up, but variations in soling require different machinery and are more difficult to achieve. Each Van Doren model was therefore built around the same basic foundation. Yet because it was a small business with manufacturing facilities in California, the company could cater directly to customers' desires and tailor the uppers accordingly; innovation focussed on those aspects of the shoe that could be altered. Shoes were produced in small numbers in response to individual whims and short-lived fashions. Stores took personalised orders and offered customers a palette of colours and fabrics. If particular combinations proved popular, larger batches were made and offered for direct sale. When Van Doren noticed browsers rejected shoes because they did not like the material used, customers were invited

190 *Thomas Turner*

to supply their own fabrics. This flexibility contributed to the company's regional success. Podiatrists recommended it because it could manufacture pairs of shoes in different widths and sizes, and a speciality was made of multi-coloured shoes for high school, cheerleading, band, and drill team uniforms.

Van Doren was ideally placed to benefit from the Californian skateboarding boom. Proximity, availability, and the company's willingness to accommodate customers' needs all contributed to their popularity. Tony Alva (cited in Palladini 2009, p. 27), for example, has said he wore them because 'there was a little shop two blocks from my junior high school . . . and we were able to buy one shoe at a time'. The influential Zephyr team of which he was a member wore the dark blue Van Doren #44 at the 1974 National Championships in part because Van Doren shoes were already popular among teenagers in the Santa Monica neighbourhood in which many of the team lived (Wentzl Ruml interviewed in Peralta 2001[2]). As Alva suggests, price was a significant factor in the company's popularity. Van Doren shoes cost less than similar alternatives, an important consideration for the disadvantaged teenagers who rode for Zephyr. Yet without realising it, Van Doren had also created a shoe that was well equipped for skateboarding. Their thick, hardwearing sole by chance provided just the right amount of grip and flexibility desired by skaters. *SkateBoarder* declared them 'fairly soft soled, which enables more "feel" of the board', and therefore almost perfectly suited to skating (Schneider 1979, p. 21).

The company, however, did little at first to court this new market. When Jim Van Doren (cited in Horowitz 1978, p. 173), Paul's brother and partner, was interviewed by *SkateBoarder* in 1978, he claimed Van Doren only 'became involved in the skateboarding industry because it became apparent [it] was already making a shoe that had proved itself with the skaters in California'. He attributed the popularity of the company's shoes 'to their long-wearing and excellent grip features – plus the fact that [skaters] could get them in different color combinations' (p. 173). Skateboarders were just another customer group. The company only began to target them directly after the Californian skateboarding boom became impossible to ignore. It did so by tailoring the shoes' uppers to skateboarders' desires. The first skateboard-specific model, the #95, was launched in 1976. Designed with Alva, it simply added foam wadding and a reinforced heel counter to the standard #44. Alva (cited in Palladini 2009, p. 27) said he 'asked for a little more padding around the ankle and some cool colors, that's all' and that he wanted to create 'a more distinctive style' for skateboarders. The Van Doren sole was the same as ever, and the shoe was sold in colour combinations of royal blue, light blue, navy, gold, red, brown, beige, black, and white. The usual 'Van Doren' heel label was replaced with a new skateboard logo with the slogan 'Off The Wall', a phrase Peralta and Alva used to describe pool skating (p. 13). Advertisements emphasised the endorsement of celebrated skaters:

> I have worn Vans most of my life, and recently designed their Skateboard shoe. They are the favorite in Santa Monica among myself and all the boyz. – TONY ALVA

Transformative improvisation 191

I wear nothing but Vans. They're dependable for critical situations.
— STACY PERALTA

They're light, comfortable, with good traction. — CHRIS CHAPUT
(Van Doren 1977).

A second skateboarding-inspired model was launched in 1978. The #36 introduced a new upper style with a 'leather cap toe and heel, leather eyelets [and a] wild leather racing stripe' but again retained Van Doren's standard rubber sole (Van Doren 1978). Nevertheless, advertising claimed the 'exclusive waffle sole design is constructed with super grip built right in' and suggested that, '[w]hen you're skating, you can feel the difference . . . the difference that makes you a champ' (Van Doren 1979). Van Doren products were given to many professional and amateur skaters before they were made more widely available. *SkateBoarder* photographs showed the #36 being worn by Peralta and other stars several months before advertisements and mail-order coupons made it available to a bigger audience. By the end of the decade, Van Doren was closely associated with skateboarding and often considered a manufacturer of specialist skateboard shoes, which had become a sizeable chunk of the company's business. Despite the company's accidental route into skateboarding, *SkateBoarder* dubbed Jim Van Doren the '[p]atron saint of skatefeet' (Horowitz 1978, p. 173).

Vans were skateboard shoes in the tradition of the Randy '720', a basic model tweaked and remarketed for a specific market segment in response to a new way of using an existing product. From a material perspective, the alterations that changed standard shoes into skateboarding shoes were minimal: slightly different upper patterns, a new heel label, a bit more padding. The transformation was more imaginative; it was because Vans shoes were thought of as skateboarding shoes that they became skateboarding shoes. This transformation relied more on collaboration between consumers and producers. Because skateboarders considered Vans skate shoes and Van Doren marketed them as such, each party reinforced and replicated the central idea, allowing basic leisure shoes to be reborn as a new type of footwear.

By echoing the imaginative transformations effected by consumers, producers legitimate shifts in use and encourage the spread of new ways of using and thinking about their products. In this way, casual shoes from California came to be seen and used as specialist skateboarding footwear by skaters elsewhere. The important role played by the producer in officialising new ways of understanding products is revealed by the parallel case of Nike, whose basketball shoes proved as popular among 1970s skateboarders as Vans. They offered the right combination of grip and feel; *SkateBoarder* put them on a level with Van Doren (Schneider 1979). Like Vans, they were worn by top skaters. In 1978, Alva wore green suede Nike Blazer shoes on a tour of Europe, in the movie *Skateboard* (Gage 1978), and during the filming of *Skateboard Kings*, a BBC documentary (Ové 1978). He called his 'high-top Nike shoes' his 'favorite safety equipment' because they protected his ankles when he fell and his board tumbled behind him (*Interview with Tony Alva* 1978, p. 79). He was not alone. Nike shoes appeared in

192 *Thomas Turner*

countless photographs in skateboard magazines and were worn by skaters around the United States. The cover illustration of the first issue of *Thrasher*, the magazine that defined 1980s underground skate culture, was of a skater wearing Nike Blazer (*Thrasher*, vol. 1, no. 1, January 1981, p. 1).

Blue Ribbon Sports (BRS), the company behind Nike, was closely associated with California. It focused initially on the West Coast and built its business in the 1960s with runners in and around Los Angeles. Its first store opened in Santa Monica in September 1966. It was not ignorant of skateboarding. Free shoes were provided for the cast of a skateboard film (Strasser & Becklund 1993, pp. 246–247), and sales of Señorita Cortez, a women's running shoe, boomed after Farah Fawcett was filmed wearing them on a skateboard in *Charlie's Angels* (McCowan 1976). Unlike Van Doren, however, BRS did little to exploit its link with skateboarding. Its shoes were not adapted for skateboarders, and no special models were produced. Advertising was not taken in skateboard magazines. Instead, during the late 1970s, promotional work concentrated on strengthening the Nike brand with college and professional basketball players and coaches (Strasser & Becklund 1993, pp. 234–243). Advertising for the Blazer concentrated on the connection with top ballplayers, not skateboarders (advertisements reproduced in Jackson 2002, pp. 22–23). As a consequence, despite their popularity, Nike shoes were perceived as basketball (or tennis) shoes that were good for skating but never quite regarded as 'true' skate shoes. Even so, the company's basketball models, notably the 1984 Air Jordan, remained popular among skateboarders and inspired shoes produced in Asia for companies like Airwalk, Etnies, and Vision (Blümlein et al. 2008 pp. 104–148, 184–191). Yet despite the company's long connection with skateboarding, in 1997, its first specialist skateboard model was greeted with suspicion and ridicule by the skateboard press (pp. 282–285). Had it endorsed the shifting use of its shoes in the late 1970s, things might have been very different.

Conclusion

As Shove and Pantzar (2005, p. 57) argue, 'products alone have no value. They do so only when integrated into practice and allied to requisite forms of competence and meaning'. Products and practice are intertwined, and the way products are understood and valued develops through practice. Goods are open to constant reinterpretation and reinvention, as existing objects are co-opted and re-evaluated by the originators of new practices. The appropriation of products from one practice to another and the use of things in new ways generates new meanings for objects, but as the example of the skateboard shoe shows, the spread and diffusion of these meanings is to a large degree dependent on them being echoed and restated by producers. The skateboard shoe developed out of shoes made for other purposes; the earliest examples were simply existing models, intended for other activities and consumer groups, given a slight makeover, and repackaged to appeal to the skate market. Yet by doing this, producers replicated and commodified what skateboarders had themselves begun. By using and thinking about existing shoes in new ways, assessing them by criteria that had not been considered by their makers, skateboarders reconceived ordinary shoes as skate shoes. Producers followed their lead. The imaginative transformation of products and the subsequent creation of new product categories and specially designed products begins with the actions of consumer-practitioners, but it is reinforced and completed with producers' complicity. As the skateboarders of the 1960s and 1970s demonstrated, by improvising with available products, the originators of practices initiate the process by which new ideas and specially designed products are established.

Notes

1. About US$90 by current prices.
2. It should be noted that the film in which the interview appears was supported financially by Vans and that the director, Stacy Peralta, was sponsored by Van Doren in the 1970s and 1980s.

References

Adams, V & Hills, G 1989, *Skateboarding is not a book*, Fantail, London.

Ball, A 1977, *How to skateboard: a beginner's guide to the world's fastest growing sport*, Kenneth Mason Publications, Homewell.

Bender, M 1962, 'Shift to low sneakers still plagues mothers', *New York Times*, 26 October, p. 48.

Black, N (director) 1965, *Skaterdater*, Byway Productions, Los Angeles.

Blümlein, J, Schmid, D, Vogel, D & von Krosigk, H 2008, *Made for skate: the illustrated history of skateboard footwear*, FauxAmi Exhibitions, Stuttgart.

Borden, I 2001, *Skateboarding, space and the city: architecture and the body*, Berg, Oxford.

Brooke, M 1999, *The concrete wave: the history of skateboarding*, Warwick Publishing, Toronto.

Bunting, G & Bunting, E, 1977, *Skateboards: how to make them how to ride them*, Harvey House, New York.

Cook, J 1966, 'Today's schoolboy and the new fashions: he hasn't lost his buttons', *New York Times*, 1 April, p. 22.

Davidson, JA 1985, 'Sport and modern technology: the rise of skateboarding, 1963–1978', *Journal of Popular Culture*, vol. 18, no. 4, pp. 145–157.

Gage, G (director) 1978, *Skateboard*, Blum Group, Los Angeles.

Hang Ten 1976, 'THE DYNAMIC DUO!', *SkateBoarder*, vol. 2, no. 5, p. 142.

Hiss, T, & Bart, S 1976, 'Free as a board', *New York Times*, 12 September, p. 211.

Horowitz, M 1978, 'Design symposium: protective equipment', *SkateBoarder*, vol. 4, no. 12, July, pp. 166–175.

'Interview with Tony Alva' 1978, *SkateBoarder*, vol. 4, no. 12, July, pp. 66–83.

Jackson, R 2002, *Sole provider: 30 years of Nike basketball*, powerHouse books, New York.

Le, J 2005, 'California dreaming: the Vans story', in S Wood (ed), *Sneaker freaker: the book 2002–05*, Riverhead Freestyle, New York, n.p.

Makaha Sportswear 1978, 'RADIALS', *SkateBoarder*, vol. 5, no. 4, November, p. 47.

McCowan G (director) 1976, *Charlie's Angels: Consenting Adults* (television broadcast), 8 December 1976, Spelling-Goldberg Productions.

McNulty, P, & Stoner, R 1965, 'International skateboard championships', *Skateboarder Magazine*, vol. 1, no. 3, August, pp. 1, 16–37.

Molotch, H 2003, *Where stuff comes from: how toasters, toilets, cars, computers and many other things come to be as they are*, Routledge, New York.

Ové, H (director) 1978, *The world about us: skateboard kings*, BBC, London.

Palladini, D 2009, *Vans off the wall: stories of sole from Vans Originals*, Abrams, New York.

Peralta, S (director) 2001, *Dogtown and Z-Boys* (DVD), Sony Pictures Classics, Culver City.

Randolph Rubber Company c.1960, Randy Mighty Mouse, rubber-soled printed canvas sneaker, Northampton Museum and Art Gallery, 2011.144.1.

Randolph Rubber Company c.1966, Randy Batman, rubber-soled printed canvas sneaker, Northampton Museum and Art Gallery, 2009.57.20.

Reiser, H 1978, *Skateboarding*, Franklin Watts, New York.

Schneider, D 1979, 'Skate shoes', *SkateBoarder*, vol. 6, no. 3, October, p. 21.

Shove, E, & Pantzar, M 2005, 'Consumers, producers and practices: understanding the invention and reinvention of Nordic walking', *Journal of Consumer Culture*, vol. 5, no. 1, pp. 43–64.

'Skateboard mania' 1965, *Life*, 14 May, pp. 125–134.

South East Bay Skateboard Club c.1965, photograph, author's collection.

Strasser, JB & Becklund, L 1993, *Swoosh: the unauthorized story of Nike and the men who played there*, HarperCollins, New York.

Van Doren c.1972, 'Footprints from The House of Van', promotional leaflet, reproduced in Palladini, D 2009, *Vans off the wall: stories of sole from Vans Originals*, Abrams, New York, p. 86.

Van Doren 1977, 'OFF THE WALL', *SkateBoarder*, vol. 3, no. 6, July, p. 135.

Van Doren 1978, 'Van's world's number one skateboard shoes', *SkateBoarder*, vol. 4, no. 9, April, p. 142.

Van Doren 1979, 'HI-POWERED HI-TOPS!', *SkateBoarder*, vol. 6, no. 4, November, p. 6.

Vita-Pakt Juice Company 1965, 'Step on it . . . it's alive!', *Skateboarder Magazine*, vol. 1, no. 3, August, p. 56.

Weintraub, B 1965, 'Skateboards take the spotlight at Wesleyan', *New York Times*, 3 May, p. 35.

Weir, L 1978, *Skateboards and skateboarding: the complete beginner's guide*, Pan Books, London.

Weiss, EM 2004, 'A reinvention of the wheel', *Washington Post*, 17 August 2004. Available from: www.washingtonpost.com/wp-dyn/articles/A6502-2004Aug16.html. [14 February 2015].

Whitter, W (director) 2005, *Rollin' through the decades*, Beaquarr Productions, London.

Index

1970s 3, 8–9, 53, 58, 73–4, 102, 105, 182, 186, 192
1980s 8, 10, 53, 60, 93, 102, 105, 140, 142, 192
1990s 7, 10, 24, 76, 141–9, 156, 172
360s 18, 20, 23, 26

action sport *see* sport
Affirmative Action: A Brisbane Skateboarding Documentary 47, 51
affordances 22–4
Alva, Tony 73–4, 182, 188, 190–1
architecture 55, 91–2, 99, 144–5, 182
A.Skate Foundation 38
authenticity 31, 34, 40–1, 65, 70, 74, 82, 85, 104, 110–1, 118, 155, 160
authorities 34, 44, 46, 53, 100, 145–6, 160, 169–70, 172–3, 177–8

Bay Area Skatepark (San Francisco) 109, 116–17, 119
Beasley Skate Park (Toronto) 152–165
blogs 45–6, 61, 65, 67, 71, 101
body, the 17–23, 26–7, 35, 76, 79, 81, 85–6, 126, 160–1, 172; bodily 19–20, 36, 38, 85–6, 147
Borden, Iain 2, 3, 5, 7, 8, 9, 35, 36, 51, 57, 60, 145, 169, 174, 180, 182, 183
bowl 30, 73–4, 80, 103–4, 110, 155
Burnside Park (Portland) 145, 162, 172–5

capitalism 5, 75, 77, 82, 85, 109, 118, 146, 153, 156–7, 160–1
citizenship 109, 118, 172, 177
city space *see* urban space
class 60, 114, 118, 131–2, 139, 147, 154
collaboration 6–7, 53, 96, 103–4, 162, 175, 183, 188

commercial exploitation 1, 102, 183
commercialization 9, 31, 40, 147, 149
commodification 3, 5, 28, 75–8, 146, 182, 192
community 23–4, 28, 37, 44, 50, 68, 77, 95, 108–9, 114, 117–19, 150, 159
co-optation 40, 139, 142, 144, 147
creative class 166
creative industries 152
creativity 4, 7, 11, 21, 23, 36, 50, 57, 61–2, 164, 178, 183
crime 34, 109, 112–13, 139, 158, 177

Delueze, Gilles 17–27
demographics 8, 45, 48–9
diversity 2, 44–6, 113, 164
DIY 2, 11, 60, 68, 114–15, 140, 145, 152, 157, 162, 172, 174, 180
do it yourself *see* DIY

economic activity 35, 145, 169
education 2, 38, 52
Eighties *see* 1980s
empowerment 2, 30, 36, 39, 52, 111, 162
entrepreneurship 2, 31, 38, 41, 109–10, 114, 118–19, 172, 175, 177
ethnicity 8, 45, 60, 114
exclusion 33, 35, 60, 68, 109, 118, 160
extreme sport *see* sport

Fanling Skatepark (Hong Kong) 30, 41
Foucault, Michel 25, 123, 129, 130, 132, 170–2
fourth wave 140–1, 144–9
fourth-wave skaters *see* fourth wave
freestyle 4, 18, 23, 26
funding 44, 46–7, 105, 108–9, 112, 116–17

196 *Index*

gender 2, 45–6, 48–9, 112, 115–16, 121–32; exclusion 119; identity 122–3; relations 112; females and femininity 2, 6, 34, 37, 44, 46, 48–51, 104, 112, 115–17, 199, 121–32, 160; males and masculinity 4, 6, 33, 44–6, 48, 50–1, 60, 74, 81, 103, 111–13, 115, 119, 125, 130, 160, 163

generational: intergenerational/multigenerational 3, 6, 11, 48–9, 50, 53, 140–1, 146, 148–50, 158–9

gentrification 2, 6, 34, 86, 152–3, 159–64, 166

globalization 75–7, 85, 157, 162

government 55, 114, 169–80

health 48–9, 51, 55, 109–11

Hungerford Bridge (London) 94, 96–101, 103–5

identity 3, 6, 47, 54, 65, 68–70, 81, 108–9, 117, 121–32, 140–50

inclusivity 1, 10–11, 30–41, 44, 46–7, 53–5, 109, 111–19

incorporation 165; commercial 1; commodity form 157; ideological form 157; spatial-temporal 6, 153–65

innovation 4, 18, 21, 23, 25–6, 28, 59, 154, 157, 164, 186, 189

JFK Plaza *see* LOVE Park

Kona Skatepark (Florida) 10, 139–51

LGBT 33, 46

lifestyle sport *see* sport

LOVE Park (Philadelphia) 24–5, 34, 100, 109

mainstream(ing) 1–3, 8, 10–11, 31, 40–1, 57, 60, 140–1, 143, 146, 148–50, 176

Makaha 8–9, 187–8

Makaha Radial 187

marginalization 35, 50, 115, 118–19, 121, 126, 129, 152

marketing 28, 75, 102, 146, 185

media 1–2, 31–2, 36–7, 45–6, 50–1, 74–5, 79, 82, 84–6, 109, 121–32; mainstream 70, 121–31; representations 1–3, 37, 44, 62, 69, 84, 121–31

Mullen, Rodney 2, 4, 17–29

neoliberal(ism) 6, 38, 108–19, 152–4, 160–4, 166, 171–2, 175, 177

Nike 31, 86, 102–4, 187–8, 191–2

Nineties *see* 1990s

ollie 23, 84, 93

Paddington Skate Park (Brisbane) 44, 47, 52

philanthropy 4, 30, 32–3, 36–7, 39–41

policy 38, 44, 46, 50, 55, 171–2, 178

politics 31–2, 35–6, 39–41, 122, 125, 153, 169, 180

pool *see* swimming pool

popular culture 45, 76, 81–2, 125

power 17, 26, 28, 58, 76–7, 86, 127, 170–1

professional skateboarder(s) 1, 4, 9–10, 34, 36–7, 39, 60, 75, 97, 99, 103, 109, 111–3, 116, 142, 191

professional skater(s) *see* professional skaterboarder(s)

pro skateboarder(s) *see* professional skaterboarder(s)

pro skater(s) *see* professional skaterboarder(s)

public space 31, 35, 44, 47, 49, 53–4, 91, 95, 97, 100–1, 110, 117–18, 169, 180

race 3, 5, 74–6, 81

ramp 10, 104, 110, 112, 114, 144–5, 149

Randy 720s 185, 196, 189, 191

rebellion 12, 40, 59, 79–80, 83, 142–3, 146, 165, 158, 178

resistance 7, 25–6, 28, 31, 39, 51, 57, 60, 86, 139, 143, 146, 165, 169–73, 175–6, 178–9

Rob Dyrdek Foundation 37, 110, 112–13, 118

Rob Dyrdek's Safe Spot Skate Spots 109–13

Seventies *see* 1970s

sexism 2, 60, 69, 128

sexuality 3, 33, 46, 121, 126–8

sexual orientation *see* sexuality

skateboarding: industry 1, 11, 35, 52, 60, 65, 68, 103; meaning of 7–11; popularity 8–9, 30–1, 36–7, 40, 44–5, 78, 139

skateboard park *see* skatepark(s)

skate culture 2–4, 11, 18, 24–5, 28–41, 61–2, 65, 68, 70, 73, 79, 111, 114–15, 117–18, 121, 125, 12930, 132, 152, 154, 157, 160, 162–3, 174, 177–8, 192; contradictions in skate culture 7, 11, 31–2, 143

Skateistan 2, 37–8, 52

Skatepark(s) 3, 5–6, 8–10, 35, 37, 39, 46–7, 49–50, 53, 73, 86, 91, 93, 103–4, 108–23, 128–9, 144–5, 152–65, 172–5, 177, 183; skater-built skateparks/DIY skateparks 162, 169, 172–5

Index 197

skate-proofing 54, 110, 112
skate stoppers 23, 47, 172
skate stopper technologies *see* skate stoppers
space(s): 24–5, 34, 47, 49, 53, 59, 68, 75,
 84, 86, 91, 93–7, 99, 109–13, 117–19,
 144–5, 157–8, 162, 169, 180; public
 space 10, 31, 35, 47, 49, 53, 96, 101,
 110, 117–18, 146, 169, 173, 180, 182;
 urban space(s) 2, 6, 41, 47, 75, 84, 91,
 96, 99, 110, 118, 157, 172, 180
sponsorship 10, 39, 62, 104, 113–14, 116,
 118, 124, 164, 166, 174, 185, 193
sport 1, 3–4, 9–11, 17–18, 25–7, 31–2,
 44–5, 50, 54, 61, 75, 102, 111–12,
 115–16, 121–4, 130–1, 139, 141, 146–50,
 158, 177, 188; action sport 38, 75, 102–3;
 extreme sport 1, 7, 10, 28, 139, 140, 178;
 lifestyle sport 11, 112, 122–3, 130
stereotypes 52, 55, 70, 121, 126, 176
street skateboarding 4, 6, 8, 10, 23–5, 35, 46,
 53, 83, 96, 98–100, 105, 109, 111, 113,
 118, 140–5, 149–50, 154–5, 160, 173, 178
street-based skateboarding *see* street
 skateboarding
street skating *see* street skateboarding
street-style skateboarding *see* street
 skateboarding
subcultural *see* subculture(s)
subculture(s) 4, 11, 44–6, 48–9, 51–2, 55,
 57, 59–60, 139–41, 143–6, 148–50,
 152–3, 157–8, 160–1, 163–6

subjectivity 79, 118, 125–6, 177
surfing 7–9, 18, 25–8, 58–9, 73, 102, 140,
 158, 182–5, 187
swimming pool 5, 7, 9, 22, 73–5, 79, 82,
 85, 103–4, 152, 155, 157, 183, 190

Tha Hood Games 113–15, 118
third wave 125–49
third-wave skaters *see* third wave
Town Park (Oakland) 113–15, 118–19
Transworld Skateboarding 7, 31, 124
Turner Skateboard Park (Ontario)
 157–59

Undercroft, the (London) 53, 91–105
urban renewal 110, 159
urban space 47, 50, 54, 84, 91, 96, 99, 110,
 117–18, 169

Van Doren 101–5, 147, 189, 190–1
Vans *see* Van Doren

X Games 10, 31, 76, 113

youth 38, 49–52, 74–80, 82–3, 85,
 113–14, 119, 140, 143, 178–9
youth culture 80–1, 83, 116, 177

Z-Boys 8–9, 18, 59
Zephyr (Skate Team) 9, 190; *see also*
 Z-Boys